ENGLISH PAINTING

Other books by R. H. Wilenski

★

R. H. WILENSKI

ENGLISH PAINTING

WITH *202* ILLUSTRATIONS

BOSTON AND NEW YORK

HALE, CUSHMAN AND FLINT

PRINTED IN THE UNITED STATES OF AMERICA

This book is
dedicated
to
A. and A. W.

CONTENTS

CONTENTS

APPENDICES

ILLUSTRATIONS

ILLUSTRATIONS

ILLUSTRATIONS

ILLUSTRATIONS

14

ILLUSTRATIONS

ILLUSTRATIONS

ILLUSTRATIONS

ILLUSTRATIONS

ILLUSTRATIONS

ILLUSTRATIONS

ILLUSTRATIONS

21

ILLUSTRATIONS

ILLUSTRATIONS

ILLUSTRATIONS

PREFACE

In two books called 'The Modern Movement in Art' and 'The Meaning of Modern Sculpture' I discussed a movement in Western European art, including English art, which began in Paris in the eighteen-eighties—roughly a half a century ago. The present book is concerned with English Painting from Gothic times to a point somewhere after the Pre-Raphaelite Movement of the eighteen-fifties and before the Cubist-Classical Renaissance discussed in the other books. It makes no pretence to be a complete history of English painting in that long period. It is more in the nature of a series of comments on English painters who seem to me of interest or consequence from the special point of view defined in the 'General Introduction' which follows this 'Preface'.

The drawings and paintings in surviving mediaeval and Gothic manuscripts are outside the subject of this book.

These survivals, with the surviving examples of embroidery and sculpture, are real evidence of mediaeval and Gothic work in these particular fields produced in England in these periods. But they can tell us no more of the appearance of the non-existing mural and panel paintings than Greek vases can tell us of the non-existing mural and panel paintings by the ancient Greeks; they can and must be separately studied, but they cannot and must not be used to fill the yawning gaps in the available knowledge of English mural and panel painting in mediaeval and Gothic times.

For the facts in regard to the surviving mural and panel paintings I went, naturally, to the antiquaries—it being their business to collect them. But to extract facts from the average antiquary is not as easy as it sounds, because all but the very best antiquaries seem ashamed of their useful profession and evidently aspire to be art historians and art critics. The real antiquary, of the highest class, acts like a serious scientist. He collects facts, puts them all down on the table without comment

25

or grouping, and leaves them there for the use of the art historian and the art critic. But the average antiquary, whom we may call the fanciful-antiquary, is not content to stop when he comes to the end of his own business. He must be for ever fiddling with his facts, trying to make them look more numerous by putting two and five, and three and four together, trying to make them look more important by invading the province of the art historian or the art critic, dragging in manuscripts when his facts relate to paintings, attaching non-existent pictures to painters of whom nothing is known but the names, clamping the cassocks of St. Albans monks to battered panels in Norway, balancing the portrait of an English king on the nose of a jeweller at Prague.

These fanciful-antiquaries make things very difficult for the art critic in search of reliable information. The critic goes to the books by the professional collectors of facts, for plain statements of the facts collected, and finds himself confronted with a *soi-disant* history of English Gothic painting which turns out to be a mosaic of a few facts and a little hearsay held together in an arbitrary pattern by a cement of surmise.

My own work in this book is addressed to the general student, the average sensible man of average education, who cares, of course, very wisely, not a button for any Master Hugh of Winchester or Master Nigel of St. Albans whose works are non-existent, and who cares equally wisely not a button for fragments of frescoes so faded that they are almost invisible and fragments of panels so damaged that their original appearance can only be discovered by guesswork, if at all.

In Chapters I and II, and their Appendices, I have therefore tried to chip away sufficient of the fanciful-antiquaries' cement to destroy their arbitrary patterns, and to put down their main unconnected facts frankly, as unconnected facts, upon the table. I have gone back, that is to say, to the point where these confusing writers would have stopped if they had been content with their own business and not aspired to be art historians and art critics.

26

Chapter III and the relevant Appendix are concerned with surviving paintings by English artists in Tudor and Stuart times. Here till recently the mosaic offered was usually based on the work of Sir Lionel Cust and on Mr. Collins Baker's 'Lely and the Stuart Painters'. Much of the necessary clarification in this field has now been done by Professor W. G. Constable and Mr. Collins Baker himself in their joint book, 'English Painting of the Sixteenth and Seventeenth Centuries', where Professor Constable has drastically removed a mass of surmise from the Tudor period. To find the facts about the Tudor survivals was thus relatively easy. But to find them in the case of the Stuart period I had to do some chipping.

For the sections on Hogarth and the English painters who followed in the eighteenth and nineteenth centuries, I have used the standard biographies and books of reference and the often very illuminating information collected in 'Artists and their Friends in England', by Mr. W. T. Whitley. I have not been through the enormous number of books about Blake. Of those which I have read I am most indebted to Darrell Figgis' 'The Paintings of William Blake' with its hundred plates and sympathetic text. For information about the lives of the artists who surrounded Blake I am mainly indebted to Mr. Laurence Binyon's 'The Followers of William Blake'.

Holding that the artist's intentions are the essence of his art I have been at pains to quote *ipsissima verba* and given what seem to me revealing extracts from letters and other writings by Hogarth, Gainsborough, Reynolds, Crome, Blake and others.

For the rest I have gone to the paintings; and, when the paintings are not accessible, to photographs from them. Most of the pictures mentioned I have seen; in the case of all the others I have had photographs before me at the time of writing.

I have to thank Mr. J. B. Manson, Director of the National Gallery of British Art, Millbank, and Mr. Martin Hardie, Keeper of the Victoria and Albert Museum, for valuable facilities; the Directors of American museums, especially of the Metropolitan Museum, New York, the Boston Museum of Fine

Arts, the Worcester Art Museum, the Chicago Art Institute, and the Cleveland Museum of Art, who have supplied me with photographs and information; the Governors of the Foundling Hospital, the Committee of the Norwich Castle Museum, and the Trustees of other collections from which pictures are reproduced.

I am also much indebted to all owners who have sent me photographs of their pictures and to those who have kindly collaborated by putting no difficulties in the way of the reproduction of photographs obtained from other sources.

I have to thank Sir Robert and Lady Witt and their librarians for much help given me in the Witt Library.

Mr. Frank Sabin kindly supplied me with photographs of drawings by Rowlandson, and Mr. Percy Moore Turner sent me photographs of Norwich School pictures, including Crome's *On the Yare* which I reproduce. Mr. Oliver Brown and Mr. Phillips of the Leicester Galleries have also kindly sent me photographs; Messrs. Agnew have done the same. Messrs. Knoedler, London and New York, allowed me to go through their extensive collection of photographs and lent me several hundred, including some of the important paintings now in America which I reproduce, and most of the examples of English sporting pictures which illustrate the chapter called 'Paintings of Outdoor Life'. Mr. W. F. Mansell has done me a similar service by lending me hundreds of photographs. A number of living artists have greatly helped me by gifts of photographs from their works. I have further had gifts of photographs from other sources. I have had these and a modest collection of photographs of my own before me during the period of writing to reinforce my memory of the pictures known to me and help me to make comparisons—as far as is possible—with others. It would have been better to have had all the pictures. But that, unfortunately, could not be done.

I am much indebted to all owners of copyright and to the photographers whose negatives are reproduced. In particular I must mention Mr. W. F. Mansell, M. Giraudon, Mr. Sydney

Newbery, Mr. Paul Laib, Mr. A. C. Cooper, Mr. Hawker of Newbury, and Mr. Alfred Cracknell, who photographed Leon Underwood's drawing *Freedom* specially for this book.

References in the text to the pictures reproduced can be located by referring to the artist's name in the Index at the end.

London, 1933.

GENERAL INTRODUCTION

'*This island seems to me worthy the consideration of a man of taste, not only because of the charm of the countryside and the beauty of the people, not only because of the outward show which appears to me most choice and to announce a people rich and happy in the bosom of peace, but also by the incredible quantity of excellent pictures, statues, and ancient inscriptions which are in this Court.*'   PETER PAUL RUBENS.

'*The ingenious Mr. Hogarth used to assert that everyone, except the connoisseur, was a judge of painting.*'   OLIVER GOLDSMITH.

'*The Enquiry in England is not whether a Man has Talents and Genius, But whether he is Passive and Polite and a Virtuous Ass and obedient to Noblemen's Opinions in Art and Science. If he is, he is a Good Man. If Not, he must be Starved.*'   WILLIAM BLAKE.

'*Habit is a form of death; intention is an aspect of life.*'
DARRELL FIGGIS.

RUBENS wrote the words quoted above when he came to England in 1629. They remain true at the present day, not only in their appreciation of the charm of the English country and of English people, but also in their observation of the English habit of collecting old pictures, sculpture and bric-à-brac. Rich Englishmen, when Rubens visited England, were not concerned with encouraging creative English painting and sculpture around them. They were concerned with acquiring examples of painting and sculpture of the past. The noble patrons of art, then, as in Blake's day, expected a native artist to be 'passive and polite' and 'obedient to noblemen's opinions in art and science'. On those opinions and the way they were formed in his time Hogarth also had a word to say:

31

'I think that young men by studying in Italy have seldom learnt much more than the names of the painters; though sometimes they have attained the amazing power of distinguishing styles, and knowing by the hue of the picture the hard name of the artist, a power which, highly as they pride themselves upon it, is little more than knowing one hand-writing from another. For this they gain great credit, and are supposed vast proficients, because they have travelled. They are gravely attended to by people of rank, with whom they claim acquaintance, and talk of the antique in a cant phraseology, made up of half or whole Italian, to the great surprise of their hearers, who become gulls, in order to pass foɪ connoisseurs, wonder with a foolish face of praise, and bestow unqualified admiration on the marvellous bad copies of marvellous bad originals, which they have brought home as trophies, and triumphantly display, to prove their discernment and taste. . . . There is another set of gentry, more noxious to the art than these, and those are your picture jobbers from abroad, who are always ready to raise a great cry in the prints, whenever they think their craft is in danger; and indeed it is their interest to depreciate every English work as hurtful to their trade of continually importing ship-loads of dead Christs, Holy Families, Madonas, and other dismal dark subjects, neither entertaining nor ornamental, on which they scrawl the terrible cramp names of some Italian masters, and fix on us poorEnglishmen the character of universal dupes. If a man, naturally a judge of painting, not bigotted to those empyrics, should cast his eye on one of their sham virtuoso pieces, he would be very apt to say, "Mr. Bubbleman, that grand Venus, as you are pleased to call it, has not beauty enough for the character of an English cook-maid."—Upon which the quack answers, with a confident air, "Sir, I find that you are no connoisseur; the picture, I assure you, is in Alesso Baldminetto's second and best manner, boldly painted, and truly sublime: the contour gracious; the air of the head in the high Greek taste; and a most divine idea it is."
—Then spitting in an obscure place, and rubbing it with a dirty handkerchief, takes a skip to t'other end of the room, and

32

1. LEON UNDERWOOD
Freedom
Private Collection, England

2. THE CHICHESTER ROUNDEL
Bishop's Palace, Chichester

screams out in raptures, "There's an amazing touch! A man should have this picture a twelvemonth in his collection before he can discover half its beauties!" The gentleman (though naturally a judge of what is beautiful, yet ashamed to be out of the fashion, by judging for himself) with this cant is struck dumb; gives a vast sum for the picture, very modestly confesses he is indeed quite ignorant of painting, and bestows a frame worth fifty pounds on a frightful thing, which, without the hard name, is not worth so many farthings.'

This has a topical ring, not only as regards England, but also as regards America. And everyone interested in the arts must take one side or the other in the dispute. No compromise is possible. We must either stand with the past-loving connoisseurs, the dealers who sell objects from the past, the rich men who buy them, and the curators who keep them dusted in museums; or with the original creative artists of our own day. We must either assume that the creative artists of the present are more important to us than the artists of the past; or that the artists of the past are more important to us than the creative artists of the present. We must put our faith in living artists or in artists who are dead.

For my own part I have always believed that the present is more important to us than the past; and that all our studies should aim at understanding the creative art around us in our own day.

I have written elsewhere: 'The study of art-history is stupid and dangerous pedantry unless it helps us to understand and appreciate the original painting of our own day.'[1] At the time when I wrote it I assumed that this desired understanding and appreciation of the present could in fact be achieved by a student who began by the study of the past. But can the past really help us to this achievement? Is it really possible to go straight to the past and extract from it any standards which apply to conditions in the world we know?

As I see things now I believe that the boot, as it were, is on the other leg; that we cannot begin to understand the past until

[1]'French Painting' by R. H. Wilenski (Medici).

33

we understand the present; that standards taken from the past cannot help us to comprehension of art that is living, but only to the over-estimation of the various kinds of contemporary production which are born dead.

'The ingenious Mr. Hogarth used to assert that everyone, except the connoisseur, was a judge of painting.' This goes, I think, too far. Hogarth had a tendency in his polemics to over-shoot the mark. But it is true, I think, to say that the connoisseur, in Hogarth's sense, is always a person whose education specially unfits him to understand and appreciate original contemporary art—the only kind of contemporary art which matters anywhere ever.

Assessments of the value of particular paintings are disguised autobiography unless they are based upon standards, and unless those standards in their turn are based upon something broader than the writer's personal psychological demands from art. The past-loving connoisseur has standards. But they are inevitably, I submit, the wrong standards, because they are always based on technical procedures which he has observed in the remains of the past. If the contemporary work which confronts him conforms to those technical procedures—if, that is to say, it is 'traditional', i.e. derivative, in technique—he can understand it and he applauds; if it does not so conform, he is not equipped to under-stand it, and he accordingly condemns.

We must go, I think, even further and say that the past-loving connoisseur is not only ill equipped to understand the present but also ill equipped to understand the past. The only real clue to the meaning of any human activity in the past is that activity as manifested in the present. The activity called art is surely no exception to this rule. The man who cannot under-stand and so appreciate the creative art of his own day cannot understand or appreciate the creative art of any time or place. The only art, which can teach us to understand art that was ever alive, is the art of living men. If we fail to understand that art we fail to understand all art—always, inevitably. Art, after all, is an aspect of life. We cannot learn to understand life by studying the surviving records of the past. Shakespeare did not learn what he knew of Cleopatra and Volumnia from the historians.

On the other hand the spectator who begins by learning to understand the original art of his own day, and to distinguish it from derivative painting and other hack procedures in works by living men, equips himself to make the same distinctions when confronted with the original, derivative, and hack painting of the past. Thus equipped, he can study the art of the past with understanding and in a useful way.

It follows that there are and can be no fixed and permanent standards for the useful assessment of the art of the past. Creative art goes on and is continually changing. While the art critic is searching the past for works that will aid comprehension of the creative standards of his own day—those standards are being changed behind his back. If he is slow he will render no service. He will arrive too late. Art will not stand still to help even the most useful art critic.

There are men who cannot face this fact; who yearn for fixed standards; who want their art-appreciation to be a drug and a habit. Such men tell us that this continual change of standard is a peculiar and disturbing characteristic of our own time, an aspect, they will say, of the restlessness of modern life. But the truth is, of course, that life has always been restless; that standards have always perpetually changed. It is a truism that every age evolves new standards as part of its adjustment to life, and that every artist who has contributed to such adjustments has been an innovator.

Darrell Figgis said: 'Habit is a form of death.' It is and it has always been so. He also said: 'Intention is an aspect of life.' And here, I think, we have the only useful type of criterion for the assessment of works of art. The study of art history, to have value, as I submitted in 'The Modern Movement in Art', must surely be the study of the attitudes, motives, and procedures of the artists—of the aspect of life which Darrell Figgis, if I read him rightly, referred to as 'intention'. And the intentions of the past can only be understood when we understand the same or similar intentions in the present.

The foregoing, I hope, explains the presence in this book of some reproductions of original works by living English artists —though the book's nominal subject is English painting from Gothic times to the Pre-Raphaelites. I have tried to assess the past by the standards of the present as I understand them; and I have done this in the hope that the past thus interpreted may help appreciation of the original English painters of to-day.

CHAPTER I

EARLY GOTHIC REMAINS
1066-1377

*

For the general student the history of English painting properly begins with Hogarth. This is not to say that there were no English painters before the beginning of the eighteenth century when Hogarth began to paint. There have always been English painters in England. But deliberate and wholesale destruction on religious grounds in the sixteenth and seventeenth centuries, and silly restorations of the surviving fragments in the nineteenth and probably the twentieth centuries, have put real knowledge of English Gothic painting irrevocably beyond our reach; and the English paintings surviving from Tudor and Stuart times are nearly all hack portraits by second or third-rate painters imitating the brilliant foreigners who worked here in that period.

We can form no general idea of English painting from the accession of William the Conqueror (1066) to the accession of Richard II (1377). No complete mural painting or easel picture known to be done by an Englishman in this period of three hundred years exists at the present time; and the condition of the surviving fragments is such as to render real knowledge of their original appearance, in almost every case, entirely impossible.

The surviving mural paintings in most cases are either so faint and fragmentary that they are not decipherable by the ordinary spectator, or else they have been 'revived' or 'restored', i.e. repainted, probably more than once, in the six or seven hundred years of their existence.

The few surviving paintings on panels are nearly all badly

damaged and to a large extent effaced, and many have been repainted.

As Professor W. G. Constable, who knows every fact known about mediaeval painting in England, has put it: 'A definitive or even a tolerably comprehensive history of English mediaeval painting is, in the present state of knowledge, impossible. It may indeed, always be impossible.' The general student may go further and change the last sentence to : 'Such a history must now remain impossible for ever.'

Patriotism, atavism, and past-loving connoisseurship find it hard to accept this situation; they find it distressing to be without a cake which their ancestors have eaten. The fanciful-antiquaries have accordingly made attempts to serve up the crumbs in the cupboard as a substantial meal. They have extolled non-existent pictures and described as masters a number of painters about whom nothing is really known except the names. As already noted in the Preface they have built up an arbitrary history of early English painting, concealing a paucity of facts by a multitude of guesses. The general student need not concern himself with the details. If they excite his curiosity he will find some of them in the Appendix to this chapter.[1]

As also stated in the Preface the drawings and paintings in the surviving manuscripts are outside my subject; and we must be careful to remember that the manuscripts which have chanced to survive do not tell us the appearance of the destroyed mural paintings and panel pictures. Of the paintings properly so called which survive from this period there is only one which calls for the general student's attention—a painting on the wall of the Chapel of the Bishop's Palace at Chichester, generally known as *The Chichester Roundel* (Pl. 2).

Nobody knows who painted this delightful Virgin and Child. If we name a nationality we are guessing, because the mediaeval Church was an international organisation, and artist-monks of different nationalities worked side by side here, as elsewhere, at that time. We all hope that the painter was English.

[1]Appendix I, pp. 261-265.

For if he was, the painting demonstrates that there was an English painter at that period who could produce a mural painting as delicately significant in design and drawing, and as exquisite in feeling, as any surviving in Italy or elsewhere.[1]

[1]We do not know the original colour of this painting. To-day it is a delicate harmony of faint tints. The Virgin's cloak is pink, her robe and the Child's robe are white. The background is blue. The censers and the embroideries on the hem of the Child's robe, formerly silver, have turned black.

CHAPTER II

LATE GOTHIC REMAINS
1377-1509

★

It is equally impossible to form any general idea of painting by English artists between the accession of Richard II (1377) and the accession of Henry VIII (1509).

The surviving fragments include the remains of mural paintings in the Chapter House, Westminster; in parish churches in East Anglia; at Ampney St. Mary in Gloucestershire, at Breage in Cornwall, Friskney in Lincolnshire, Pickering in Yorkshire, and elsewhere.

The paintings in the Chapter House, Westminster, are the remains of pictures which formerly filled five arched compartments. Some of the heads resemble Italian or Avignon painting of the period. The painter, since he was employed at Westminster, was doubtless regarded as an important artist. But nobody now knows his nationality or name.

The remains of fourteenth-century mural paintings in the parish churches seem village workmanship. Some are interesting as records of the social unrest which culminated in the Rebellion of Wat Tyler. The subjects seem to have been democratic protests. The remains at Ampney St. Mary, Gloucestershire, and Breage in Cornwall, for example, represent Christ as Piers Plowman, the Oppressed Labourer—a nude figure displaying wounds which, at Breage, cover the whole body.

The remains of fifteenth-century mural paintings in parish churches, of which the largely repainted frescoes at Pickering in Yorkshire are examples, seem originally to have depicted scenes from sacred and legendary history, and moralities. St. Christopher seems to have been a favourite subject.

40

3. THE WILTON DIPTYCH
Left-hand panel
National Gallery, London

4. THE WILTON DIPTYCH
Right-hand panel
National Gallery, London

From the late fourteenth and the fifteenth century we have really only three surviving works of importance: *The Westminster Portrait of Richard II*, the *Wilton Diptych* (Pls. 3, 4 and 5), and the *Eton Chapel Frescoes* (Pl. 6). The curious will find notes on some other remains in the Appendix to this chapter.[1] The general student can confine his attention to these three.

In the *Westminster Portrait of Richard II* the king, a full-length life-size figure, holds orb and sceptre and is seated on a throne. The picture was originally painted in distemper on gesso. At some time a stucco diaper was imposed over the original background which is now flat gold.

We do not know the original appearance of this picture. A record of 1732 tells us that the lower part had been defaced by the backs of people using the stalls in the Abbey Choir, behind which it hung, and that it was then repainted in oil by 'one Broome, a printseller'. In 1823 it was 'cleaned'. In 1866 it was 'cleaned' again, and the oil painting of 1732 was removed. We also do not know the nationality or name of the artist. Richard II had close relations with the Continent. Some antiquaries guess that the painter was a Parisian or one of the Franco-Flemish artists who worked for the Duke of Burgundy and the Duke of Berri. More patriotic antiquaries guess that the painter was English. For my own part I am not tempted here to indulge in guesswork. I am content to confess quite simply that I do not know.

The same applies to the celebrated *Wilton Diptych*. This shows in one panel Richard II, with St. John the Baptist, St. Edward the Confessor, and St. Edmund (Pl. 3), and in the other the Virgin and Child surrounded with angels (Pl. 4). The panels at the back are decorated in one case with the arms of Richard impaled with those of Edward the Confessor, and in the other with a white hart, which was the King's device (Pl. 5). No one knows the nationality or name of the artist. The antiquaries have indulged in prolonged and repeated orgies of guessing about both. The general student need not follow them.

[1]Cf. Appendix II, pp. 266-268.

This picture does not seem to have been very much or often repainted. As it appears at present, it is pretty in colour, prettily drawn, and delicate in feeling. But it is clearly not the work of an artist of great original powers. The creative spirit in Europe at the time when it was painted had already produced Giotto, Duccio and the Lorenzetti; we must set the *Wilton Diptych* in relation to the achievements of those masters and rank the painter—whether English, French, Franco-Flemish, Avignon School, Bohemian, or Italian—with a minor artist of charm like Gentile da Fabriano who was then doing much the same sort of thing in Florence.

In the *Eton Chapel Frescoes* (Pl. 6) we have considerable remains of paintings by an artist whose name is known. The College accounts tell us that the artist who painted these *Miracles of the Virgin* on the walls of the College Chapel between 1479 and 1488 was called William Baker. The paintings have an obviously Flemish character and Baker may have been Baecker phonetically spelt. But he may also have been Baker. So Baker he shall be. Nothing else is known about him.

The paintings as we know them to-day are in grey monochrome with touches of colour. They originally covered both walls of the chapel with two rows of subjects painted in some oil or wax medium over earlier decorative painting in distemper. In 1561 the College barber was paid six and eightpence 'for wypinge oute the Imagery Worke uppon the walles of the Church'. This 'wypinge out' was presumably done with plaster or whitewash and most of the painted area was then covered with panelling, an organ, seats and so forth. In 1847 the panelling and seats were moved, and the existence of the paintings was discovered; the 'wypinge out' substance was removed; and the paintings, described as 'terribly mutilated' re-emerged. The destruction of all the paintings was then ordered; and the top row of pictures was chipped and scraped away. But for some reason or other the destruction was stopped before it had been completed; the lower paintings which had not been scraped away were covered with oak stalls and remained so covered till they

5. THE WILTON DIPTYĆH
Exterior of right-hand panel

6. WILLIAM BAKER
Miracles of the Virgin—Detail
Eton College Chapel

emerged once more at the bidding of Dr. Montague James in 1923.

In their present condition, gloomy in colour, and dull in design, they suggest that William Baker was an artist of no great account. They provide no evidence that he could or did contribute to the creative art of his own time. They reveal no Renaissance curiosity, no Renaissance urge towards experiment, no shafts of imagination, no intense observation, no passionate feeling, no great architectural powers. We can discover here and there a figure which has a certain liveliness or grace, but the concept of form is not consistent in the various parts. The paintings—if the inconsistency is not due to repainting—suggest that Baker was a derivative artist with eclectic tastes. I guess that he was a travelled man who had been to Flanders, Germany and Italy and thus had contact with many types of art; but that he was not a man who would have understood the most original of his contemporaries; that he would have admired Ghirlandaio, for example, more than Leonardo da Vinci, Signorelli, Botticelli and Piero dei Franceschi. Most of all, quite evidently, he admired the Flemish painters of the age before his own—Dirck Bouts and Roger van der Weyden—who were both dead before he began the paintings at Eton.

43

CHAPTER III

TUDOR AND STUART PAINTING
1509-1702

*

The destruction which has left us with nothing but odds and ends of English Gothic painting was begun by Henry VIII (1509-1547), continued under his successor Edward VI (1547-1553), and completed under the Commonwealth (1649-1660).

Henry VIII's attack on the Church organisation set out to suppress alleged exploitation of the people by the Church, and to nationalise the Church's wealth. The destruction of images in churches was said to be necessary because the images were credited with magic powers by ignorant peasants, and because 'relics vying with each other in grotesque pretensions' were said to have been used as instruments to mislead the people. Henry was not a man to do things by halves. His Commissioners had to go about their work in earnest. At Bury St. Edmunds, for example, where they dismantled the shrine of St. Edmund—(a monument in form like a church, made of wood, covered with plates of silver gilt, surmounted with gold cresting, and with a gold relief of Christ in Glory at the western end and figures in niches along the sides)—the images were found 'very cumbrous to deface'; but defaced they had to be to save the Commissioners' heads. The Commissioners published lists of miracles which they alleged had been worked by jugglery, and they destroyed shrine after shrine and painting after painting in countless places.

Cromwell's agents were no less conscientious. They had to deal with paintings and sculpture which had escaped the earlier iconoclasm and also, presumably, with new images imported in the Romanist revivals. They were Protestants, whose fathers had suffered persecution, who remembered the burnings by Queen Mary in England, the burnings in Spain under the Inquisition, the St. Bartholomew massacre in France, and the burnings, throttlings, tongue-tearings and breakings-on-the-wheel in the Netherlands. They were Protestants who also knew that in Piedmont in their own time the Protestants were being persecuted in the old spirit. They were fanatics who destroyed works of art as a gesture against the cruelties associated in their minds with the faith which had produced these paintings. They worked in the spirit of the Dutch iconoclasts who felt that they were striking Alva and Titelmann when they drew their knives across a painting or knocked off a statue's head. Their iconoclasm was not a crime comparable with the destruction of human bodies and the torture of human souls by persecution. We cannot condemn such action emanating from a revulsion against cruelty. And I am far from certain that we need very seriously deplore it in this case. For it is possible to have too large an artistic heritage. It may be that, in spite of iconoclasms, we have more relics of the past to-day than are really good for us.

Henry VIII's destruction of religious pictures might have been the signal for the creation of a new secular art if conditions had been favourable. But he not only reorganised the Church, he also reorganised the body politic. He transferred much of the wealth which he acquired from the Church to the gentry, thus creating a new plutocracy, which soon became coarse, selfish, and arrogant, unwilling to enlarge its experience by contact with original art, willing to employ artists solely as ministers to its own pride and vanity. A plutocracy of this character makes artistic creativity impossible and reduces art to face-painting and clothes-painting, unless the artist is big enough and assured enough to fight his patrons, impose his own will upon them, and use them as material for his art. No English artist of this stature, as far as we know, was forthcoming in Tudor England. The patrons called the tune. They knew what they wanted—a likeness and detailed imitation of fine clothes—and they were

45

determined to get it. When the German, Hans Holbein, appeared they found their man.

Holbein worked in England from 1526 to 1528, and again from 1532 (with occasional foreign journeys) to 1543. He became Court Painter to Henry VIII in 1536. He gave his sitters no trouble, as he painted his oil pictures from drawings which he made at one or at most two sittings, and he started a fashion for miniature portraits which soon became widespread.

It is difficult to-day to assess Holbein as an artist. Judged by standards of intention he seems, in most of his work, very cautious and derivative, an artist who, at the climax of Renaissance curiosity, experiment, and science, in the age of Michelangelo, Raphael, Titian, and Dürer, remained sheltered within the familiar experience of Gothic art, making patient still-life imitations of textures and features, fingers and rings. Judged by scientific standards of drawing he seems an artist with small constructional ability, who could rarely place the far eye in a three-quarter view with anatomical correctness. To appreciate him to-day we have to judge him by the romantic standard of the nineteenth century; to look upon him as a recorder of emotive fragments, a man more concerned with the differences between faces than with scientific realism or imaginative experience or architectural form; a man who, at his best, could draw a romantically emotional portrait.

At Henry VIII's Court he was applauded as a face-painter who could produce a likeness and faithfully depict fine jewels and elaborate clothes; and the applause was so loud that face-painting in the Holbein manner by native and other foreign artists in England became for long the order of the day.

Some of these imitations of Holbein have survived. But we do not know if the painters were English or foreign. An exception is the *Portrait of Edmund Butts*, son of Henry VIII's physician, which is now in the National Gallery, London. This picture is inscribed *'faict par Johann Bettes Anglois'* and is dated 1545. No other surviving picture is known to be the work of this John Betts and nothing else is known about him.

7. ISAAC OLIVER
Sir Anthony Mildmay
Cleveland Museum, Ohio, U.S.A.

8. PORTRAIT ASCRIBED TO GHAERAEDTS
Private Collection, U.S.A.

The Dutch painter Antonio Moro (1512-1576) came to England in 1553 to paint for Philip II the celebrated portrait of Queen Mary.

A Flemish or Dutch painter who signed with a monogram *HE* was at work in England from 1545 or thereabouts to 1573. His name is shown by records to have been HANS EWORTS or Eworth or Ewotter. His monogram occurs not only on portraits but also on a picture called *Queen Elizabeth and the Goddesses*. In this curious picture, the Queen is seen with Juno, Minerva and Venus who are represented as thunderstruck by her beauty and majesty; Juno to express her sentiments throws down her sceptre; Minerva is *bouche béante*; Venus, with Cupid in attendance, throws down her roses, symbol of her own power; Windsor Castle figures in the background. On the frame we read:

> *Juno potens sceptris et mentis acumine Pallas*
> *Et roseo Veneris fulget in ore decus;*
> *Adfuit Elizabeth: Juno perculsa refugit;*
> *Obstupuit Pallas erubuitque Venus.*

A number of portraits—in addition to those which bear his monogram—are now ascribed to Eworts by antiquaries. The general student must remember that these ascriptions are supposition. In his early work this artist seems to have imitated Moro. In his later work, in the reign of Queen Elizabeth, he may have been influenced by the Holbein tradition which then came back into fashion.

For Elizabeth (1558-1603) had pronounced views on portrait painting and tried to set the clock back to the Holbein-Gothic style. The essence of that formula, as the Queen saw it, was the absence of dark shadows in the face. In the age of Tintoretto and El Greco, the Carracci, Caravaggio and Rubens, the Queen objected to the new-fangled use of shadows, and she made this plain to the portrait painters of her Court.

In particular she made it plain to the miniature painters who had Court patronage—the Englishman Nicholas Hilliard and his pupil Isaac Oliver.

NICHOLAS HILLIARD (1537-1619) was an artist of skill and spirit who felt a decided urge to use shadows for the suggestion of relief. But the Queen, as Hilliard himself tells us, gave him a lecture on the subject and completely converted him. The Italians she said who 'had the name to be cunningest and to drawe best shadowed not'—which shows that her attitude to Italian painting was much behind the times. The best light for a portrait, she told him, was the open air—where presumably she thought she looked her best. And she took him for the sitting to 'the open ally of a goodly garden where no tree was neere nor any shadowe at all, save that as the heaven is lighter than the earthe soe must that littel shadowe that was from the earthe'. Hilliard was amazed at the Queen's intelligence: 'This Her Majestie's curiouse demand', he wrote afterwards, 'hath greatly bettered my jugment, besids divers other like questions in art by her most excelent Majestie, which to speak or writ of weare fitter for a better clarke.' And he then lays it down that—as the Queen doubtless also suggested—dark shadows in a portrait indicate that some blemish in the sitter must be covered up or else that the painter's eyesight was so bad that he could not 'diserne his shadowes, except they weare grosse' or else that he had worked in a bad light 'to high or to lowe or to littel'.

ISAAC OLIVER (1556-1617) was a Frenchman, who is presumed to have been brought to England as a Huguenot refugee in 1562. He continued the Hilliard tradition in miniatures and seems to have avoided shadows when painting members of the Court. His miniatures are heads and occasionally full-length figures. I reproduce his portrait of *Sir Anthony Mildmay* (Pl. 7) which measures $9\frac{1}{4} \times 6\frac{7}{8}$ inches and is painted in a scheme of blue, ivory, and grey. The sitter was connected with Queen Elizabeth's Court from his childhood; he began his career by reciting, as a child, a poem of welcome on one of her Progresses, and was rewarded by an official statement that the Queen was 'pleased graciously to commend its expression and felicitous delivery'; in 1596 he was appointed ambassador to Henri IV and was then knighted—this picture being subsequent to the knighthood. Another large miniature by Isaac Oliver represents three gentlemen named Browne with their servant, all full length. In his later work he seems to have shadowed with some vigour. He had a son Peter Oliver (1601-1660) who also painted miniatures.

Though Queen Elizabeth's taste in pictorial art was *arriéré*, and she showed no sympathy with the creative painting of her age, she was not a woman without taste. She had quite evidently aesthetic feeling which betrayed itself in her passion for embroidered clothes. She liked floral patterns on a light ground; and the lovely Elizabethan embroideries can doubtless be ascribed to her influence in this field. This had its effect on the paintings of the period. Many of the portraits produced in her reign acquired a certain decorative charm from the beauty of the elaborately embroidered dresses copied with infinite patience by studio hacks. This seems to have continued into the reign of James I (1603-1625), because Elizabeth left so many expensive dresses when she died that James is said to have ordered his own Queen to wear them out, and it was thus correct for some time at his Court to appear in the fashions of the previous reign (Pl. 8).

A good many Elizabethan and Jacobean portraits survive. They are for the most part neat and archaistic in execution, in no sense contributions to the creative spirit of the moment which produced Caravaggio, Rubens and Franz Hals. In most cases it is not known who painted them. Foreign portrait painters who had reputations in England at this time included Marc Ghaeraedts, Paul Van Somer, and John de Critz; the English painters included Robert Peake and an amateur named Sir Nathaniel Bacon. I add, for the curious, some notes about these and other practitioners of the period in Appendix III.[1]

When we get to the reign of Charles I (1625-1649) we find Rubens here in 1629, and Van Dyck in 1620 and again from 1635 to 1641. Other foreign artists patronised were Daniel Mytens and Gerard Honthorst.

[1]Cf. pp. 269, 270.

Charles I as everyone knows was a collector of old pictures. But he was not only a collector; he was also alive to the genius of Rubens and the brilliant talents of Van Dyck. He was twenty-one, and still Prince, when Van Dyck paid his first visit. Van Dyck was also twenty-one and had just finished his training with Rubens. As Van Dyck remained here only for a short time and then went to Italy, Charles had to content himself with Mytens and Honthorst. Mytens was a native of The Hague who had come to England some years earlier. Charles sat to him in 1623, gave him a house and garden in St. Martin's Lane, and on his accession made him his 'Picture-drawer' for life with an annual allowance. Charles invited Honthorst to England in 1628, paid him handsomely for portraits of himself and Queen Henrietta Maria, and granted him a pension—though he was only in England for six months.[1]

Rubens came to England in 1629 not as artist but as diplomatic envoy to negotiate peace between England and Spain. This and Rubens' other activities in diplomacy are so well known that we almost forget how strange it was, on the one hand, that the most powerful sovereigns of the moment should have employed an artist in such negotiations, and on the other that Rubens, who was then over fifty and at the height of his powers, with a studio in Antwerp full of commissions, should have absented himself for months at a time in such a capacity in Spain and England. For the legend that he only 'played at diplomacy' is quite untrue. He took the mission which brought him to England most seriously, and his letters show that he not only attended to business but succeeded in spite of Spanish procrastinations in achieving a result. I have already quoted from his impressions of England.[2] Another letter written on this English visit shows that he could see beneath the social surface and scent trouble ahead: 'The greatest lords lead a sumptuous life and spend enormously, so that most of them are heavily in debt. . . . The . . . lords and ministers . . . for the most part, have insufficient revenues to support their rank, and are obliged to fulfil

[1]Cf. Appendix III, p. 271.　　　　　　　　　　[2]Cf. above, p. 31.

their needs as best they can, and that is why both private and public interests are sold here for cash down.'[1]

Rubens was received by the King the day after his arrival and cordial relations were soon established. Before he left nine months later he had been commissioned to decorate the ceiling of the banqueting room at Whitehall (eventually completed from his sketches by his pupils in 1635), and he had painted for the King and given him as a souvenir of the occasion of their acquaintance *War and Peace* and *St. George*, where Charles is depicted as the valiant saint.

These pictures painted in England by a living artist must have had a staggering effect. The English Court had been prepared for the pageant aspect of the pictures by the Masques designed by Inigo Jones (1573-1652), which in turn had precedent in the pageants arranged for Queen Elizabeth on her Progresses. But they were not prepared to see the art of Titian and Veronese carried to a climax by a living man; nor were they prepared for the open landscape in the *St. George* with its views of the Thames and Richmond Castle in the background. Rubens had set a standard which made all the painters working in England seem little more than pigmies.

And indeed, compared with Rubens, very minor painters they all veritably were—foreigners and Englishmen alike—till Van Dyck returned. I have already mentioned some of the foreign portrait painters. The Englishmen were John Hoskins (1600?-1665?) a miniature painter to whom Charles sat; Cornelius Johnson (1593-*c.* 1664) who painted both James I and Charles; and some others to whom hardly any works can be with certainty ascribed. Here again, the curious will find some notes in Appendix III.[2]

When Van Dyck returned to England in 1632, at the height of his powers, all the small fry were undone. Johnson went into the country to paint portraits of local gentry, who knew nothing of Van Dyck, and he eventually retired to Holland. Mytens

[1]From 'Sir Peter-Paul Rubens' by Anthony Bertram (Davies, 1928).
[2]Cf. pp. 269-273.

immediately offered Charles the resignation of his post as
'Picture-drawer to the King for life'; Charles, unwilling to hurt
his feelings, urged him to retain the post, and Mytens supported
the ordeal for several years; but then he, like Johnson, went to
Holland and worked there for the remainder of his life.

This was inevitable. Van Dyck carried all the guns for great
success in this environment. He was a real creative artist, with
the moral power to impose his will upon his sitters, and an engaging personality that disguised his will. He was never the servant
of his patrons; he made them the servants of his art. The elegance
of Charles I's Court, and the brilliant entertainments in private
houses, which Rubens describes with astonishment, were there
to provide Van Dyck with material for his paintings. At this
Court, which was so soon to vanish, there was a real interest in
decorative effect; Charles loved the arts; and the love of art was
therefore fashionable. Queen Henrietta's eyebrow was a jet
black line on an ivory face, and her hair was disposed in oiled
geometric ringlets; she made her face a decorative pattern and
the Court ladies followed her lead. Van Dyck set out to exploit
this material and he was still exploiting it superbly when he died
nine years later, in 1641. He had established in England not only
a standard of sumptuous decorative portraiture but also a standard of sumptuous living for the fashionable portrait painter.
He had a magnificent studio, a collection of Old Masters,
numerous pupils and assistants. He entertained handsomely and
gave his sitters the minimum of trouble. He asked them, I fancy,
for only two or three short sittings for the head; and a month
later the full-length picture was sent home—everything but the
head having been painted from studio models by pupil-assistants
working under his direction.[1]

One of his pupil-assistants, an Englishman, and a gentleman
by birth, named WILLIAM DOBSON (1610-1646), aspired to
the position which he vacated. Dobson was taken up by the
King (who made him Serjeant Painter and sat to him) and
he obtained a good many commissions for portraits which he

[1]Cf. below, pp. 103-107, 139, 140.

painted 'in the manner' of Van Dyck. He seems to have imitated Van Dyck's extravagance, and to have lived for a while in state. But times were changed. The Civil War had begun. And Dobson was not Van Dyck. He became involved in financial difficulties, was imprisoned for debt, and died at the age of thirty-six. Few pictures certainly by his hand survive. A signed work, *Henry Mordaunt, 2nd Earl of Peterborough*, represents the earl about to don armour supplied to him by an angel. The portraits of *Sir Richard Fanshawe*, *Thomas Simon*, and *Sir William Farmor* may show him at his best.

ROBERT WALKER (*c.* 1600-1658), another imitator of Van Dyck, painted the well-known picture *Oliver Cromwell with his Squire*. In this limp work the Protector is fitted into a Van Dyck studio posture and the face is flattered.

Cromwell was also painted by SAMUEL COOPER (1609?-1672) who had been the leading miniature painter since about 1642. Cooper was a nephew of the miniature painter Hoskins and he seems to have worked as assistant to his uncle till that date. His miniature portrait of Cromwell, reproducing the celebrated warts, gives us some idea of a face which, like that of the late Lord Oxford and Asquith, no artist except Rembrandt could have mastered. Rembrandt was at the height of his power during the Commonwealth; and we can set Walker and Cooper in the rank where they belong when we imagine what the painter of *Jan Six* (1654), the Ross *Man's Portrait* (1655) and the Frick *Self-portrait* (1658) might have left us as a record of Oliver Cromwell's head.[1]

JOHN HAYLS or Hales or Hailes or Jan Hals (1600?-1679) was another portrait painter in England from the later years of the Commonwealth onwards. He is known to have been a pupil of the Hague portrait painter Miereveldt (1567-1641) and I guess that he was a Dutchman, perhaps of the family of Franz Hals. We know nothing about his life except that he visited Italy, that he painted Pepys and Mrs. Pepys and Pepys' father, and that he died of heart failure at his home in Long Acre

[1]But cf. below, p. 107.

'coming from the necessary house drest in a velvet suit for the Lord Mayor's feast' in 1679.

The only picture that can be with any certainty ascribed to him is the portrait of Pepys. The portraits of the diarist's wife and father have disappeared. The Pepys portrait which is in the National Portrait Gallery, London, shows that the artist had been impressed by Rembrandt's 'shadowing'; but it does not suggest that he had any notable powers. Here are some of Pepys' diary entries for 1666, the year in which these portraits were painted:

'February 15: Mr. Hales begun my wife's portrait in the posture we saw one of my Lady Peters, like a St. Catherine. While he painted, Knipp and Mercer and I sang.

'March 3: To Hales's, and there saw my wife sit; and I do like her picture mightily and very like it will be, and a brave piece of work; but he do complain that her nose hath cost him as much work as another's face, and he hath done it finely indeed.

'March 17: This day I began to sit and he will make me, I think, a very fine picture. He promises it shall be as good as my wife's, and I to sit to have it full of shadows, and do almost break my neck looking over my shoulder to make the posture for him to work by. Home, having a great cold; so to bed, drinking butter ale.

'March 24: I had occasion to follow the Duke into his lodgings, into a chamber where the Duchess was sitting to have her picture drawn by Lilly who was then at work. But I was well pleased to see that there was nothing near so much resemblance of her face in his work, which is now the second, if not the third time, as there was of my wife's at the very first time. Nor do I think at last it can be like, the lines not being in proportion to those of her face.

'March 30: Up, and away goes Alce, our cook-maid, whom we loved and did well by her, and she an excellent servant, but would not bear being told of any fault in the fewest and kindest words, and would go away of her own accord, after having given her mistress warning fickly. . . . To Hales's and there sat till almost quite dark upon working my gowne, which I hired to be drawn in; an Indian gowne.

'April 11: To Hales's, where there was nothing found to be done more to my picture, but the musique, which now pleases me mightily, it being painted true.

'March 25, 1667: Called at Mr. Lilly's who was working; and indeed his pictures are without doubt much beyond Mr. Hales's, I think I may say I am convinced: but a mighty proud man he is, and full of state.'

'Lilly' was, of course, the Dutchman Peter Lely (1618-1680) who had arrived in England the year that Van Dyck died, and scattered all the small fry to odd corners as Van Dyck had done before. He had painted the Duke of York for Charles I soon after his arrival in 1641; he had continued to paint portraits all through the Commonwealth; and he became Court painter without a rival at the Restoration. His methods were those of Van Dyck. He had a magnificent studio, a collection of Old Masters (he had been a buyer when Charles I's collection was dispersed), a staff of pupil-assistants, and the same arrangements for the convenience of his sitters. Lely's talents were not equal to Van Dyck's. He was more superficial and he had less facility; his eye was not so sure and his hand was not so wonderfully swift; and he had not worked, as Van Dyck worked, in the studio of Rubens. But at his best he was an adventurous and personal colourist, a brilliant manufacturer of decorative portraits, able to make women look luxurious and voluptuous without silly naughtiness, and able to make men look capable without brutality. He knew how to impose his will upon his sitters and he held Van Dyck's position, as he deserved to, till he died.

James II (1685-1689) at first extended his patronage to an English painter JOHN RILEY (1646-1691) who had been taken up by Charles II and then dropped, because Charles when he saw the portrait which Riley produced of him exclaimed: 'Odds fish then I am an ugly fellow!' which suggests that the portrait was too like. That indeed must have been a difficulty for all painters of Charles II. Nobody could have produced a likeness of Cromwell except Rembrandt; but nobody could have avoided catching a likeness of Charles II; the task was how to steer clear of too resembling a record of this striking face. Riley had sensibility, honesty, and a good eye. He was evidently fascinated by the type of face which seems to register a satisfied weariness after long sensual indulgences and disillusionment without bitterness; in his *John Maitland, 1st Duke of Lauderdale*, where, as in the case of the King, he was confronted with a subject of this kind, he has left us a most faithful and sympathetic record; and we have only to compare with it the portrait of the same sitter by an obscure painter of the period, named Edmund Ashfield, to realise how completely Riley here imposed his will; but we can hardly doubt that the Duke was no more pleased with the picture than Charles was with his. When Riley had his second chance at James II's Court he was destined to fare no better. His *John Maitland, 1st Duke of Lauderdale*, shows that he could dominate his sitter when he stood at his easel, but contemporary accounts make it clear that he was a shy neurotic who could not stand up to them in business or social intercourse; one of his pupils tells us that business interviews with his patrons reduced him to a condition that we should call 'a state of nerves'; and, unlike Hayls and Lely, he would never work with any visitor or even a pupil in the room.

Such a man was destined to go down before a pretentious German called Gottfried Kneller, who arrived in England about 1674, determined to rival the careers of Van Dyck and Lely and to be knighted, as they were.

Kneller (1646-1723) had neglected no preliminary stages for the enterprise. On his arrival he posed as a cosmopolitan celebrity and talked of his student days in Amsterdam under Bol (one of the most successful of Rembrandt's pupils)—which was calculated to impress those who remembered that Lely had been trained in Holland. He also said that he had looked in for a while at the studio of Rembrandt (who was not admired in England at that time) and he spoke of him with scorn as of a man in whose works 'true proportion and exact design were wanting'.

Then he vaunted studies in Rome (where Carlo Maratti was then the approved master), in Naples, and in Venice; and he talked of the distinguished Venetian families whose members he had painted—which was calculated to impress those who remembered that Van Dyck had painted all the Genoese patricians before he established himself in England. He had—if the story be true—the effrontery to challenge Lely to a contest to paint a head of James II as Duke of York against him; and Lely, who was then sixty, is said to have generously submitted to the contest and applauded his young rival's picture.

The portraits turned out in the mass-production factory which Kneller soon established were the expression of his intentions. The Van Dyck-Lely tradition was, of course, observed. Kneller arranged the maximum of impressive luxury in his studio, he collected Old Masters, and he had an unprecedented army of assistants, mainly German, each charged with some particular function—drapery, lace, hands, etc. His sitters, who are said to have sometimes numbered as many as fourteen in one day, were put to the minimum of trouble and only asked to sit for chalk drawings for their faces—which was reassuring to those who had suffered like Pepys from painters who required them to 'keep the posture' in long sittings.

The material success which Kneller had determined to capture was won by the beginning of James II's reign; and it continued, ever growing, through the reigns of William and Mary (1689-1702), Queen Anne (1702-1714), and into the Georgian age. He achieved his knighthood in 1692, became richer and richer, built the country mansion at Whitton near Hounslow which is now the training school for British Army bandsmen, kept troops of liveried servants, and drove between his town house in Lincoln's Inn Fields and Hounslow in a coach-and-six. He died in the year in which Reynolds was born, when Hogarth was twenty-six.

This date, 1723, marks the end of the domination of foreign artists in England which had persisted from Holbein's success at the Court of Henry VIII. Kneller's triumphs were undeserved.

But Holbein, in his environment, was obviously irresistible; and both Van Dyck and Lely won and held their positions by their merits.

Nothing can be gained by attempting to disguise the low average level of the works which the imitators of these brilliant invaders produced. Mr. Collins Baker in the opening chapter of his well-known book, 'Lely and the Stuart Portrait Painters', praises the minor seventeenth-century painters for using a stereotyped technique and then says: 'It must be a common experience for those who have seen large private galleries of English portraiture to notice how flimsy and how clumsy even the most brilliant of our modern portrait painters appear in comparison with good examples of the lesser seventeenth-century artists.' This experience has not been mine. I know no portrait by any of the lesser seventeenth-century artists in England which would make *The Smiling Woman* (Pl. 9), by Augustus John, seem flimsy and uncertain.

For the curious I add some further notes, in Appendix III, on these lesser painters of Stuart times.[1] The general student need not concern himself with their productions. For him, as I have said, English painting really begins with Hogarth, to whose life and achievements we now turn.

[1]Cf. Appendix III, pp. 269-273.

9. AUGUSTUS JOHN
The Smiling Woman
National Gallery, Millbank, London

10. WILLIAM HOGARTH
The Price Family
Metropolitan Museum, New York

CHAPTER IV

HOGARTH
1697-1764

★

1. HOGARTH'S LIFE

WILLIAM HOGARTH was born in London, the son of a schoolmaster who had come South from Westmoreland. We have a glimpse of his childhood in his own words: 'As I had naturally a good eye and a fondness for drawing, *shows* of all sorts gave me uncommon pleasure when an infant; and mimicry, common to all children, was remarkable in me. An early access to a neighbouring painter drew my attention from play; and I was, at every possible opportunity, employed in making drawings. I picked up an acquaintance of the same turn, and soon learnt to draw the alphabet with great correctness. My exercises when at school were more remarkable for the ornaments which adorned them than for the exercise itself. In the former, I soon found that blockheads with better memories could much surpass me; but for the latter I was particularly distinguished.'[1]

At the age of fifteen he was apprenticed to a silver-plate engraver from whom he learned to engrave tankards and so forth with heraldic designs and decorative motifs in the French *rocaille*, *grotesque* and *arabesque* traditions.[2] He then learned to engrave on copper and began to design bookplates, showcards

[1]Hogarth at his death left notes for an autobiography which came into the possession of one John Ireland at the end of the eighteenth century and were assembled and published by him. This autobiography, with some miscellaneous writings by Hogarth, was printed in 'Anecdotes of William Hogarth' by J. B. Nicholls (1833). Hogarth's 'Analysis of Beauty' was published in his lifetime.

[2]Cf. my 'French Painting' (Medici, 1931), notes, pp. 110 and 122.

and illustrations for books. In 1720, at the age of twenty-three, he started work as an independent engraver and illustrator for the booksellers, producing notably two sets of illustrations to Butler's *Hudibras*. He maintained himself in this way, and by some satirical prints of no particular importance, for some seven or eight years. When he could spare the time he worked in an 'academy' conducted by SIR JAMES THORNHILL (1676-1734) a decorative painter in the Italian baroque tradition who painted the cupola of St. Paul's Cathedral, altarpieces for several Oxford colleges, and ceilings at Greenwich Hospital and Blenheim Palace. In this academy—or, as we should say, life-class—which Hogarth later conducted himself, he soon acquired facility in oil painting. By the age of thirty he had painted a number of oil pictures including several scenes from *The Beggar's Opera*. Then at thirty-two he ran away with Thornhill's daughter and married her.

There is a tradition that Thornhill at first objected to the marriage and relented on seeing *A Harlot's Progress*. If there was a breach, it was soon closed, and Hogarth was employed the year after his marriage in assisting his father-in-law in decorative commissions. At the same time he started to make money by painting portrait heads and small portrait groups which established the tradition of the Conversation Portrait Group in English art.

He was not however temperamentally equipped to be a portrait painter; and his attempt to maintain his home in this way soon proved itself a failure. 'As I could not bring myself to act like some of my brethren', he wrote later, 'and make it a sort of manufactory, to be carried on by the help of background and drapery painters, it was not sufficiently profitable to pay the expences my family required. I therefore turned my thoughts to painting and engraving modern moral subjects, a field not broken up in any country or any age.'

A Harlot's Progress was the first of these 'modern moral subjects' by means of which he now set out to make money. He painted the six pictures in 1731; he engraved them and published the prints in 1732. These prints were a great success. There were several pirated editions and the story was made into a Ballad Opera and into a Pantomime Entertainment performed at Drury Lane.

As a result, Hogarth established himself in the fashionable Leicester Fields, and, as often done at the time, he hung a Golden Head outside his door to indicate his profession as artist. The sign in his case was a head of Van Dyck which he had made out of cork. In a moment of disappointment, later, he took it down. But for some time he enjoyed good fortune and he was always able to maintain this house in London and eventually a country house at Chiswick as well.

A Harlot's Progress was followed by a series of engraved pictures commenting on contemporary social life. These included *Southwark Fair* (1733), *Strolling Actresses in a Barn* (1738), *The Four Times of the Day* (1738), and the series known as *A Rake's Progress* (1735).

Meanwhile he tried his hand at 'history painting' and produced two large mural compositions, *The Pool of Bethesda* and *The Good Samaritan*, which he presented to St. Bartholomew's Hospital in 1736 in order, he tells us, 'to show that were there an inclination in England for encouraging historical pictures, such a first essay might prove the painting them more easily attainable than is generally imagined'. Then in 1739 he challenged the leading portrait painters of the day with the full-length life-size portrait *Captain Coram* (Pl. 69b). The sitter was the founder of the Foundling Hospital, and the artist presented the portrait to the Charity.

The dilettanti and connoisseurs of the day refused to recognise Hogarth as either a 'history painter' or a portrait painter of account. They laughed at his panels in St. Bartholomew's Hospital and saw no merit in his *Captain Coram*. He in his turn was never weary of abusing the gentlemen who pretended to connoisseurship on the strength of a tour in Italy, and the art dealers who battened upon them.[1] There was a continuous feud be-

[1]Cf. above, pp. 31-33, and below, pp. 69-75.

tween him and these groups of *soi-disant* art-lovers. As a result he always had difficulty in selling his paintings (though the prints from his 'modern moral subjects' always provided him with the necessities of life). Thus it came that in 1745 his studio still contained the original paintings of *A Harlot's Progress*, *A Rake's Progress*, *Strolling Actresses in a Barn* and *The Four Times of the Day*; and he determined to sell them personally by auction. The conditions of the sale were singular and of his own invention; the bidders were to register their names and addresses, and their bids, and to receive a ticket in exchange; at the stated time the pictures were to be deemed sold to the ticket with the highest bid. This procedure was successful. He sold all the pictures and made the equivalent of something over £2500 in present money.[1]

The series of engraved pictures called *Marriage A-la-Mode* was published soon after this sale in 1745, and in the following year he painted *Garrick as Richard III* and *Simon Fraser Lord Lovat*. The latter was the result of an interview at St. Albans where Lovat was in captivity and on his journey to the gallows. From the drawing then produced Hogarth painted his picture, and he also made an etching which was sold at a shilling and brought him for some time £12 a week—the equivalent of perhaps £60 a week in present money.[2]

[1] The actual sum realised was £427 made up of £273 for the two 'Progresses' and the balance for the others. This total is habitually described by Hogarth's biographers as dramatically small. But the changed value of money must be borne in mind. The £184 made by *A Rake's Progress*, for example, must be thought of as the equivalent of something in the region of £1000 in present money.

[2] The explanation of this success is that Lovat was very much 'in the news' at the moment. The story of his life was then on every man's tongue; his early adventures in the Highlands when he tried to become Laird of the Frasers by audacity and force; his reputed outrage on the Dowager Lady Lovat; his intrigues with the Court at St. Germain; his treacheries and long exile followed by his reign as tyrant of the Frasers; and the final collapse of his fortunes in the 1745 Rebellion when he was guilty of the basest treachery to both sides and to his own son—all this was being told and retold with a hundred embellishments on every hand when Hogarth published his print exhibiting to the curious—in the only way possible before photography—the physical features of this villain of the hour.

11a. WILLIAM HOGARTH
Family Group
National Gallery, London

11b. JOSEPH HIGHMORE
Mr. B. finds Pamela writing
National Gallery, Millbank, London

12a. BENJAMIN WILSON
Portrait in an Interior
Private Collection, U.S.A.

12b. HENRY TONKS
Evening in the Vale
National Gallery, Millbank, London

Between 1747 and 1751 he produced the series of prints called *Industry and Idleness* and also *Gin Lane, Beer Street* and *The Four Stages of Cruelty*, which were sold at low prices to place them within reach of the people to whom they were specifically addressed as 'moralities'; and he painted two 'history pictures'—*Paul before Felix* for Lincoln's Inn and *Moses brought to Pharaoh's Daughter* for the Foundling Hospital. The picture known as *Calais Gate: The Roast Beef of Old England* was the result of a visit to France in 1749.

After 1750 the tide of his fortunes began to turn. In that year he painted an episode of the 1745 Rebellion showing the Guards concentrating at Finchley for the march to Scotland—commonly called *The March to Finchley*. This is a scene of disorder where some of the soldiers are shown taking leave of women, drinking, and so forth. Hogarth had the singular notion of wishing to dedicate the print of this picture to the King. George II, who took no interest in the arts, was very naturally offended at the proposal to inscribe his name beneath such a representation of his soldiers in a recent campaign; he refused permission for the dedication, and is reported to have said: 'What! a painter burlesque a soldier? He deserves to be picketed for his insolence, Take his trumpery out of my sight.' After this first error of tact the artist made a second; when the engraving appeared it was found to be dedicated to the King of Prussia 'an encourager of Arts and Sciences'.

In 1751 he decided to sell the oil paintings of *Marriage A-la-Mode* by another auction in his studio. He advertised the conditions as before, adding that no picture dealers would be permitted to bid. The time fixed for reception of the last written offer was noon on the specified date. Shortly before the hour a Mr. Lane of Hillingdon—who lives in history from the circumstance—appeared in Hogarth's studio and found no one there but the artist and a friend. He was informed that the highest bid received was £120 and he immediately bid a hundred and twenty guineas, offering at the same time a delay of an hour or so in case further bidders might put in an appearance. An hour later, no one having appeared, Hogarth turned to him and said, 'If you are satisfied with the purchase, I am abundantly so with the purchaser'; and the six pictures became Lane's property for £126, including the frames which had cost £25. Even allowing for the difference in the value of money between Hogarth's day and our own (which would make the sum for the actual pictures at least £500), there can be no doubt that the artist had ground for disappointment—especially as *A Rake's Progress* had been sold for nearly twice the sum. And in fact he was bitterly chagrined. He restrained his disappointment in farewell words of courtesy to the purchaser, whose own courtesy had been faultless. But when the door was closed he rose into passionate rage against the public and the connoisseurs who had failed to respond to the auction; and the next morning, as a gesture, he took down the Golden Head that had hung as his artist's sign for nearly twenty years outside his house.

Six years earlier he had painted his own portrait with his favourite dog. In the foreground of this picture he had placed a palette with a serpentine line drawn upon it and the words, 'The Line of Beauty and Grace' written beneath. When he published a print from this picture he was frequently asked to explain the significance of this detail, but had always refused to do so. In 1753 he provided the explanation by publishing a book called 'The Analysis of Beauty' written and illustrated by himself; I refer to the argument of this most interesting essay in Appendix IV.[1] Here I need only note that although it was seriously discussed by Lessing in the 'Vossische Zeitung' in 1754, by Burke in 'The Sublime and the Beautiful' in 1756, by Goethe in 'Der Sammler und die Seinigen', and by Sterne and Bishop Warburton—it was received with contempt by the small fry of the art world at the time. The connoisseurs and the little artists, who were jealous of Hogarth's originality and independence of thought, greeted it with insolent derision. Hogarth, they said, was completely ignorant in the field of art properly so called and completely without letters; some pointed with delight to spell-

[1]Cf. below, pp. 274-279.

13. WILLIAM HOGARTH
William James
Worcester Museum, Mass., U.S.A.

14. WILLIAM HOGARTH
A Rake's Progress. Scene 3.

ing mistakes in the text; others said that the book was not really his own work; and he was told to stick to his popular satires, where ugliness abounded, and leave questions of 'Beauty' to cultured people who knew all about it. Paul Sandby, a topographical draughtsman to whom I refer later,[1] was among the most contemptible of these detractors; in addition to written attacks he produced an etching called *The Author run Mad* showing Hogarth in a lunatic asylum, with a mahlstick in the shape of 'The Line of Beauty', an ink bottle on his head, and straws in his hair. Hogarth at once set out to defy these attacks which he accurately described as the 'buzzing' of a 'cloud of insects'. He decided to produce no more prints of social subjects and to devote himself instead to 'history painting' and to portraiture and thus force his detractors to acknowledge his power in the fields which they suggested were outside his comprehension.

In 1756, accordingly, he painted a series of pictures of religious subjects for St. Mary Redcliffe in Bristol. Then, at the beginning of 1757 he made a public announcement of his return to portrait painting and he soon obtained a number of commissions. But this second attempt at a career as a portrait painter was no more successful than the first. He was now sixty and even less disposed than formerly to subordinate his will to his sitters and turn his studio into a portrait factory. He had now moreover against him the competition of young Joshua Reynolds who had returned from Italy in 1752 and had immediately impressed his powers upon the fashionable world.

With the failure of his second attempt at the career of a portrait painter he entered upon the last period of his life when he suffered further disappointments and encountered still more venomous hostilities.

In 1758 he was commissioned by Lord Charlemont to paint a picture. The patron left both the choice of subject and the price to the artist's discretion. Hogarth painted the picture known as *The Lady's last Stake*, showing a young and virtuous married lady, who, by playing at cards with an officer, loses her

[1]Cf. p. 179.

money, watch and jewels, and is wondering whether it might not be well to take the officer as her lover—he having offered to return her property if this were done. Lord Charlemont was delighted with the picture, and one of his friends, Sir Richard Grosvenor, who saw it, gave the artist a second commission on the same terms. But this time the result was different. A picture ascribed to Correggio representing *Boccaccio's Sigismonda weeping over the Heart of her murdered Lover* had recently been sold in London for £400 (say £2000 in present money). Hogarth doubtless regarded it as a worthless picture (the attribution to Correggio was later admitted to be false) and he took the opportunity of the commission to try and demonstrate that he, a living artist, could paint a finer picture of the same subject. The gesture was admirable and Hogarth might well have produced something of more value than a third-rate painting in the manner of Correggio—if he had painted it uninfluenced by Italian pictures. But unfortunately he tried to imitate the art which he was challenging; and thus brought himself down to the level of other imitators. The picture done, he informed Sir Richard Grosvenor that the price must be the same as the so-called 'Correggio' of the same subject, i.e. £400 (though he had only asked Lord Charlemont £100 for *The Lady's last Stake*) and he invited him to come and see his challenge to the 'black masters'. Sir Richard was dismayed by the price and still more dismayed when he saw the picture. He had hoped doubtless that Hogarth would have painted for him the solution to the situation depicted in *The Lady's last Stake* and he had doubtless expected a companion picture called *Virtue triumphant* or *Insult punished*. He and his friends may even have registered bets at the club on the painter's probable solution of the lady's dilemma. But what he saw in Hogarth's studio was a dull and pretentious picture 'in the Italian manner' representing a subject which, as he truly remarked, 'would be too often occasioning melancholy ideas to arise in one's mind'. When Hogarth offered to release him from the bargain he thankfully accepted and retired. But Hogarth was enraged. He exhibited the picture in the hope of

15a. WILLIAM HOGARTH
A Harlot's Progress. Scene 1—Engraving

15b. WILLIAM HOGARTH
A Harlot's Progress. Scene 2—Engraving

16a. WILLIAM HOGARTH
A Harlot's Progress. Scene 4—Engraving

16b. WILLIAM HOGARTH
A Rake's Progress. Scene 8—Engraving

establishing its merits. But he only met with more rebuffs. The connoisseurs fell upon it. Horace Walpole described it as 'the representation of a maudlin strumpet just turned out of keeping, and, with eyes red with rage and usquebaugh, tearing off the ornaments her keeper had given her'—a passage of astounding bad taste from a man who knew that the model for Sigismonda was said to be the artist's harmless and respectable wife. The failure of the *Sigismonda* was complete. Hogarth was never able to sell it and when he died three years later it was still in his studio.

There was nothing for it but the production of more prints appealing to the public at large. Unfortunately, Hogarth tells us, it was a moment 'when war abroad and contention at home engrossed everyone's mind' so that the print market was in a state of 'stagnation'. He tried accordingly to force the pace, as it were, in order to attract attention, and he published first a religious satire called *Credulity, Superstition and Fanaticism* and then a topical political satire called *The Times* attacking the warmongers of the moment, Pitt, Temple, Wilkes (then editing 'The North Briton') and Churchill the henchman of Wilkes. Hogarth had known Wilkes for many years. The two men may have met in connection with the Foundling Hospital of which Hogarth was a Governor and Wilkes was at one time the Treasurer. J. T. Smith tells us that both Wilkes and Churchill at one period were the artist's boon companions; and Hogarth afterwards spoke of Wilkes as 'till then rather my friend and flatterer'. When Wilkes heard that Hogarth was about to attack him, he sent mutual friends to remonstrate and point out that 'such a proceeding would not only be unfriendly in the highest degree but extremely injudicious'; that Hogarth's pencil ought as heretofore to be 'universal and moral, to speak to all ages and all nations, not to be dipped in the dirt of the faction of a day, of an insignificant part of the country, when it might command the admiration of the whole'. Hogarth replied that neither Wilkes nor Churchill were attacked in his print though Pitt and Temple were. This was scarcely accurate because parcels of 'The

North Briton' are represented as fuel for the Fire of War in Hogarth's design. Wilkes then sent a further remonstrance and warning. He would not think it worth while, he said, to take notice of any reflections on himself, but when his friends were attacked he 'found himself wounded in the most sensible part'; if the print appeared he would immediately take retaliatory steps in 'The North Briton'. And in fact as soon as the print was published Wilkes and Churchill attacked the artist with fury. They described him as bought by Bute; as a miserable, vain, weak creature, jealous of the Old Masters, who left 'his own peculiar walk of humour to paint history pictures and portraits which were considered as almost beneath all criticism'; he was a painter, Wilkes wrote, incapable of 'a single idea of beauty, grace or elegance', a painter whose *Sigismonda* represented nothing ever seen on earth but his own wife in an agony of passion —'but of what passion no connoisseur could guess'; a man for whom avarice and vanity had been the guiding principles through life. Wilkes repented later of these attacks and excused himself by saying that he was drunk when he wrote them. But Hogarth, who was now very ill, was not willing to accept this excuse. He replied with caricature-prints of Wilkes and Churchill. 'The pleasure, and pecuniary advantage,' he tells us, 'which I derived from these two engravings, together with occasional riding on horseback, restored me to as much health as can be expected at my time of life.' But he was actually sixty-seven and his illness was more serious than he knew. In October 1764 he left his country house at Chiswick for his house in Leicester Fields, and there, soon after his arrival, he died suddenly from the bursting of an aneurism.[1]

His last autobiographical note reads as follows: 'Thus have I gone through the principal circumstances of a life, which, till lately, past pretty much to my own satisfaction, and, I hope, in no respect injurious to any other man. This I can safely assert, I

[1]Churchill who was brutally attacking him to the last moment, and had referred to him contemptuously as already a dead man, himself died a few days later.

have invariably endeavoured to make those about me tolerably happy, and my greatest enemy cannot say I ever did an intentional injury; though without ostentation, I could produce many instances of men that have been essentially benefited by me. What may follow, God knows.'

2. HOGARTH'S CHARACTER

HOGARTH was a fine upstanding outspoken fellow in a society which poured gold into the lap of Kneller. He was also a fine upstanding outspoken fellow in a city which was still the London of Ned Ward.[1] At the same time he was a man of sensibility, much affected by the coarse blows aimed at him at various times; a man with a deep hatred of cruelty; a man of considerable intelligence, not without letters, capable of theoretic thought, who made disastrous blunders deriving from a complex that was almost an obsession.

His lifelong war against the rich dilettanti and the past-loving connoisseurs had roots in a desire to be applauded as a great artist by these particular groups. He was neither an amateur indifferent to outside opinion because he could afford to ignore it, nor an original artist of the rank which disdains to concern itself with the reactions of spectators. He lacked the grand self-confidence of the supreme type of creative artist. He proclaimed his own merits because secretly he doubted them. He talked against the dilettanti and the connoisseurs, he wrote against them, he played practical jokes upon them with faked Rembrandt etchings, he made satirical engravings showing Time smoking a picture, and a dressed-up monkey watering the dead plants of the past while the living plant of the present is neglected—and he did all this because secretly he longed for the applause and admiration of the dilettanti and the connoisseurs.

He began his engravings of 'modern moral subjects' because portrait painting as he practised it was 'not sufficiently

[1]Ward lived till 1731.

profitable', and all his life he produced and published his engravings to make money. But he cared nothing for the applause of the man in the street who bought his engravings. From the time of *A Harlot's Progress* he knew that he could please and intrigue the general public whenever he desired to do so; and when he set out to do this he neglected no component of success. But because this success was so assured to nim he always secretly despised it. The success he coveted was the success which he could not win.

He always made easily the money he required; as he grew older the revenue from his numerous prints became, as he tells us, 'a kind of an estate', and in his last period, after the death of his brother-in-law, the last holder, he obtained the office of 'Serjeant Painter of all his Majesty's works, as well belonging to his Royal Palaces or houses, as to his great Wardrobe or otherwise'—an office which, he tells us, brought him, with its various perquisites, the equivalent of something like a thousand pounds a year in the values of to-day.[1] It was thus not the rich men's money that he coveted. He was not a victim of financial distresses, his tastes were simple, he had no desire to rival the coach and six of Sir Gottfried Kneller. What he sought to extract from the dilettanti and the dealers in Old Masters was a gesture discounting his popular prints as pot-boilers, and proclaiming him an artist whose portraits and 'history pictures' ranked him with the masters of the past.

He defended his pictorial comedies to support his own morale: 'Comedy,' he said, 'in painting as well as writing, ought to be allotted the first place . . . though *the sublime*, as it is called, has been opposed to it.' But he tried again and again to excel in 'the sublime'. Again and again he attempted 'history painting', imitating the art of the past and thus degrading himself to the level of a derivative artist, in the vain hope of bringing his haughty opponents to their knees. This man, who had painted dozens of original pictures, longed above all things for praise of his derivative works 'in the Grand Manner'. A contemporary,

[1]Two hundred pounds a year is the figure given by Hogarth. For the office of Serjeant Painter, cf. p. 52.

17. WILLIAM HOGARTH
A Rake's Progress. Scene 8—Detail
Soane Museum, London

18a. UNKNOWN ARTIST
Victorian Interior
Private Collection, London

18b. WILLIAM HOGARTH
Marriage A-la-Mode. Scene 2
National Gallery, Millbank, London

who himself succeeded in the manœuvre, tells us that a word in favour of his *Sigismonda* would command a proof print 'or force an original sketch from him'. He was equally anxious to win praise by his portraits. He turned repeatedly to portraiture as a means of attack on the fortress which refused to admit him. His *Captain Coram* (Pl. 69b) was a special effort, the portrait which he painted 'with most pleasure' and in which he 'particularly wished to excel'. But, he tells us, 'the current remark was that portraits were not my province.'

This 'current remark', he persuaded himself, was inspired by a conspiracy of dealers, dilettanti, connoisseurs, and art-dealing portrait painters: 'For men who drudge in this [portrait painting] merely for gain,' he wrote, 'to commence dealers in pictures is natural. . . . They stand in the catalogue of painters, and having little to study in their own way, become great connoisseurs; not in the points where real perfection lies, for there they must be deficient, as their ideas have been confined to the oval; but their great inquiry is, how the old masters stand in the public estimation, that they may regulate their prices accordingly, both in buying and selling. You may know these painter-dealers by their constant attendance at auctions. They collect under pretence of a love for the arts; but sell, knowing the reputation they have stamped on the commodity, they have once purchased, in the opinion of the ignorant admirer of pictures, drawings, and prints; which thus warranted, almost invariably produce them treble their original purchase-money, and treble their real worth. Unsanctioned by their authority, and unascertained by tradition, the best preserved and highest finished picture (though it should have been painted by Raphael) will not, at a public auction, produce five shillings; while a despicable, damaged, and repaired old canvas, sanctioned by their praise, shall be purchased at any price, and find a place in the noblest collections. All this is very well understood by the dealers.'

There was good foundation for this charge of dealing against portrait painters. Lely, Kneller and Reynolds were all associated with the trade in 'Old Masters'; the minor portrait painters in the seventeenth and eighteenth centuries also habitually dabbled in art dealing; many were copiers if not indeed fakers of old pictures; one of Kneller's assistants—John Peeters—was known among the art dealers as 'the Doctor' for his skill in working up poor old drawings to give them an 'air of quality' to which the connoisseurs added the appropriate names. Marchi, a young Italian whom Reynolds brought back with him from Italy, was an expert copyist, taught by Reynolds 'how to give the copy an old appearance so that few even amongst connoisseurs shall distinguish the difference'.[1] But we cannot of course ascribe Hogarth's failure to win material success as a portrait painter to a conspiracy between the dealer-portrait painters and the dealers against him. He really failed, as he knew, because he did not flatter his sitters—and this explains his bitter accounts of portrait painting in England which I quote in another place.[2]

The disdain with which secretly he treated his pictorial comedies is the explanation of the increase in didactic tone in them as the years went on. In *A Harlot's Progress* and *A Rake's Progress*, as I point out below, the didactic note is restricted to certain plates in each series. But later, despising the easy success of comedy, he sought to justify the work, which he looked on as his pot-boiling, by adopting the procedures of the moralist.

'My father', writes J. T. Smith in his 'Life of Nollekens', 'knew Hogarth well, and I have often heard him declare, that he revelled in the company of the drunken and the profligate.' We need not, of course, assume from this that Hogarth was drunken and profligate. It is true that we have only to look at his prints to know that in the early part of his life he certainly went everywhere in Ned Ward's London 'catching strokes of nature' as Gainsborough put it.[3] We have specific record of a visit to Moll King's disreputable tavern in the company of the painter Hayman, who, tradition has it, led Gainsborough astray. We can guess that in his younger years he often got drunk in such places

[1]Cf. below, p. 144.   [2]Cf. below, pp. 103, 104.
[3]Cf. below, p. 114.

19. WILLIAM HOGARTH
Shrimp Girl
National Gallery, London

20. RICHARD WILSON
View in Italy
National Gallery, London

and that his relations with the women who frequented them were not invariably platonic. But no concept of him as a man habitually addicted to drink and loose living can be entertained for a moment by any person of sense and experience. And, indeed, it is recorded that in his later years his haunts were Slaughter's Coffee House in St. Martin's Lane and the Turk's Head in Gerrard Street, Soho—both respectable taverns where artists habitually forgathered.

We have to picture him as a man who kept apart from the pretentious world where Kneller and later Reynolds lived in state; as a man whose friends were mainly minor painters— fellows whom he liked because they were goodnatured, and good company, willing to drink a glass with him, and share his interest in the kaleidoscope of life, and jeer with him at his particular *bêtes noires*.

His circle in fact included SAMUEL SCOTT (*c.* 1710-1772) who painted topographical pictures of London; THOMAS HUDSON (1701-1779) a portrait painter and the master of Reynolds; JOSEPH HIGHMORE (1692-1780) the painter of charming illustrations to Richardson's *Pamela* (Pl. 11b), who could also paint a portrait at one sitting, and talk of his visits to Düsseldorf and Flanders; BENJAMIN WILSON (1721-1788) a successful portrait painter (to whom he proposed a partnership in portrait painting in 1757) and an artist capable of spacial composition of the kind which interests so many artists in our day—Henry Tonks, for example, whose *Evening in the Vale* (Pl. 12b) is a more complex and scientific excursion into the field explored by Wilson in *Portrait in an Interior* (Pl. 12a); HUBERT GRAVELOT (1699-1773), the French engraver, a lively and adventurous man with tales to tell of Paris and the West Indies, who was in London from 1733 to 1745 and conducted an art school in which Gainsborough was a pupil. In the earlier period and probably later it is clear that Hogarth also knew FRANCIS HAYMAN (1708-1776) a Jew, or of Jewish extraction, who played a considerable part in all the politics of the art world at the time. Hayman was intimate with all the London artists, and was probably the second master of Gainsborough. He was with Hogarth at Moll King's Tavern and saw the woman spitting gin at her rival which Hogarth recorded in the tavern scene in *A Rake's Progress* (Pl. 14). He was also with Hogarth, as was Hudson, on the visit to France in 1749 when Hogarth was arrested for sketching Calais Gate—an episode recorded in *Calais Gate: The Roast Beef of Old England*. He passed his youth in painting scenery for theatres and in decorative undertakings of various kinds; he then had some success as a portrait painter. Active in the negotiations and intrigues which eventuated in the foundation of the Royal Academy four years after Hogarth's death, he was one of the original Academicians and Librarian of the Academy from 1771-1775. It has been frequently said that he was a drunkard and addicted to loose living. But there is no more evidence for this than in the case of Hogarth. His career suggests that he was respectable at any rate in his later years. But we may perhaps accept the legend that he was a glutton and that people in the restaurants he frequented were amazed at the quantity of food which he devoured.

To these convivial spirits we must add Captain MARCELLUS LAROON, a strange personality, adventurer, actor, singer, soldier and painter by turns, who sang at Covent Garden 'with a noble strong voice', served in Flanders, was at Oudenarde, and was taken prisoner in Spain. When in London he was frequently seen in the Drury Lane taverns and almost as frequently was carried before the justices for escapades when he was 'drunk and disorderly'. It is recorded that he was excellent company and I can well believe it. As an artist he was far from negligible. He painted with a rather French daintiness and with his light touch anticipates Gainsborough himself (Pls. 32, 33a and 33b).[1]

In this circle Hogarth was the central personality and the leading intellect. It is true that he was insular and had a prejudice against foreigners; but this prejudice—due partly to his complex

[1]The most ambitious and attractive painting by Laroon with which I am acquainted belongs to Mr. Osbert Sitwell. This represents a number of figures riding to a village wedding or something of that kind.

21a. ROBERT ADAM
Landscape Composition
Victoria and Albert Museum, London

21b. BENJAMIN BARKER
Landscape with Stormy Effect
Victoria and Albert Museum, London

22. J. C. IBBETSON
Robert Burns
Private Collection

in regard to the dilettanti who worshipped so blindly what he called 'exoticks'—is comprehensible in a man whose only attempt at foreign travel had landed him in jail; and it is the only evidence of weakness in his mind. Everything he wrote is shrewd and interesting. 'The Analysis of Beauty' was one of his attacks on the opposing fortress, but it was also quite evidently the result of much reflection and more letters than are commonly assigned to him. Its theory, which only his more intelligent contemporaries could follow, is closely related to the art theories of to-day; and for that reason I discuss it briefly in Appendix IV.[1]

3. HOGARTH'S ART

HOGARTH was not the inventor of the Conversation Portrait Group. Portraits of family groups were well known in Holland in the seventeenth century. When the Dutch bourgeois came into his own after the defeat of the Spaniards he employed artists to record himself, his family and his surroundings, and thus created a form of art which was destined to be further developed in England. *The Geeling Family*[2] by Metsu (1629-1667) is a typical ancestor of the English Conversation Group.

The earliest portrait group by Hogarth, with which I am acquainted, is *The Price Family* (Pl. 10). This was probably painted before his marriage, about the same time as the *Scene in the Beggar's Opera* and a year or two before the *Performance of the Indian Emperor or The Conquest of Mexico*. The student will detect the influence of Watteau in these paintings, and there can be no doubt that Hogarth had some acquaintance with the Frenchman's work. He probably encountered engravings after Watteau's *arabesque* and *grotesque* decorations at an early age,

[1] Cf. Appendix IV, pp. 274-279.
[2] This picture is reproduced as Pl. 106 in my 'Introduction to Dutch Art'.

when he was still apprenticed to the silversmith, and later he doubtless studied the engravings from Watteau's pictures which de Jullienne published regularly from 1721.[1] He also probably saw the paintings by Watteau owned by Dr. Mead who had treated Watteau for consumption when he came to England in 1719. Mead, a friend of Captain Coram, was connected, as Hogarth was, with the Foundling Hospital to which he presented his portrait by Allan Ramsay[2]; he kept open house to artists and allowed them to copy what they pleased in his considerable collection of pictures. Hogarth and his circle, I imagine, all went there; and it is interesting to note that the collection included some paintings by Canaletto.

This perhaps explains why in *The Price Family* (Pl. 10) we observe a linear arabesque and abstract rhythm that recall Watteau and Watteau's studies in Crozat's house.[3] But these features soon give place in Hogarth's work to a more domestic concept of the Conversation Group (Pl. 11a); and the formality in the portraiture, which is also a feature in *The Price Family*, is soon abandoned for franker and more vigorous characterisation. When we look on his portrait of *William James* (Pl. 13) we can understand why he failed to win material success in portraiture. He could not and he would not flatter his sitter. In 1757 he painted one Dr. Hay, and Chancellor Hoadley wrote: 'I should not like to meet that figure alive in the fields going to Chelsea for fear of laying that night in a ditch with twenty gashes in my crown.' He himself regarded his *Captain Coram* (Pl. 69b) as his finest achievement in portraiture; and the modern student will support the assessment. It would be a severe test of any portrait to set it by John's *Smiling Woman* (Pl. 9); but *Captain Coram* would survive the ordeal.

In the Ashmolean Museum in Oxford there is a sketch for a Conversation Group where the handling of pigment resembles the sketches of portrait groups by Largillière (1656-1746) who was a pupil of Lely. And Hogarth's manner of painting—both

[1]Cf. my 'French Painting', pp. 108, 110 and 122.   [2]Cf. p. 155.
[3]Cf. my 'French Painting', pp. 101, 102 and 112.

in his sketches and his finished pictures—had its roots in the Lely tradition. His technical procedures were not original. We meet them elsewhere at the time. But no one used them more skilfully than he did, especially in the *Marriage A-la-Mode* series and in some of his portraits.

We do not know when he painted the *Shrimp Girl* (Pl. 19). It was in his studio when he died and is possibly of the period round 1757 when he was painting *Garrick and his Wife*. As we now see the *Shrimp Girl*, it is a shadow of its former self. Painted evidently in three-quarters of an hour, with thin flowing paint, which was immediately almost absorbed by the canvas, a large part of its vitality has gone; also it has become yellow—either as a result of the quantity of oil used by the artist to make the paint fluid or as a result of varnish used by restorers in attempts to revive it. But, when Hogarth laid down his brush, the *Shrimp Girl* must have been an irresistible production—vivid, full of expression, quivering with light and colour, supremely economical in machinery—a spontaneous gesture comparable only with the head of the Princess in *Las Meninas* which Velasquez had painted in an hour about a hundred years earlier, or with the most brilliant Impressionist sketches of the age before our own.

Hogarth claimed to have invented the painting of pictorial comedies. He turned his thoughts, he tells us, 'to painting and engraving modern moral subjects, a field not broken up in any country or any age'. But this again was an exaggeration. Pictorial comedy in engravings had been known all over Europe all through the Renaissance; and the Dutch had painted hundreds of genre chronicles with caricature-comment all through the seventeenth century. Hogarth was certainly acquainted with engravings after Dutch paintings of this kind—in particular he evidently knew prints from paintings by Jan Steen (1626-1679). The tavern scene in *A Rake's Progress* (Pl. 14) is a direct descendant of the Dutch 'Prodigal Son' tavern scenes where pocket-picking so frequently appears. 'I have endeavoured', Hogarth tells us, 'to treat my subjects as a dramatic writer: my picture is my stage, and men and women my players, who by means of certain actions and gestures, are to exhibit a dumb show'; in this the Dutch popular genre painters had already led the way.[1]

Nevertheless it was in his pictorial comedies and later in his didactic engravings that he made his most personal and his most valuable gestures. The dilettanti and the connoisseurs of his own day underrated his portraits. But they all admitted that he had made an original contribution in the field of popular art.

'I should never think', writes J. T. Smith, 'of exhibiting a portfolio of his prints to the youthful inquirer.' How far is this judgment justified? In what sense and how far was Hogarth a moralist? How far and in what sense did he adopt a moralist's procedures in his art?

The question is pertinent because in these pictures, painted for engravings, he was not primarily concerned with decorative art, or descriptive art, or romantic art or architectural art. He did not paint them as studies in 'plasticity' or 'tone values' or 'significant form'. He was concerned first and foremost, as his own words tell us, with the action and gestures of the figures which were 'to exhibit a dumb show'; and that dumb show purported to have a moral aim.

The moralist to carry conviction must adopt one of two methods. He must either base himself on some widely accepted religious or ethical precepts and recall the precepts to obtain his effect. Or he must concentrate on the observance and non-observance of the precepts and obtain his effect by the *in terrorem* process of exhibiting the inevitably pleasant consequences of the one and the inevitably dreadful consequences of the other. Hogarth as moralist used the second procedure. But it was some time before he mastered it. He did not completely realise the form or put it completely into practice till he produced the series known as *Industry and Idleness: or The Industrious and the Idle Apprentice* at the age of fifty. Here all his machinery is assembled and set in order; but this series nevertheless always

[1]Cf. my 'Dutch Painting' (pp. 181-244 with accompanying plates).

23a. AMBROSE McEVOY
The Thunderstorm
Private Collection, England

23b. THOMAS GAINSBOROUGH
The Woodman
Private Collection, England

24. THOMAS GAINSBOROUGH
The Cottage Door
Private Collection, U.S.A.

strikes me as hack work compared with *A Harlot's Progress, A Rake's Progress, Marriage A-la-Mode, Gin Lane* and *Beer Street* and *The Four Stages of Cruelty.*

He was thirty-four when he produced *A Harlot's Progress,* and at that time, though not a drunkard or a rake, he had, as I have said, no objection to the company of drunkards and no horror of young women of easy virtue. He was working on *A Harlot's Progress* at a time when he was also painting two little pictures called *Before* and *After* which are rather broader in their humour than the average French *estampe galante,* and make it clear that the girl's lapses in the opening scenes of *A Harlot's Progress* were not such as would have roused him to indignation. The subject of this series, if the moral was to be pointed by the *in terrorem* procedure, is one which demands an uncompromising attitude in the author from the beginning to the end. The sinner must be shown sinning and then the victim of a series of disasters following logically and inevitably as the result of her sin. And the initial sin must be of the sinner's own volition, because if it be shown as the result of accident or misfortune the sinner becomes a victim of circumstance and not wholly, or even principally, responsible for the results.

But Hogarth did not really set out as a moralist when he began *A Harlot's Progress.* He set out to make money, as he has told us himself.[1] He composed the first picture as an illustration of two well-known scandals of the moment. The scene shows a girl just arrived in London from the country about to yield to the wiles of a woman employed by an old rake; the man stands in the doorway of a house awaiting the result (Pl. 15a). The figures of the man and the woman were portraits of individuals —a Mrs. Needham and a Colonel Charteris—who were notorious villains and prominently 'in the news' at the time the prints were published. The first picture of the series was thus, as he wrote later of another publication, 'a timed thing'.[2]

[1] Cf. above, p. 60.
[2] Mrs. Needham had been recently exposed in the pillory for activities of the kind depicted in Hogarth's print. Her conduct had been so scan-

But how was it as the first scene of a morality play called
A Harlot's Progress? Surely quite inadequate, seeing that the girl

dalous that the enraged populace attacked her during the punishment
and inflicted such injuries that she died as the result.

Colonel Charteris was some species of maniac who had an astonishing
career. A gentleman by birth he went into the army as a youth and was
drummed out for repeated cheating at cards and dice. He procured
another commission, and being entrusted with money for raising recruits
he gambled it away and then recovered part of it by staying at an inn,
burning his breeches in the night, and extorting £100 or thereabouts
from the innkeeper for alleged theft of the breeches which, he said, had
contained sixty guineas and a gold watch. Later, in Edinburgh, in a
dispute with a miller in the market-place, he had fallen upon the man and
bitten off his nose. He built up a large fortune by clever speculations, by
investments in land, and by his methods at cards and dice. It was his
custom to lend back his winnings on the security of the loser's property;
and before he was forty he had thus secured a number of valuable estates
in various parts of England and Scotland. In spite of his conduct he was
always received in good society, and at the age of twenty-seven he had
married a lady of good position. But he spent little time in his wife's
company and seems to have devoted himself more and more to the
satisfaction of an ever-growing mania for promiscuous intercourse with
young women. Wherever he went tales were told of him. He was
credited with intrigues with girls of the upper classes and with the employment of a number of women—including Mrs. Needham—to seduce
young girls coming from the country. His libertinage was so conspicuous
that it was sufficient on one occasion for a woman to spread a rumour that
her sister had been taken to his house for the mob to break in and demand
her release—only to be met angrily, not by Charteris but by the girl, who
protested that she had no desire to be released. In a moment of generosity
he projected a charity school for his natural children and a group of almshouses for women who claimed to have been ruined by their association
with him; he proposed to advertise for the children, and carried the
scheme to the stage of employing an architect to draw plans for the
almshouses. At the age of forty-six he was accused of the rape of a woman
whom he had met in a country lane near Edinburgh; condemned to
death, he procured a pardon from George I. In 1730, at the age of fifty-
five, he had again been accused of rape—this time by a servant girl, who
alleged that she had been decoyed to his house by a woman, and he was
again condemned to death. His friends, who included his son-in-law the
Earl of Wemyss and Robert Walpole, rallied round him; the case was
referred to the Privy Council, and he obtained a pardon from George II.
When he died two years later, on one of his estates, the people of the
neighbourhood pelted the hearse with garbage, tried to tear the body
from the coffin, and threw carcases of dogs and cats into the tomb.

25. J. M. W. TURNER
Dido and Aeneas: The Morning of the Chase
National Gallery, Millbank, London

26. RICHARD WILSON
The Thames at Twickenham

is here obviously a victim of two criminals experienced in vice. The effective morality play would have followed this first picture with Mrs. Needham in the pillory and peasants casting garbage into the old rake's grave.

But in Hogarth's second scene the girl has passed from Charteris to a rich protector who has installed her in an elegant apartment complete with maid and butler and a negro page; in a fit of silly hyper-confident ill temper she kicks the tea-tray into her protector's lap (Pl. 15b). As a result she is, in Horace Walpole's phrase, 'turned out of keeping',[1] and in Scene 3 we see her, as a public woman, arrested for stealing a watch, by one Sir John Gonson who was widely known and detested at the period for savage punishment of women of this class.

In the second scene, it will be observed, the girl is brought down not by her sin but by her 'tantrums', and in the third she falls into the power of a notorious bully as the result not of her unchastity but of her theft. No moralist of course would have told the story in this way. Hogarth told it thus because in these pictures he was not really a moralist but a man depicting and commenting on life.

In the fourth picture the girl is beating hemp in Bridewell (Pl. 16a). Here once more she is shown as the victim of circumstance; and Hogarth here is protesting not against her sins but against the obscene cruelties that were practised in the place. Women in his day were flogged in this House of Correction and the public were admitted to witness a scene so disgusting that it had turned even Ned Ward's stomach. Hogarth had no objection to young women of easy virtue but he detested cruelty in all its forms. This picture in which he really appears for the first time as a moralist, or more accurately as a social reformer, was his first protest against cruelty and foul social conditions in his day; and it was soon to be followed by others as bitter and more violently expressed.

In *A Rake's Progress* there are only two scenes of a truly didactic kind—the scene in the Fleet prison and the scene in

[1]Cf. above, p. 67.

Bedlam. In the other scenes the rake's misfortunes are not shown in the moralist's way as the inevitable consequences, to everyone, of particular sins, but as the results of mistakes made and bad luck encountered by one particular, and particularly foolish, young man.

In the first picture of this series Tom Rakewell has been recalled from Oxford on the death of his father—an old miser who had hidden his gold behind the cornice, and noted in his diary that he has at last got rid of a bad shilling. Tom suddenly finds himself rich; he makes a settlement on Sarah Young, a girl of the people who is in love with him and has been till now his mistress, and he sets out to spend his money and see life.

A real moralist of course would not thus have excused Tom's outbreak into extravagance by suggesting in this way that he had suffered in the past from a miserly father; he would have shown the father as a man who had passed his life to extreme old age in arduous toil that he might provide his son with comfort and security. And if the moralist had drawn the first scene in this manner he would have made the desertion of Sarah—the only part of the scene which can be construed as sin by Tom—the cause of a series of subsequent disasters arising obviously and inevitably from it; as Sarah was wronged by Tom it would have been Sarah whom the moralist would have made the instrument of Tom's destruction.

But Hogarth has not proceeded in this way. In the second scene, which is caricature-comment, Tom amuses himself in the acquisition of fashionable airs and graces and is appropriately exploited by fencing masters, dancing masters, picture dealers, horse dealers and so forth in the Molière tradition. In the third scene he is drunk in a Drury Lane tavern, where one of the women of the establishment has stolen his watch (Pl. 14). And in the fourth he is arrested for debt.

It is impossible to construe these episodes as inevitable retribution for the desertion of Sarah. And not only this. In the fourth picture Hogarth has actually brought Sarah on the scene

27a. RICHARD WILSON
On the Wye
National Gallery, London

27b. JOHN CROME
The Slate Quarries
National Gallery, Millbank, London

28. FRANCIS TOWNE
Mountains
Victoria and Albert Museum, London

—not as the avenging instrument but as the instrument of escape from disaster; she has husbanded the settlement that Tom made upon her, and she now pays down sufficient to keep him from prison.

In the fifth scene Hogarth goes back to the beginning and tries again to make his story a morality play. He shows Tom being married to a wealthy one-eyed old lady—a scene which might well have been the second in the series, seeing that the young man here again renounces Sarah for the pleasures which money can buy. But as a morality play the story breaks down again in the next plate. Here Tom, at White's Club, has gambled and lost heavily—in no sense an evitable result of the casting off of Sarah, and less a crime than a misfortune seeing that he might with equal chance have won. In the seventh scene, as a result not of vice or dishonesty but of this bad luck at White's, Tom is in a debtor's prison. In the last scene he is, for no apparent reason, in Bedlam and raving mad; and there Sarah is brought once more upon the stage—again not, in the moralist's way, as the instrument of destruction but as the angel of pity kneeling by his side.

But the prison scene and the Bedlam scene are here again protests against cruelty and social conditions. The prison scene indicts the Fleet as the prison scene in *A Harlot's Progress* had indicted Bridewell. And in the Bedlam scene, where we see a fashionable woman and her maid visiting the men's quarters (Pls. 16b and 17), the indictment is yet fiercer and more bitter. In Hogarth's day, as in Ned Ward's a few years earlier, Bedlam was open to the public, who went to giggle and titter at the inmates and talk to them and take obscene delight in their obscenities. Ned Ward has described the horrible procedure in a passage which concludes as follows: 'Having pretty well tir'd our selves with the Frantic Humours and Rambling Ejaculations of the Mad-Folks, we took a turn to make some few Remarks upon the Looseness of the Spectators, amongst whom we Observ'd abundance of Intriguing. Every fresh comer was soon engaged in an Amour; though they came in Single they went out by

Pairs. . . .' Hogarth's picture attacked these conditions, which were in fact put a stop to some twenty-five years later.

In *Marriage A-la-Mode*, painted in 1745, we have again a story which purports to be a morality. In the first scene an insolvent Earl and a rich bourgeois make a shameful bargain. The Earl sells his son and the bourgeois sells his daughter. The young Viscount and the girl are obviously quite innocent parties in this first scene. The villains are the fathers, and it is on them that the real moralist would accordingly have brought disaster. Hogarth has made no attempt to build the story in this way. He concentrates on the difficulties of the situation for the young people who have no affection for one another, and no interests in common, and who both seek substitute satisfactions to replace the happiness of conjugal life. The second picture shows us the interior of their home at noon. The young Lord has been out all night; he has returned exhausted; a girl's lace cap protrudes from his pocket. Her Ladyship, in a négligé, has just come down from her bedroom to drink coffee. She too is exhausted by the night's attempt to forget unhappiness in pleasure. She has entertained a company in the saloon till the small hours; there has been gambling and music and silly talk about the elegant bibe-lots of the apartment which her money has furnished with rows of saints by 'Old Masters', and rows of statuettes, etc., from Italy, Africa and China. She makes a sarcastic comment to her husband as she yawns and stretches (Pl. 18b). The third scene is an interlude to which I shall return in a minute. The fourth, known as *The Toilet of the Countess*, is a pendant to the scene where Tom Rakewell is exploited by the fencing masters, horse vendors and so forth. The Countess at her levée is exploited by actors, singers, musicians, dealers in sham antiquities, etc., while a young lawyer, who had appeared in the first scene, is arranging an assignation at a forthcoming ball. In the fifth scene she has been surprised with her lover; her husband in blind rage has drawn his sword against a naked man who has picked up his own sword in self-defence and mortally wounded the aggressor. In the last scene the Countess dies and her father, who had sold her, commits a last infamy by removing from her finger a valuable ring—all that remains of the fortune he had provided to secure a son-in-law with a title.

This series contains only one didactic scene—the third picture which I have called an interlude. Here we are transported to premises occupied by a quack doctor and his wife who perform secret operations and provide alleged remedies for secret diseases. The young Lord has come here with the owner of the lace cap which protruded from his pocket in the second picture—a girl still clearly in her teens; and the artist has made us share his horror at the contact of these two young people with the sinister inhabitants of this dark house.

Protests against cruelty and prevailing social conditions are again made in *Gin Lane* and *The Four Stages of Cruelty*. Hogarth himself wrote down his purposes in *Gin Lane* and *Beer Street*: 'When these two prints were designed and engraved,' he tells us, 'the dreadful consequences of gin-drinking appeared in every street. In *Gin Lane*, every circumstance of its horrid effects is brought to view *in terrorem*. Idleness, poverty, misery, and distress, which drives even to madness and death, are the only objects that are to be seen; and not a house in tolerable condition but the pawnbroker's and Gin-shop. *Beer Street*, its companion, was given as a contrast, where that invigorating liquor is recommended, in order to drive the other out of vogue. Here all is joyous and thriving. Industry and jollity go hand in hand. In this happy place, the pawnbroker's is the only house going to ruin; and even the small quantity of porter that he can procure is taken in at the wicket, for fear of further distress.'

He also wrote his purpose in *The Four Stages of Cruelty*: 'The leading points in these, as well as the two preceding prints, were made as obvious as possible, in the hope that their tendency might be seen by men of the lowest rank. Neither minute accuracy of design, nor fine engraving, was deemed necessary, as the latter would render them too expensive for the persons to whom they were intended to be useful. And the fact is, that the passions may be more forcibly expressed by a strong bold stroke, than by the most delicate engraving. To expressing them as I felt them, I have paid the utmost attention, and as they were addressed to hard hearts, have rather preferred leaving them hard, and giving the effect, by a quick touch, to rendering them languid and feeble by fine strokes and soft engraving. . . . The prints were engraved with the hope of, in some degree, correcting that barbarous treatment of animals, the very sight of which renders the streets of our metropolis so distressing to every feeling mind. If they have had this effect, and checked the progress of cruelty, I am more proud of having been the author, than I should be of having painted Raphael's Cartoons.'

There we can leave the aspect of intention in Hogarth's art, and pay tribute to his special equipment for its fulfilment. His special gift was an exceptional visual memory which he tells us he always cultivated assiduously. He could retain visual impressions with exceptional clearness, and paint figures and scenes from notes in a sketch book or from literally thumbnail sketches—since he had a habit in public places of making sketches on his thumb. He seems to have asked a friend sometimes to pose for an attitude—Hayman is traditionally said to have posed for the Viscount in the second picture of *Marriage A-la-Mode* (Pl. 18b); but it is obvious that his pictures were not painted from a series of posturing models like the *tableau-vivant* 'subject pictures' of the nineteenth century.

I have described his scenes as comments on life; and this distinguishes them from the work of the men whom he himself stigmatised as 'still-life painters'. In his didactic plates of the later years he is so obviously using the distortions and exaggerations of the *in terrorem* method that we are not likely to mistake his presentations for categoric statements. But in his comedy scenes we are tempted to assume that we are looking on accurate delineations of the customs, clothes and apartments of the time. To do this is to fall into error. Everything in Hogarth's work is stressed and distorted for his purpose—caricatured, in the first sense of the word—i.e. a 'loaded' or 'charged' (*caricata*) presen-

29. J. S. COTMAN
Viaduct
Victoria and Albert Museum, London

30. J. S. COTMAN
The Baggage Waggon
Castle Museum, Norwich

tation.[1] Thus the second scene in *Marriage A-la-Mode* (Pl. 18b) depicts a room in Arlington Street then occupied by Horace Walpole. But we must not assume that Hogarth made a still-life copy of the room and its equipment in the same way that the unknown Victorian artist made a still-life copy of an interior in the picture which I reproduce (Pl. 18a). The Victorian painter has produced an elaborate piece of purely descriptive painting. Hogarth has bent his room as it were to his intention as a social satirist. He has filled it with bric-à-brac of his invention all contributing to the idea which is the real subject of the picture. And so it is with the clothes and the way they are worn in his pictures. At a certain distance of time we cannot distinguish all the subtle differences in clothes and gestures which mean so much to contemporaries. The coat that spells the fop, or the vulgarian, or the gentleman, at the time, is merely a coat of the period a hundred or even fifty years later. We cannot now follow the significance of a sword held so or so or of a snuffbox handled in this way or that. All these details in Hogarth's pictures are charged and stressed; they are all caricature-comments and were recognised as such by spectators in his day, though to our eyes they are apt to seem nothing but still-life painting.

We must also observe that the crowding of incident and detail in Hogarth's pictures is in itself a procedure of emphasis. He asks us to read his pictures from corner to corner, inch by inch, because the sum of the parts in his pictures is intended to contribute to their product, i.e. to the central idea as social comment.

His pictures, as pictures, suffer from this procedure; they all obviously contain much that destroys them as pictorial designs. But we are surely ungrateful if we quarrel with him on this score. For without the accumulation of these reinforcements we might find it much harder to follow his 'dumb show'.

From the standpoint of the modern student Hogarth's most important contribution is his protest against cruelty; and in saying this we do him no injustice seeing that he has told us that

[1]Cf. below, pp. 165-177.

he would rather have checked the progress of cruelty than been the author of Raphael's Cartoons.[1]

His second contribution is in the field of caricature-comment where he adopted the procedure of stress by accumulation of details which as we shall see has since been used not only in the field of caricature-comment but also in other aspects of English painting.[2]

[1]Cf. above, p. 86.   [2]Cf. below, pp. 165-177.

31. THOMAS GAINSBOROUGH
Lady Innes
Private Collection, U.S.A.

32. MARCELLUS LAROON
Conversation in a Wood

CHAPTER V

PICTURESQUE LANDSCAPE

*

RICHARD WILSON (1714-1782) is commonly referred to as 'the father of English landscape'; and the title is not undeserved.

The son of a Welsh parson, he came early to London, and started as a painter of portraits and landscapes. He seems to have had some success, and at the age of thirty-five he went to Italy —either at his own expense or with the assistance of a patron. In Italy he frequented the landscape painters of the time; the Frenchman Joseph Vernet (1714-1789) and the Venetian Zuccarelli (1704-1788) were among his friends; and to them he owed his acquaintance with the various aspects of the picturesque tradition in landscape as it survived on the Continent at that date.

I say 'survived' because in the middle of the eighteenth century, when Wilson arrived in Italy, the triple picturesque tradition in landscape, which had been created at the beginning of the seventeenth century by the foreign artists resident in Rome, was already more than a century old. I have discussed the genesis of this triple tradition in my books on Dutch and French painting.[1] Here I need only very briefly recapitulate.

The foreign artists in Rome, about a hundred and twenty years before Wilson arrived there, were divided into three colonies—German, Netherland, and French. The German colony was grouped round Elsheimer (1578-1610) and his Dutch pupil Lastman (1583-1633) the master of Rembrandt;

[1]'An Introduction to Dutch Art', pp. 55-71, 135-158, 172-176; 'French Painting', pp. 56-73.

the Netherland colony, grouped at first round Paul Bril (1554-1626), and later round Jan Both (1610-1652), influenced Cornelis van Poelenburgh (1586-1667), Nicholas Berchem (1620-1683), Adam Pynacker (1622-1673), and Pieter van Laer, known as Bamboche (1595-1660); the French colony was led by Nicholas Poussin (1594-1665) and Claude le Lorrain (1600-1682). The picturesque-classical landscape was created by Poussin and rendered more obviously attractive by Claude. The picturesque-genre landscape was largely the invention of Bamboche, from whom it passed to Wouverman (1619-1668) and Watteau (1684-1721). The picturesque-romantic variation, which influenced Rembrandt (1606-1669) and Salvator Rosa (1615-1673), seems to have been created in the first instance by Elsheimer.

All these artists had been impressed by the grandeur of Mediterranean scenery and by the remains of a civilisation much older than their own. When they walked in the country round Rome—which Laurence Binyon has described as 'the Campagna, with its wide plain bordered by noble hills, its lakes lying in wooded hollows, its majestic remains of Roman monuments, its broken aqueducts and tombs; a serene and ordered landscape, perfumed with associations, breathing of a great past'—they indulged in an imaginative escape into antiquity; and partly by means of this escape they created the three types of picturesque picture.

As created by Poussin the picturesque-classical landscape (which was only part of his tremendous achievement) was an aspect of great art—an aspect which the modern student is well equipped to appreciate. In the eyes of a generation surfeited with the still-life-imitative, the romantic, and the impressionist landscape painting of the nineteenth century, even the feeblest *pastiche* in Poussin's tradition has a quality of conscious order which brings it, as it were, to our side of the Rubicon. Poussin himself is intensely admired by modern students because he ignored the incidental, the temporary, and the accidental. His picturesque landscapes are works of architecture realised with marvellous completeness; they are microcosmic symbols, records of the true classical attitude to art.

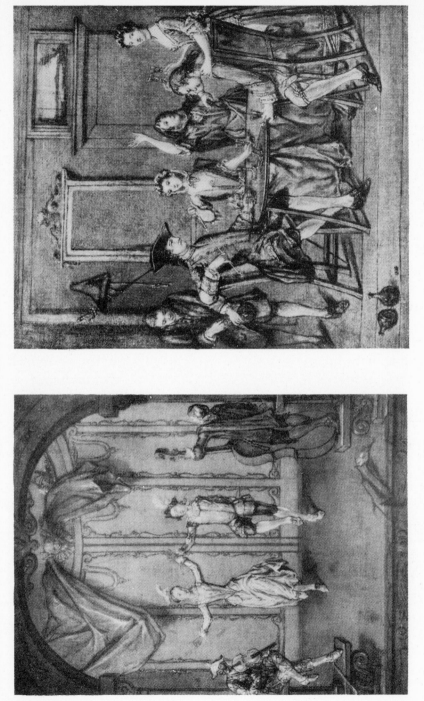

33b. MARCELLUS LAROON
Tavern Scene
National Gallery, Millbank, London

33a. MARCELLUS LAROON
Dancers and Musicians

34a. ARTHUR DEVIS
Lady Tyrconnel

34b. ARTHUR DEVIS
Lord Tyrconnel

Claude converted Poussin's microcosmic landscapes into objects of luxury. Poussin's pictures are properly at home only in some Temple of Wisdom. Claude constructed his landscapes on Poussin's architectural principles, but as his mind was relatively trivial, and his intention mainly decorative, the result is a series of elegant decorations for elegant private rooms. His pictures are furniture-pictures, of the highest class it is true, but furniture-pictures all the same.

Owners of elegant apartments, and art dealers all over Europe, were quick to recognise the attractions of Claude's domestication of Poussin's austere achievements; and there arose accordingly an international trade in pictures of this kind, from which the dealers derived much profit for two hundred years.

The dealers had similar success with picturesque-genre productions in the style invented by Bamboche. Rich men everywhere bought this type of picture as well as the Claudian type all through the seventeenth and the eighteenth centuries. Dutch gentlemen who neglected Hals and Rembrandt and despised the Dutch genre and naturalistic landscape painters, covered their walls with picturesque landscapes by Berchem and Both. Elsewhere Italian and French works in both these styles were also continuously collected.

By the middle of the eighteenth century the picturesque-classical tradition was already worn almost threadbare. Lifeless formulae had taken the place of the classical principle; and a pseudo-classical air was provided by stock arrangements of the stock symbols for the stock ingredients—mountains, trees, waterfalls, ruined towers and fallen pillars—which we find collected in the drawing by the English architect, Robert Adam (1728-1792) which I reproduce (Pl. 21a). The artists put these compositions together in the studio, using engravings after pictures by other people, and also occasionally sketches of their own. They made no effort to enlarge their experience and their art degenerated more and more. But as the art degenerated the trade in it increased. More and more gentlemen in all countries were persuaded that their walls were inadequately furnished without picturesque landscapes—preferably imported from abroad. In the eighteenth century every Russian nobleman of standing bought pictures of Roman ruins by the Frenchman Hubert Robert (1733-1808); and rich Englishmen furnished their living rooms with pictures by the Italians Zuccarelli and Panini.

In the eighteenth century both picturesque-classical and picturesque-genre landscapes were so well known in England that the word 'picturesque' appeared in the English language to describe them. It was used not only of these picturesque-classical and picturesque-genre compositions but also to describe effects admired in nature because they recalled such pictures—the word 'beautiful' being reserved for Raphaelesque and baroque compositions in the 'Grand Manner'. At the same time Burke popularised the word 'sublime' to describe the picturesque-romantic compositions in the Salvator Rosa manner, and this word was also used of effects in nature, admired with a pleasant sensation of horror, which recalled these compositions.

It was this atmosphere that Wilson found when he returned to England from Italy at the age of forty-one in 1755. He had become proficient in the composition of picturesque-classical landscapes in the approved formulae and with the approved ingredients; he had been encouraged and applauded in Rome; and he had every reason to expect success in England.

But success did not come to him. He was always able to sell a certain number of Italian landscapes with ruins, etc.; but though he was made a Foundation Member of the Royal Academy in 1768, and later Librarian, he seems never to have had more than two or three patrons, and it never became fashionable to collect his work. He lived for the remainder of his life in poverty, became much embittered, and often found consolation in the bottle. When he was about sixty-two he inherited a small property in Wales; there he painted his last pictures and died at the age of sixty-eight—so removed from the world of celebrities that no newspaper troubled to chronicle his death.

How came it that Wilson's pictures failed to bring him material success when the stage seemed set for just such pictures to achieve it? The failure I think must be ascribed to several causes.

In the first place he does not seem to have had a temperament contributing to material success. An amiable disposition—or the appearance thereof—is a factor in an artist's career as in all others. Wilson appears to have been unamiable, outspoken, difficult, and liable to fits of bad temper. He had Court patronage both before he went to Italy and for some years after his return. But he lost his temper in connection with a Court commission and offended the King. He was jealous of his contemporaries and spoke of Gainsborough's landscapes as 'fried parsley'. When he was on the Hanging Committee of the Academy he covered brightly coloured pictures by other artists with a mixture of Indian ink and Spanish liquorice to bring them down to the tonality of his own. And in his later years he was rendered still more difficult by disappointment.

In the second place the fact that he was not a foreigner was against him. English gentlemen, in the second half of the eighteenth century, were willing to employ native artists as face-painters, but very few were willing to hang a landscape or a picture properly so called by a native artist in their rooms. They were persuaded, as other gentlemen were persuaded elsewhere, that it was more distinguished to import their wall-furniture from abroad. Gainsborough himself always had difficulty in selling his landscapes.

But we must not exaggerate this obstacle. It is possible that if Wilson had been an Italian the English collectors might have bought his work, as they bought that of Panini and Zuccarelli. But it is far more likely that even so they would still have treated him exactly as they did. Because there was a third factor which impeded his material success. He was not content to give the gentlemen exactly the pictures which they had seen before.

Wilson, at bottom, was an original artist. He used the picturesque formulae which he had acquired; but his pictures, except when he was deliberately pot-boiling, contained an element of originality which those who expected painters to work within their own familiar experience of pictures were not willing to accept. We have but to compare Robert Adam's *Landscape Composition* (Pl. 21a) with Wilson's pictures (Pls. 20, 26, 27a and 110b) to know why those who liked the first felt ill at ease with the second.

Wilson was never really happy with the picturesque-classical tradition. He was born a hundred years after Poussin and Claude, and he had within him the original artist's urge towards enlargement of his experience. Reynolds described his landscapes as 'near common nature'; and he thereby showed his discernment. For Wilson broke the mould of the tradition within which he worked. As he was fundamentally an original artist he was in tune with the cultural discontents of his age and unconsciously he was in tune with the nineteenth-century attitudes that were about to be. He had learned to admire and understand Claude and Poussin. But secretly he loved the Dutchmen who were about to influence so many English landscape painters. It is not surprising to read that he always spoke in terms of enthusiasm about Cuyp who was then quite neglected in the salerooms.

Little is known of the landscapes which he painted before he went to Italy. But there seems to be some evidence that they were nearer to the Dutch than to the Italian tradition. And in his later period—except when he was pot-boiling—he showed a decided tendency to break away from the approved constructions of the picturesque style, and to make his pictures record his emotional reactions to effects in nature in the romantic way. We see this in his *Cader Idris* and his *River Scene* (Pl. 110b). And we get the intermediate stage of the still-life descriptive Dutch approach—which made Reynolds say that his pictures were 'near common nature'—in *The Thames at Twickenham* (Pl. 26).[1]

Wilson was understood by Turner, Constable and Crome, who all admired him. He showed Turner the possibility of regenerating the exhausted picturesque-classical tradition (Pls.

[1]Cf. below, pp. 203-207.

94

35. ARTHUR DEVIS
Members of the Walpole Family
Private Collection, U.S.A.

36a. THOMAS GAINSBOROUGH
Robert Andrews and his Wife
Private Collection, England

36b. THOMAS GAINSBOROUGH
Heneage Lloyd and his Sister
Fitzwilliam Museum, Cambridge

25 and 105). He taught Cotman not only his picturesque patterning (Pl. 29) but also helped him in his richer and more significant works (Pls. 30, 106 and 118). He led Crome to the romantic attitude of his most affective pictures. And he made a gesture which Constable continued in *Weymouth Bay* (Pl. 116a) and *On the Stour near Dedham* (Pl. 116b).

Nevertheless, it is accurate, I think, to say that Wilson fell between two stools. The constitution of his character and mind, and the effects of the necessity of pot-boiling, caused him to attempt a compromise between his experience as an original artist and the contemporary dilettanti's familiar experience of art, which represented then as always the taste of the time as distinguished from its culture. His work was both too original and not original enough to achieve material success. He could produce neither the complete *pastiche* demanded by the dilettanti nor work of that driving originality which forces the spectator to evolve a new standard to make room for it.

As a painter he used a creamy texture which is 'fatter' than that of Claude or Poussin or Cuyp; and those who like this 'quality' find it an additional attraction in his pictures.

When the nineteenth century arrived the picturesque tradition, in its old forms, had run its course. Turner, as we shall see, explored and abandoned it as he explored and abandoned all traditions; Cotman flirted with it and learned a great deal from the principles behind it. But with these exceptions the cultural attitude of the new romantic-individualist age reacted against it; and eventually it became a habit among landscape painters to look upon it with contempt.

Before the romantic-naturalism of the nineteenth century won through, there were, however, a number of minor English artists, painting for the most part in watercolours, who worked within the picturesque field. Of these Alexander Cozens, Francis Towne and John White Abbot are the most interesting to modern students, and John Robert Cozens is the best known.

ALEXANDER COZENS (*c.* 1698-1786) was long believed to be and may possibly have been a natural son of Peter the

Great. He was born in Russia, or went there in early life. He visited Italy, and came to England before 1742. He became drawing master at Christ's Hospital and subsequently conducted a drawing class at Eton where George III, when Prince of Wales, and Sir George Beaumont, collector and amateur artist, were among his pupils. He also taught drawing at one time to the fashionable world at Bath. He made landscape compositions in sepia some of which are in the picturesque-classical tradition while others have a curious rather Chinese air. He was evidently an ingenious man, much interested in landscape composition and in theories of beauty; and he wrote books which were subscribed for by prominent figures in the fashionable world and by well-known artists including Reynolds. One book was entitled 'Principles of Beauty relative to the Human Head'; this was illustrated by profile heads with ears but no hair—the hair being drawn on loose sheets of tissue paper making it possible to see the effect of different arrangements of hair on the same face. He also published a treatise on landscape composition discussing the vexed difference between 'Beauty' and 'Sublimity'. His most celebrated publication was an essay on a method of composition which he described as 'Blot-drawing'. In this method the artist makes casual 'blots' of sepia or Indian ink on paper, then crumples the paper, and accepts the result as the basis for a composition to be deliberately completed by brush or pen. Cozens practised this method and taught it to his pupils; and examples of the results are preserved in the London Victoria and Albert Museum. Rivals in his day treated the procedure and the treatise with derision and spoke of Cozens as 'Blotmaster to the Town'. But in so far as the procedure postulates that the business of a painter is to compose a picture, and not to imitate the temporary appearance of some particular fragment of life, it is of course in line with the classical tradition. Moreover, analogous procedures have illustrious authority, for we read in the writings of Leonardo da Vinci: 'A painter cannot be said to aim at universality in the art unless he love equally every species of that art. For instance, if he delight only in landscape his can

37. THOMAS GAINSBOROUGH
Mr. and Mrs. Brown of Trent Hall
Private Collection, England

38. THOMAS GAINSBOROUGH
The Artist with his Wife and Child
Private Collection, England

be esteemed only as a simple investigation; and, as our friend Botticello remarks, is but a vain study since by throwing a sponge impregnated with various colours against a wall, it leaves some spots upon it which appear like a landscape. It is true, also, that a variety of compositions may be seen in such spots, according to the disposition of mind with which they are considered; such as heads of men, various animals, battles, rocky scenes, seas, clouds, woods and the like. It may be compared to the sound of bells, which may seem to say whatever we choose to imagine.' And we read in the writings of Sung Ti, a Chinese artist who worked in the eleventh century: 'You should choose an old tumble-down wall and throw over it a piece of white silk. The morning and evening you should gaze at it, until at length you can see the ruin through the silk—its prominences, its levels, its zig-zags and its cleavages, storing them up in the mind and fixing them in the eye. Make the prominence your mountains, the lower parts your water, the hollows your ravines, the cracks your streams, the lighter parts your nearer points, the darker parts your more distant points. Get all these thoroughly into you, and soon you will see men, birds, plants and trees, flying and moving among them. You may then ply your brush according to your fancy and the result will be of heaven, not of men.'

Alexander Cozens is thus a personality of interest to modern students who are so deeply concerned with theories of artistic creation; and though his actual compositions seem amateurish and tentative in comparison with modern achievements they appeal to-day by reason of the artist's experimental attitude and intentions.

This is also true, incidentally, of the work of GILES HUSSEY (1710-1788) who though not a landscape painter may conveniently be mentioned at this point. Hussey was born a gentleman and studied in Italy on an allowance from his father. He recognised that the boundless esteem in which Graeco-Roman statues were then held had set up bad standards and noxious prejudices as a standard of beauty; and he came to the conclusion that 'ideal form' must be mathematically evolved. He tried to work out a theory of 'Beauty' on a mathematical basis, and talked so much about it to his friends that they all regarded him as mad. As he showed no signs of being able to make money by his art his father stopped his allowance; and thereafter he seems to have had an unsuccessful career in spite of help and encouragement from various patrons when he returned to England. He seems to have been disinherited by his father but to have succeeded to the family property on the death of his brother. Five years later when he was sixty-eight he resigned all his property to a relation and led what is described as 'a retired and religious life' till he died in Devonshire at the age of seventy-eight. Very few of his works seem to have survived. The print room of the British Museum has some drawings including a red chalk head and shoulders of a young man executed with great precision of hand and very deliberate stylisation, and a curious profile drawn with pronounced use of semicircular lines, said to be from an antique gem.[1] It is clear that both as a theoretician and an artist Hussey belongs more to the twentieth century than his own.

The same applies to FRANCIS TOWNE (1740-1816) whose drawings in intention are strangely close to certain aspects of twentieth-century art. He too seems to have been an amateur, and his work, also, is rare. He was born in Devon, and worked in Wales, Italy and Switzerland. We can now appreciate his drawings easily because we are familiar with similar intentions more completely realised by modern artists. Weary of the stock ingredients of the picturesque landscape tradition Towne looked intensively at specific structure and sought thus to give new life to the picturesque tradition. His Italian drawings are clearly the result of personal experience. In Switzerland he was interested both in the geological and the architectural structure of the mountains (Pl. 28). Some of his drawings are expressed in a language that is as deliberately symbolic and geometrical as the *Still Life* (Pl. 160) by Paul Nash.

From our experience of modern English achievements in

[1]Reproduced in Whitley's 'Artists and their Friends in England'.

39. THOMAS GAINSBOROUGH
Miss Juliet Mott
Private Collection, U.S.A.

40. THOMAS GAINSBOROUGH
'Perdita': Mrs. Robinson—so-called 'Sketch'
Royal Collection, England
By gracious permission of His Majesty the King

watercolour, where acute observation of specific form and architectural structure are skilfully combined—as in the drawing by John Nash I reproduce (Pl. 107a)—we have learned to appreciate also the tree drawing by JOHN WHITE ABBOT (1763-1851) who attempted the combination in his watercolours. Till recently this artist was entirely forgotten—or confused with the portrait painter Francis Lemuel Abbott (1760-1803) who painted the best known portrait of Nelson. To-day he seems to us almost as interesting as Alexander Cozens or Francis Towne.

JOHN ROBERT COZENS (1752-1799), son of Alexander Cozens, travelled in Italy and Switzerland, on one occasion with Richard Payne Knight, collector and critic, and on another with Beckford, the author of 'Vathek'. He went mad at the age of forty-two and died five years later. He was attended in his last illness by a Dr. Monro, to whom I refer again in connection with Girtin and Turner.[1]

Most of J. R. Cozens' watercolours were topographical drawings or pretty little picturesque compositions in the prevailing formulae. But he also made some drawings, admired by Turner, Constable and Girtin, which reveal personal reactions to the architecture of both mountain and plain forms. In these drawings he heralds in a tentative way the modern attitude to landscape. His work has a hard task when confronted with landscapes produced since the Cubist-Classical Renaissance which has taught artists to concentrate on architectural form. Compared with modern artists his powers of analysis and synthesis seem rudimentary. But we must not forget that drawings like his *Elba* and *Campagna* were original at the time they were produced.

The work of all the landscape artists hitherto mentioned was related to the picturesque-classical tradition. Other English artists in the eighteenth century produced landscape paintings and drawings related to the picturesque-romantic tradition. I reproduce an example of this type of picturesque picture in its last phase—the *Landscape with Stormy Effect* (Pl. 21b) by Benjamin Barker (1776-1838). In the second half of the eighteenth

[1]Cf. below, pp. 179, 180, 182.

99

century the 'sublimity' of such picturesque-romantic compositions was in fashion among English collectors, and picturesque
stormy effects on the plain or in mountainous regions were much
in demand. This tradition substituted the concept of an un-
kempt, untamed 'nature' with trees struck by lightning, or in
senile decay, for the ordered concept of the picturesque-classical
formula; and it is mainly remarkable, as far as the modern
student is concerned, because it had an influence, doubtless viâ
his friend de Loutherbourg, on Gainsborough (Pls. 23b, 24, 49).

PHILIPPE DE LOUTHERBOURG (1740-1812), an exceptionally handsome man (witness his portrait by Gainsborough
in the Dulwich Gallery), was born at Strasbourg and settled in
England in 1771. He began as a scene painter, and worked both
for Garrick and Sheridan. He then became an eclectic exponent
of all the picturesque styles, and painted a number of landscapes
with oncoming storms. He also painted various London scenes,
and a very curious picture of a heath with a Methodist preaching
to a casual congregation who all seem to have strayed from
Rowlandson's drawings. In 1781 he painted and exhibited a
moving panorama called an Eidophusikon where changing
lights suggested changes of day and weather on scenes called 'A
View of London from Greenwich Park', 'The Port of Tangier',
'The Bay of Naples', 'The Rising of the Moon contrasted with
an Effect of Fire on the Mediterranean', 'Storm and Shipwreck at
Sea', 'The Cataract of Niagara', 'Satan and his Legions on the
Banks of the Fiery Lake', etc. Both Reynolds and Gainsborough
went to de Loutherbourg's Eidophusikon. Reynolds is said to
have approved of the performance and Gainsborough to have
been so enthusiastic that he went night after night and made a
miniature Eidophusikon with painted glass slides of his own.
In 1789 de Loutherbourg became a Faith Healer; and Hammersmith Terrace where he lived was so continuously crowded with
all kinds of invalids and cripples that the neighbours protested
and eventually attacked the house. The artist was thus constrained
to abandon his Faith Healing for which incidentally, he always
refused, it is said, to accept money.

It is here that we can place most properly the well-known figure GEORGE MORLAND (1763-1804) who has also a connection with the painters of outdoor life whose work I discuss later.[1] Morland produced some picturesque-romantic compositions; but his main contribution was a development of picturesque-genre with ragged-nature elements taken from the picturesque-romantic tradition. He was a direct descendant of Bamboche and the Dutchmen of the seventeenth century; his scenes of English village life translate the Dutch popular genre pictures into English, and imbue them with a sentimental character. The village maidens he portrayed are luscious and attractive; and his way of painting was luscious and attractive too.

Born in London he began with hack work for a dealer and soon evolved his characteristic style. He made money easily, spent it fast, drank a great deal, and was continually embarrassed in the later years by debt. At one time he had a house at Paddington where he kept foxes, goats, pigs, dogs, monkeys, squirrels, guineapigs, and dormice in addition to a donkey and a horse. Later he lived for some time on the Isle of Wight where he painted a number of coast scenes. Then he returned to London and was harassed by his creditors till he had a fit of apoplexy and died in a sponging house at the age of forty-one.

In the last eight years of his life he is said to have painted seven hundred and ninety-two pictures and made a thousand drawings in desperate attempts to escape from his debts. The success of his work continued after his death and dealers have made a great deal of money from it. His pictures and engravings appealed at the beginning of the nineteenth century because Rousseauism was then in fashion in England and France. Morland's representation of a contented picturesque English peasantry pleased the rich Englishmen of the period, who were afraid of revolution, just as Greuze's pictures of a contented picturesque French peasantry had pleased rich Frenchmen in the reign of Louis XVI. Later in the century, when Victorian architects had cut down thousands of trees and covered England with

[1] Cf. below, Ch. IX.

slate-roofed cottages in rows of fifty to a hundred, the thatched cottages beneath oak trees in Morland's pictures took on a romantic-emotive 'old world' flavour and made a new appeal which in turn became a source of profit to the dealers. At the present time the romantic appeal of these pictures has considerably declined in power owing to the healthy distrust of romantic misrepresentations which has been steadily growing among all honest people for the last fifty years; and the modern student thus finds little to admire in Morland's pictures.

As a painter Morland adapted the 'fat' creamy texture of Wilson's picturesque-classical pictures to his own purpose of picturesque-genre; and the rapidity of his execution gives an air of bravura to his work. I reproduce his *Hunting Mishap* (Pl. 79a) which, as a subject, is rather unusual in his *œuvre* but shows the technical attractions of his handling.

Mention must also be made here of JULIUS CAESAR IBBETSON (1759-1817) who was known in his day as 'The Berchem of England'. Ibbetson, a Yorkshireman, was a ship painter, then a scene painter, and then a dealers' hack in London. He went to China, returned to London, wrote a book on painting, took to drink, became enormously fat, and died in the village of Masham where he was born. He painted a great many pictures, was very eclectic within the range of the picturesque, and was a frequent exhibitor at the Royal Academy. I reproduce his portrait of the poet Burns with a picturesque landscape disposed as a background (Pl. 22). In the days when he was employed by the dealers Ibbetson produced numerous fakes ascribed to Berchem, Poelenburgh, Teniers, and others; and one of his fakes is said to have deceived the dealer Desenfans who formed, it will be recalled, the collection, now preserved in the Dulwich Gallery, as the nucleus of a National Gallery for Poland.

41. THOMAS GAINSBOROUGH
The Duke of Clarence
Private Collection, U.S.A.

42. THOMAS GAINSBOROUGH
Mrs. Elliott—Grace Dalrymple
Private Collection, England —Frick, N.Y.

CHAPTER VI

PORTRAIT PAINTING

*

'Of what consequence is it to the Arts what a Portrait Painter does?'
WILLIAM BLAKE.

'As to portrait painting, the chief branch of the art by which a painter can procure himself a tolerable livelihood, and the only one by which a lover of money can get a fortune, a man of very moderate talents may have great success in it, as the artifice and address of a mercer is infinitely more useful than the abilities of a painter. By the manner in which the present race of professors in England conduct it that . . . becomes still life. . . . Mere correctness . . . in still life, from an apple to a rose, to the face, nay, even the whole figure, if you take it merely as it presents itself, requires only an exact eye and an adroit hand. . . . Admitting that the artist has no further view than merely copying the figure, this must be admitted to its full extent; for the sitter ought to be still as a statue—and no one will dispute a statue being as much still life as fruit, flowers, a gallipot, or a broken earthen pan. It must, indeed, be acknowledged, they do not seem ashamed of the title, for their figures are frequently so executed as to be as still as a post. Posture and drapery, as it is called, is usually supplied by a journeyman, who puts a coat, &c. on a wooden figure, like a jointed doll, which they call a layman, and copies it in every fold as it chances to come; and all this is done at so easy a rate, as enables the principal to get more money in a week than a man of the first professional talents can in three months. If they have a sufficient quantity of silks, satins, and velvets to dress their laymen, they may thus carry on a very profitable manufactory, without a ray of genius. . . . By perpetual attention to this branch only, one should imagine they would attain a certain stroke—quite the reverse—for, though the whole business lies in an oval of four inches long, which they have before them, they are obliged to repeat and alter the eyes, mouth, and nose, three or four times, before they can make it what they think right. The little praise due to their productions ought, in most cases, to be given to the drapery man, whose pay is only one part in ten, while the other nine, as well as all the reputation, is

engrossed by the master phiz-monger, for a proportion which he may complete in five or six hours; and even this, little as it is, gives him so much importance in his own eyes, that he assumes a consequential air, sets his arms akimbo, and, strutting among the historical artists, cries—"How we apples swim!.." Whoever would succeed in this branch, must adopt the mode recommended in one of Gay's fables, and make divinities of all who sit to him. Whether or not this childish affectation will ever be done away, is a doubtful question; none of those who have attempted to reform it have yet succeeded; nor, unless portrait painters in general become more honest, and their customers less vain, is there much reason to expect they ever will. . . . In Holland, selfishness is the ruling passion; in England, vanity is united with it. Portrait painting therefore ever has, and ever will succeed better in this Country than in any other; the demand will be as constant as new faces arise; and with this we must be contented, for it will be in vain to attempt to force what can never be accomplished . . . or at least can never be accomplished by such institutions as Royal Academies. . . . Upon the whole, it must be acknowledged that the artists and the age are fitted for each other. If hereafter the times alter, the arts, like water, will find their level.'
WILLIAM HOGARTH.

We now arrive chronologically at the period of Gainsborough and Reynolds whom we habitually think of as portrait painters—though Gainsborough as all the world knows was also a landscape painter and Reynolds painted a number of 'subject' pictures. It is convenient therefore to reflect for a moment on portrait painting in general at this point.

The quotations set above make it clear that in Blake's opinion portrait painting has no connection with the fine arts; and that in Hogarth's opinion portraiture as practised in England by the conspicuously successful professors of his day—Kneller at first and then Reynolds—was a pretty contemptible affair. Hogarth's dictum was written at the end of his life somewhere about 1760 when Reynolds was already established as a leading practitioner; Blake's dictum, one of his annotations to Reynold's 'Discourses', was written when Reynolds had been dead some fifteen years. Both writers thus had Reynolds, among others, in their minds.

43. AMBROSE McEVOY
Portrait Group
Private Collection, England

44. THOMAS GAINSBOROUGH
Prince Alfred
Royal Collection, England
By gracious permission of His Majesty the King

To an extent, of course, we must discount both pronouncements. The basic attitudes of Blake and Reynolds were so widely
different, and their scales of values were so wholly opposed,
that it is hardly fair on Reynolds to subject his central activity to
Blake's view. And Hogarth did not write on this subject as a
detached observer—since he had himself failed to win material
success in portraiture.[1]

Nevertheless both dicta provide material for reflection in an
age where the camera's portraits confront us on every hand.

It is hard for the modern student to realise what portraiture
has meant to artists and sitters at different periods of the past. To
Holbein it meant a romantic individualised record of peculiar
features. But to his sitters it meant a likeness—nothing more and
nothing less. In Holbein's day men had to call in an artist when
they desired a likeness. There was no camera at hand.
Henry VIII, as is well known, sent Holbein to draw more than
one unknown lady whom he proposed to marry, that he might
discover as far as possible her form and features. And before that
when Henry VII contemplated marriage with the Queen of
Naples he sent three ambassadors to 'survey her person' and
instructed them to 'enquere for some conyng paynter having
good experience in making and paynting of visages and portre-
tures' who was to 'draw a picture of the visage and semblance of
the said young Quine, as like unto her as it can or may be conveniently doon'; if the painter 'at the furst or second making
thereof hath not made the same perfaite to her similytude and
likeness' or had 'omitted any feture or circumstance' then he or
another 'most conyng painter' was 'soo oftentimes to renewe and
reforme the same picture till it be made perfaite, and agreeable in
every behalfe, with the very image and visage of the said Quine'.[2]

It will be observed that the artist is here instructed to *draw*
not to paint from the sitter; and he is required to have the double

[1] The words 'whoever would succeed in this branch' in the above
quotation are, in fact, preceded by 'I found by mortifying experience
that' in the passage as a whole.

[2] Quoted from Bacon's 'History of the Reign of Henry VII' in *Portrait Painting* by Herbert Furst.

skill of 'making' and 'painting' in portraiture. The distinction was made because all through the Renaissance the artists made only *drawings* from the sitters, and painted the pictures later from the drawings. This was the procedure of the Clouets at the Court of François I and, as noted, it was Holbein's procedure in England. Replicas were often made both of the drawings and the paintings; and the portrait drawings were often put into albums just as people put photographs in albums in the nineteenth century. Portraiture in the time of Henry VIII and Elizabeth was thus portrait drawing; and a drawing surviving from this period may be the first stage of a painting, or it may be a drawing which was intended to serve as a cheaper form of likeness in itself. The elaborately painted clothes and accessories in the portraits of this period must be regarded as hack painting, done by studio assistants if the artist was prosperous, and by the artist himself if he was not.

I do not know exactly when or where *painting* from the sitters actually started. Franz Hals, I fancy, was the first outstanding pioneer. In England Van Dyck was probably the first habitually to confront his sitters with brush and canvas instead of paper and chalk. But when working from the sitters he did not usually paint on the canvas which was eventually the picture. He often made sketches in oil on a small canvas which took no longer than a drawing by a less gifted man; he worked on a grey ground and built up the head in lighter and darker tints; in the final pictures he painted only the heads, the rest as noted being done in the studio from his design.[1]

After Van Dyck many English portrait painters used brush and canvas from the start. But unless they were very successful they could not afford to employ assistants and had themselves to do all the hack work—clothes, drapery and so forth. Also, of course, unless they were really gifted they could not sketch a head from life in a couple of hours; and thus numerous, long, and arduous sittings were demanded by the minor artists, as Pepys found out to his discomfort.[2]

[1] Cf. above, p. 52.   [2] Cf. above, p. 54.

45. AMBROSE McEVOY
Daphne
Private Collection, England

Van Dyck's procedure can only give us portraiture of value when the painter is Van Dyck or Lely or Reynolds.[1] It involves special talents and powers of concentration beyond the reach of less gifted and self-controlled men. It is a procedure impossible for the second-rate artist. Most of the seventeenth-century followers of Van Dyck in England who tried to work in his way produced faces that mean almost nothing.

This procedure was also impossible for a profound original romantic like Rembrandt, who was probably the first important artist to paint his portraits entirely from the sitters. And it was doubtless largely because he painted in this way that he failed to win material success in portraiture. As time went on he found it ever more difficult to persuade people to endure the innumerable sittings he required; and at the end he was himself almost the only person disposed to stand the strain.

We have to bear all this in mind when we look at portraits by Van Dyck and Lely and their imitators, and by Gainsborough and Reynolds. The professional portrait painter who captures material success has always been, and always must be, the man whose procedures make small demands upon his sitters. I said above that we can get the measure of Cromwell's portraitists by imagining what Rembrandt, their contemporary, would have made of Cromwell's face.[2] But the comparison really is not quite fair. It is true that neither Walker nor Cooper could have painted Cromwell in forty sittings as Rembrandt would have painted him in the same number. But it is also true that if Walker or Cooper had asked the Protector for forty sittings, or even four, they would, in all probability, have lost the commission at the start.

The effect of physical conditions of this kind on the actual appearance of portraits is rarely considered by spectators or writers about art who have had no experience of portrait painting as a profession. Nor do spectators habitually remember that every portrait as we see it records a conflict—a real battle—between the painter and the man or woman before him. A painted

[1]Cf. below, pp. 139, 140.　　　　　　　　[2]Cf. above, p. 53.

portrait is always the result of a conflict of wills, a fight between two concepts of the eventual work. In some cases the artist, in others the sitter, is the victor. In most cases there is a makeshift compromise and it is this compromise that the portrait records.

Sitters and artists all go the way of all flesh; then the portraits which record the victory of the artist survive as works of art; those which record the victory of the sitter survive as material for historians and antiquaries; and the makeshift compromise portraits survive, if at all, as objects of interest only to past-loving connoisseurs and dealers.

Both Gainsborough and Reynolds were victors in this conflict—Reynolds, I shall submit, by means of exceptional moral strength, Gainsborough as a result of a saving weakness. Their portraits survive as works of art because the intentions they record are their own intentions and not the intentions of the men who paid the bill. The most conspicuous survivals in the opposite category in this period are the portraits by Zoffany—a painter as contemptible in his way as Kneller and one who has had a much more sinister influence on portraiture in England.

JOHANN ZOFFANY (1733-1810) was a German who came to England at the age of twenty-five. When he arrived the art of the Conversation Portrait Group, launched here by Hogarth, was being practised by Arthur Devis (1708-1787) in dainty pictures revealing a personal vision (Pls. 34a, 34b, 35). Zoffany picked up this pleasant form of portraiture—which appealed to Hogarth and Devis by the opportunities it provided for subjective comment and arrangement—and made it a machine to record the self-satisfaction of his patrons and his own servility. He was quite content to act as the servant of his employers; his pictures are essentially their work; his own role is purely executive. He received his instructions from rich people of the upper and upper middle classes who wished the appearance of their faces and the appearance of their clothes and their belongings to be recorded; and he carried out his instructions without comment. He recorded Mr. and Mrs. or Lord and Lady Tomnoddy and their families in the Tomnoddy dining-room with the

Tomnoddy silver on the sideboard and the Tomnoddy pictures in handsome frames upon the walls. If Lord Charles played the violoncello he painted him with an expensive instrument between his knees; if the family liked cards he portrayed them indulging in this drug; if a new country house was about to be built for them he painted the plan thrown conspicuously upon the table. All the small things which smug and comfortable people think important were painted as important things by this slavish German who was purely a still-life painter, in Hogarth's sense, and who set standards in servility and mechanical efficiency which English bourgeois patrons have demanded from portrait painters ever since. His pictures provide information for historians and antiquaries; but, with one or two exceptions, they are merely lumber in galleries of art.

The painter, like Zoffany, who records faces as still-life, in Hogarth's sense, and merely copies features, provides far less information about the sitters than might be supposed by the unreflecting. He tells us the colour of hair and eyes and the shapes of foreheads and noses. But the face he provides is inevitably the same kind of riddle as a living face in a tram or omnibus—a riddle which each spectator will solve in a different way.

We all tend to believe that we can deduce far more from human features than we really can. All human knowledge in this field has been empirically acquired; the knowledge of the specialist in physiognomy is only a collection of empirical data; and few of us know even the little known by professional physiognomists. When the ordinary man assumes that certain forms indicate certain characters, his assumptions are partly based on hearsay (emanating in the first place from physiognomists) but mainly on his own past experience; and thus features which one man, as a result of his past experience, finds assuring, another for the same reason distrusts. Furthermore, our own faces inevitably affect these assumptions. The ideas we associate with particular features generally have some relation to our own forehead or nose.[1]

[1] Cf. below, p. 235.

When, therefore, writers about art and others discuss a still-life portrait by Zoffany or some other painter of the kind, and speak of the commanding brow or cruel mouth or determined chin recorded by the artist, we must not take them too seriously, seeing that the painted features really reveal no more than the features of the unknown man in the omnibus, that the value of the writer's comment depends on the extent and nature of his own experience, and that even the man of the widest experience is really guessing when he associates this or that character with this or that nose or eye.

Real knowledge—by which in this connection I mean intuitive comprehension—can only come when the features, in life or picture, assume an expression. Here we are not confined to guessing on the basis of our own past experience, but we can capture by a process of spiritual contact a new experience truly revealing something of the man. And the more often this process is repeated, especially when the expressions observed are related to different circumstances, the more we can learn.

It follows that we can find out far more about a man from watching his face in relation to a series of circumstances than we can from his individual features or from their still-life portrayal in a picture. It also follows that the portrait painter who, by any means, however slight, suggests an expression, is really telling us something more precise than the still-life portrait painter who copies features with mechanical accuracy and completeness.

But it also follows that the portrait painter at best can tell us little. In the first place he can only record *one* expression though that expression, it is true, can be not only of the face but of the whole body; and in the second he can only relate the expression to one type of circumstance. In most portraits the expression of face and body is related to nothing but the circumstance of sitting for the picture. Sometimes some incident or accessory is inserted to suggest a different relation. It is only the masters who are able—with or without incident or accessory—to suggest a more significant relation between expression and circumstance. Van Dyck was able to do this; and so were Gainsborough and

47. THOMAS GAINSBOROUGH
The Mall
Private Collection, U.S.A.

48. THOMAS GAINSBOROUGH
The Mall—Detail

Reynolds. And if Rembrandt be in truth the most intriguing and impressive of all portrait painters it is because the more he elaborated his portraits the less he described the physical features and the more he transformed them to vehicles of expression.

Nevertheless how little even the great portrait painters really tell us that we can unreservedly believe. Here is a verbal portrait:

'There is something exclusive of the clear and deep understanding of that gentleman [Mr. Dunning] most exceedingly pleasing to me. He seems the only man who talks as Giardini plays, if you know what I mean; he puts no more motion than what goes to the real performance, which constitutes that ease and gentility peculiar to damned clever fellows, each in their way. I observe his forehead jets out, and mine runs back a good deal more than common, which accounts for some difference betwixt our parts. No doubt with me but that he has an uncommon share of brains, and those disposed to overlook all the rest of his parts, let them be ever so powerful. He is an amazing compact man in every respect, and as we get a sight of everything by comparison, only think of the difference betwixt Mr. Dunning almost motionless, with a mind brandishing like lightning from corner to corner of the earth, whilst a long cross-made fellow only flings his arms about like thrashing flails without half an idea of what he would be at—and besides this neatness in outward appearance, his storeroom seems cleared of all French ornaments and gingerbread work, everything is simplicity and elegance and in its proper place, no disorder or confusion in the furniture, as if he was going to remove. Sober sense and great acuteness are marked very strong in his face, but if those were all I should only admire him as a great lawyer, but there is genius (in our sense of the word). It shines in all he says.'

Has Gainsborough, who wrote this, told us more of anyone in any of his painted portraits?

The painted portrait is often surpassed by the verbal portrait because the painter can use no progression. The painter can write one sentence in one picture but no more.

It is for this reason of course that Lely and Reynolds always paid great attention to the decorative design of their portraits. In so far as they concerned themselves at all with the character and personality of the sitter it was a concern with some expression which seemed to them interesting or emotive in itself or in relation to some circumstance. When they could find no such expression, or could not be troubled to look for one, they invented one for the occasion or brought one down, as it were, from stock. They were usually not interested in the sitter's features. They made pictures which were so attractive as pictorial form that it hardly mattered what face was fitted in or what happened inside what Hogarth called 'the oval'. They concentrated on pictorial form because there they felt themselves on terra firma in a country of their own; because they knew that there at any rate they were engaged in an activity which the brush could accomplish and the pen could not.

49. THOMAS GAINSBOROUGH
The Mall—Detail

50. THOMAS GAINSBOROUGH
Mrs. Graham
National Gallery of Scotland, Edinburgh

CHAPTER VII

GAINSBOROUGH
1727-1788

★

1. GAINSBOROUGH'S LIFE

THOMAS GAINSBOROUGH was born in the village of Sudbury in Suffolk. His father was an unsuccessful cloth merchant who held the office of postmaster at Sudbury in his later years and died in 1748. His mother is said to have been a woman of some parts and an amateur artist. He was the third of nine children and educated at Sudbury Grammar School where his mother's brother, a parson, was the teacher.

As a schoolboy he was lively and mischievous and soon began to draw and paint. His talents impressed his parents and when he was about fourteen they sent him to London and apprenticed him to a silversmith. In London he was discovered by the French illustrator and engraver, Hubert Gravelot. He became Gravelot's pupil and assistant when he was fifteen in 1742, and he remained with him for about three years. Gravelot, as noted, conducted an art school, and was a friend of Hogarth and his friends. Gainsborough at this time may have met Hogarth, Highmore, Hudson and Laroon, and he certainly met Hayman, who, tradition has it, took him 'about town' and taught him to sow wild oats.[1]

In 1745—the year when Gravelot returned to France—Gainsborough established himself in a studio of his own in Hatton Garden. There he painted some portraits and landscape compositions and modelled animals in clay. The material results were disappointing, perhaps because, under Hayman's tuition or on his own initiative, he spent too much time in the sowing of the wild oats. That at any rate is the impression left by a letter

[1]Cf. above, pp. 73 and 74.

113

which he wrote some thirty years later to a young actor: 'Don't run about London streets, fancying you are catching strokes of *nature*, at the hazard of your constitution. It was my first school, and deeply read in petticoats I am, therefore you may allow me to caution you.' This is obviously sincere. And it may well be that the petticoats were responsible for Gainsborough's failure to win material success in London at this time. He was only able to maintain the Hatton Garden studio for something less than a year. In 1746 at the age of nineteen he was back in Sudbury.

I imagine him gay, good-looking, with the aura of London experience around him, with tales to tell of Vauxhall and Bartholomew Fair, of Gravelot and Hogarth, Hayman and Laroon, the centre of attraction in his native village and an object of wonder to the village maidens. He seemed clearly one who would continue to flit from flower to flower; impossible to think of him as one destined, like other village youths, to be a husband and father. And yet six months later he announced that he was married—and produced a girl of sixteen as his bride.

No one seems to have known who the girl was or where she came from; and no biographer of Gainsborough has ever solved the mystery. Allan Cunningham, writing in 1829, states that the artist met her in a wood where he was sketching. Her name was Margaret Burr—that is known. One other fact is also known: she had an income, equivalent to something like £1000 a year in present money, which was paid to her through a London banker from a mysterious source that has never been discovered.[1]

The young couple soon established themselves at Ipswich, the nearest county town. There, the financial problem being

[1] The amount was £200. The bank was Messrs. Hoare. Gainsborough himself was in the habit of drawing the money. There is a tradition that Margaret Burr was the natural child of the third Duke of Bedford and another that she was a daughter of one of the exiled princes. Thicknesse, Gainsborough's first patron—who disliked her—says: 'She was a pretty Scots girl, of low birth, who, by the luck of the day, had an annuity settled upon her for life of two hundred pounds.' It is probable, of course, that Gainsborough had met her in London.

51. THOMAS GAINSBOROUGH
Drawing for Landscape Composition
Private Collection, England

52. THOMAS GAINSBOROUGH
Drawing for Portrait Group—The Duke and Duchess of Cumberland
British Museum

solved by his wife's annuity, Gainsborough was free to devote himself to painting; and there for the next few years he found some employment as a portrait painter to the neighbouring gentry, and also painted landscapes for his pleasure. One of his earliest patrons in Ipswich was Philip Thicknesse, Lieutenant-Governor of Landguard Fort, who eventually suggested that he should try his fortune as a portrait painter among the fashionable folk in Bath, and offered him introductions for the purpose. Gainsborough took the advice and left Ipswich at the end of 1759—as we know from an advertisement in the 'Ipswich Journal' dated October 20 of that year:

'To be Sold, Opposite the Shire Hall, Ipswich. On Monday and Tuesday next the 22nd and 23rd inst. All the HOUSEHOLD GOODS OF MR. THOMAS GAINSBOROUGH with some PICTURES and original DRAWINGS in the Landskip way by his own hand, which, as he is desirous of leaving them among his friends, will have the lowest prices set upon them. The house to be let immediately.'

When he arrived in Bath he was thirty-three, and he remained there, with occasional visits to London, till he was forty-seven. His success there as a portrait painter both of men and women seems to have been immediate. He soon had as many commissions as he could execute, charging the equivalent of about £200 in present money for a head and shoulders and of £500 for a full-length picture.[1] He sent many of these portraits to exhibitions in London and thus acquired a London reputation while still living in Bath. When the Academy was established he joined as a Foundation Member on the invitation of Reynolds.

The famous story of Wiltshire the Bath carrier, who is said to have transported Gainsborough's pictures to London without payment, and to have exchanged an old horse with the artist for *The Harvest Waggon*, arose in connection with the sending of these pictures to the London exhibitions. But the story is considerably less 'romantic' than is commonly supposed. Wiltshire was no yokel who trundled to London behind an old grey mare.

[1]Forty and a hundred guineas respectively.

He was a carrier with a flourishing business and a fleet of waggons which transported property to and from London. A man of means, he was at one time Mayor of Bath; he owned an estate outside the city, collected pictures, and was an early purchaser of works by Gainsborough. When Gainsborough eventually left Bath for London he wished to take with him an old grey horse, which Wiltshire had lent him, and which he had been accustomed to ride. He offered Wiltshire fifty guineas for the horse; Wiltshire replied by offering it to him as a present and souvenir of Bath; and Gainsborough, not to be outdone in courtesy, sent his old friend and patron *The Harvest Waggon* in exchange.

This move to London took place in 1774. Gainsborough established himself in part of Schomberg House in Pall Mall and prepared to challenge Reynolds, then at the height of his success. He had quarrelled with the Academy the year before he left Bath and he now fitted up his new quarters to display portraits, and the landscapes painted in the Bath period, many of which were still unsold. He does not appear to have had any immediate success in London though, as he had become acquainted with most of the fashionable world in Bath, he was certainly able to get in touch with the same world in town. He sent no pictures to the Academy and exhibited only in his own house.

About 1776 (possibly because he had by then obtained commissions from some members of the Royal Family, and etiquette may have forced the Academy to invite the pictures for the exhibitions) the quarrel with the Academy was temporarily adjusted, and thereafter for a few years his portraits competed regularly with those by Reynolds. He was now the favourite painter of the Court; his other sitters, like those of Reynolds, included leading ladies in Society and the *demi-monde*. Several, in both worlds, sat both to him and to Reynolds. The Hanging Committees seem always to have placed his work badly—or at any rate not to his satisfaction; and in 1784 he had a second and final quarrel with the Academy about a matter of hanging and withdrew all his pictures, refusing ever afterwards to exhibit there.

In his later years he had a country house at Richmond and there he found the model for one of his last pictures, *The Woodman* (Pl. 23b). In February 1788 at the age of sixty-one he was attacked by some malignant tumour or cancer at the back of his neck; and in August of that year he died.

Some days before his death he wrote a celebrated letter to Reynolds: 'I am just to write what I fear you will not read,—after lying in a dying state for six months. The extreme affection which I am informed by a Friend which Sir Joshua has expresd induces me to beg a last favour, which is to come once under my Roof and look at my things, my woodman you never saw, if what I ask now is not disagreeable to your feeling that I may have the honour to speak to you. I can from a sincere Heart say that I have always admired and sincerely loved Sir Joshua Reynolds.'

Reynolds had long been jealous of him as a portrait painter. He had referred to him somewhere as 'the first landscape painter in Europe' and had been reproved by Wilson who added, 'and the first portrait painter too'. He had tried both to restrain and to conceal his jealousy. He had bought Gainsborough's *Girl with Pigs* in 1782, sent him a letter full of elegant compliments (and then tried to exchange it for a damaged picture by Titian[1]); he had also given him a sitting for a portrait which was never completed partly because he had a serious illness after this first sitting and partly perhaps because Gainsborough on his side may have been unwilling to continue the picture because Reynolds had not returned the compliment of asking him to sit; Northcote, Reynolds' pupil and biographer, states that his master said in his hearing, 'I suppose he expects me to ask him to sit to me; I shall do no such thing.'

Gainsborough's letter just quoted could not be in decency ignored. Reynolds went to the studio, and the dying Gainsborough had some unfinished pictures brought to his bedside and talked about his plans for finishing them.

Reynolds devoted his Fourteenth Discourse to an obituary of his rival. 'I cannot', he said, 'prevail on myself to suppress

[1] Cf. below, p. 145.

117

that I was not connected with him by any habits of familiarity: if any little jealousies had subsisted between us, they were forgotten in those moments of sincerity; and he turned towards me as one who was engrossed by the same pursuits, and who deserved his good opinion, by being sensible of his excellence. Without entering into a detail of what passed at this last interview, the impression of it upon my mind was that his regret at losing life was principally the regret of leaving his art; and more especially as he now began, he said, to see what his deficiencies were; which, he said, he flattered himself in his last works were in some measure supplied. When such a man as Gainsborough arrives to great fame, without the assistance of an academical education, without travelling to Italy, or any of those preparatory studies which have been so often recommended, he is produced as an instance how little such studies are necessary. . . . This is an inference not warranted by the success of any individual. . . . However we may apologise for the deficiencies of Gainsborough (I mean particularly his want of precision and finishing), who so ingeniously contrived to cover his defects by his beauties; and who cultivated that department of art in which such defects are more easily excused; you are to remember, that no apology can be made for this deficiency in that style which this Academy teaches, and which ought to be the object of your pursuit. . . .'

2. GAINSBOROUGH'S CHARACTER

GAINSBOROUGH was evidently a neurotic of neurotic stock. Two of his brothers had that passion for inventing mechanical contrivances which is so often found in mental cases. Both his daughters died insane. He exhibited at all times a marked mobility of interest, great sensibility, and great susceptibility to impressions. Reynolds, in the Obituary Discourse, said of him: 'He had a habit of continually remarking to those who happened to be about him whatever peculiarity of

53. SIR JOSHUA REYNOLDS
Drawing in a Pocket Book
British Museum

54. TILLY KETTLE
Robert Sewell
Private Collection, U.S.A.

countenance, whatever accidental combination of figures, or happy effects of light and shadow, occurred in prospects, in the sky, in walking the streets, or in company.' It is also related that after he had dined one night with Dr. Johnson he was affected for some time after with Johnson's involuntary twitches and gesticulations.

All the evidence points, I think, to a highly strung, impulsive, irritable personality, with a lively intelligence, a good deal of courage, great charm, a complete absence of snobbery and conceit, and no patience with any type of empty pretension. We see all this in his letters to the musician William Jackson of Exeter from which I must quote some passages:

'I'm a rogue in talking upon Painting and love to *seem* to take things wrong . . . let me then throw aside that damned *grinning* trick of mine for a moment, and be as serious and stupid as a Horse. Mark then, that ever since I have been quite clear in your being a real genius, so long have I been of opinion that you are dayly throwing away your gift upon *Gentlemen*, and only studying how you shall become the *Gentleman* too. Now, damn gentlemen; there is not such a set of enemies to a real artist in the world as they are if not kept at a proper distance. They think (and so may you for a while) that they reward your merit by their Company and notice; but I, who blow away all the chaff, and, by God, in their eyes too if they don't stand clear, know that they have but one part worth looking at, and that is their Purse; their Hearts are seldom near enough the right place to get a sight of it. If any gentlemen come to my house my man asks them if they want me (provided they don't seem satisfied with seeing the pictures) and then he asks *what* they would please to want with me; if they say "a picture, Sir"—"please to walk this way and my master will speak to you"; but if they only want me to bow and compliment—"Sir, my master is walk'd out"—and so, my dear, I trick them. Now if a *Lady*, a handsome Lady comes, 'tis as much as his life is worth to send her away so . . .'

'I'm sick of Portraits and wish very much to take my viol-da-gamba and walk off to some sweet village where I can paint landskips and enjoy the fag-end of life in quietness and ease. But these fine ladies and their tea-drinkings, dancings, husband-huntings, etc. etc. etc. will fob me out of the last ten years, and I fear miss getting husbands too. But . . . we must jogg on and be content with the jingling of the bells, only, damn it, I hate a dust, the kicking up a dust, and being confined in harness to follow the track while others ride in a waggon, under cover, stretching their legs in the straw at ease, and gazing at green trees and blue skies with half my *Taste*. That's damned hard. My comfort is I have five viols-da-gamba . . .'

'I must own your calculations and comparison betwixt our different professions to be just, provided you remember that in mine a man may do great things and starve in a garret if he does not conquer his passions and conform to the common eye in chusing that branch which they will encourage and pay for. . . . Perhaps you don't know that whilst a face painter is harassed to death the drapery painter sits and earns five or six hundred a year and laughs all the while. Your next will be to tell me what I know as well as yourself viz. that I am an impertinent coxcomb. This I know, and will speak out if you kill me, for you are too modest, too diffident, too sensible and too honest ever to push in music. . . .'

Here we have the real Gainsborough, a man who delighted in listening to music, and was able to perform tolerably on several instruments; and who delighted equally in painting landscape compositions though he spent most of his time in portrait painting to provide a large establishment and a coach and fashionable amusements for his wife and daughters. He spoke of himself as 'dissipated'; Thicknesse tells us that he had to be well wined before he would perform to his friends on the viol-da-gamba. We can interpret these dicta as we please. To me they mean no more than a man fond of the petticoats, good company, and a good talker when he had drunk his bottle or was otherwise 'keyed up'.

Jackson, the recipient of the letters quoted, tells us that Gainsborough's conversation was 'sprightly' and 'licentious',

55 . THOMAS PATCH
A Group in Florence
Private Collection, England

56. SIR JOSHUA REYNOLDS
Admiral Keppel
National Gallery, Millbank, London

that he hated both 'ordinary topics' and those 'of a superior cast'. Another friend discovered in his ideas and expressions 'a mind full of rich fancies and elegant truths' and a 'pregnant imagination'. His conversation, we may take it, was exactly like his letters. He was surely bored with bourgeois small talk, with fashionable affectations, and with pretentious harangues from professional men who had not 'genius in our sense of the word'. He detested the world in which Reynolds was so conspicuous and so successful, and he never went near it. Unstable in Trotter's use of the term,[1] he travelled not in the herd but outside it, relieving his neuroses by cursing and swearing, by talking nonsense because it amused him and talking sense because he couldn't help it, by playing the viol-da-gamba—and by painting some of the most exquisite pictures of the English School.

3. GAINSBOROUGH'S ART

GAINSBOROUGH was not an educated or an intellectual artist. The past, as the past, meant nothing to him. He never went to Italy, nor, as far as we know, had he any desire to do so. Such knowledge as he acquired of the work of other artists was knowledge which chanced to come his way. As an artist he developed his own resources, from first to last, on the line of least resistance at the moment.

He accepted countless portrait commissions as 'pot-boilers'. But he could rarely pot-boil all through a picture. The point generally came when he began to enjoy himself—partly because his pot-boiling was not really pot-boiling but luxury-cooking (thanks to his wife's income), but still more because he lacked the moral power to force himself for long to disagreeable endeavour. He made the world his debtor by this weakness. Some artists have enriched the world by their moral power to work against the grain, by their sustained control of their natural in-

[1]W. Trotter, 'Instincts of the Herd in Peace and War'.

clinations as painters, their refusal to give themselves, as painters, a good time; Reynolds was an artist of this calibre; Picasso, who has denied himself the pleasure of indulging his romantic instincts and declined the delight of painting for painting's sake, is a conspicuous example in our own day. But on the other hand there are artists who have enriched the world mainly by their artistic self-indulgence; Gainsborough was one of them; Manet was another; Matisse, as I see things, is an example at the present time. Gainsborough often set out to pot-boil; he placed his sitters in ready-made conventional postures—the lovely and sexual Mrs. Graham, for example, in the same attitude, by the same pillar (Pl. 50), as the desiccated philanthropist John Eld, Founder of the Staffordshire General Infirmary, because when he began the portraits he looked on the commissions as hack work and thought of the sitters as 'gentry' who had nothing of interest about them but their money—as we have seen in his letters. But then, as the pictures grew beneath his hand, he forgot his boredom and contempt and his resolution to get the work done as quickly as possible; and the time generally came when he only remembered that he was painting and that painting after all was a pleasant occupation—as pleasant as riding about the country on an old grey horse or playing the viol-da-gamba.

Then, too, there were days when he began work on pictures of his own free will. In such work his self-indulgence had full play. And the results are gay spontaneous performances which communicate the painter's pleasure to everyone who looks at them.

To understand the technical development of Gainsborough's art we must remember, in the first place, that it emerged from the Hogarthian entourage; and that Gainsborough in his youth doubtless had contact with French eighteenth-century engravings through his master Gravelot, and with the Dutch seventeenth-century landscapes which were in many private houses in East Anglia. His early landscapes were built on the Dutch model—their resemblance to the work of Wynants in particular has often been observed—and his early portraits were based on

57. SIR JOSHUA REYNOLDS
The Snake in the Grass, or Love unbinding the Zone of Beauty
National Gallery, Millbank, London

58. SIR JOSHUA REYNOLDS
Pick-a-Back—Mrs. Payne and Son
Private Collection, U.S.A.

the Conversation Groups which Hogarth, Hayman, and Devis were producing at the time (Pls. 11a, 34a, 34b, 35).

These elements explain the character of such early pictures as *Robert Andrews and his Wife* (Pl. 36a), *Heneage Lloyd and his Sister* (Pl. 36b), *Mr. and Mrs. Brown of Trent Hall* (Pl. 37) and *Lady Innes* (Pl. 31). But even at this early stage Gainsborough's personality comes through. In the Ipswich Bicentenary Memorial Exhibition (1927) a portrait group of this period, *John Joshua Kirby and his Wife*, was hung next to a group, very similar in arrangement, by Hayman; and it was interesting to note that Gainsborough—who doubtless remembered the French engravings shown him by Gravelot, and perhaps some paintings by Marcellus Laroon (Pls. 32, 33a, 33b)—by elongating the neck and narrowing the shoulders of Mrs. Kirby had endowed her with a certain *chic* which made the Hayman lady—in spite of affected posture of the hands—seem heavy and *bourgeoise*.

Gainsborough's individuality comes through still more in the early group representing *The Artist with his Wife and Child* (Pl. 38) which again makes interesting comparison with the work of Marcellus Laroon. The student will detect in Gainsborough's picture—as in Laroon's *Conversation in a Wood* (Pl. 32)—the influence of Watteau; and it is possible, though we have no evidence for it, that Gainsborough, who doubtless saw engravings after Watteau's pictures in Gravelot's studio, may also have seen the paintings by Watteau in the collection of Dr. Mead.[1] But there is more of Gainsborough than of Watteau in this picture; and it is very prophetic of his later style.

His manner in the early years at Bath is seen in the pretty portrait of *Miss Juliet Mott* (Pl. 39); and it was at Bath—when something within him had been awakened by contact with the pictures by Rubens and Van Dyck in the mansions round about—that he developed the characteristic technique of his subsequent work which a critic of his day described as 'a scratchy, thunder-and-lightning form of art', but which the modern

[1] Cf. above, p. 76.

student, prepared for it by the technique of the French Impressionists, finds attractive, not merely as a method of painting—for one method of painting is, in itself, psychologically speaking as good as another—but as the spontaneous expression of the painter's sensibility.

To the student of our day it is the pictures which are lightest and most free in handling which are the most seductive and significant of Gainsborough's works. The *Sketch for the Portrait of 'Perdita': Mrs. Robinson* (Pl. 40), for example, means more to us than the celebrated finished portrait painted from it; and the sketch *Prince Alfred* (Pl. 44) more than the elaborately finished portrait *Mrs. Siddons*. These so-called 'sketches' really appeal to us because we know them to be more essentially truthful than his so-called 'finished' pictures. They contain nothing but records of his personal experience without any extraneous additions. It is really the 'sketch' which should be labelled *'Perdita': Mrs. Robinson* and looked on as the finished picture; and the so-called 'finished' picture should be labelled *Elaborated Version of 'Perdita': Mrs. Robinson*.[1]

Gainsborough's lightness of touch does not reappear in English painting till we get to W. Q. Orchardson (1835-1910) in whose hand it was merely a method of painting in the service of a commonplace mind. What it could become again in the hands of a great artist we see in the pictures of Orchardson's French contemporary—Auguste Renoir (1841-1919).

With this lightness of touch Gainsborough gave us frequently the most charming orchestration of colour. In his finished portraits he seems to have worked on the so-called 'Old Master' system of preparing for final glazes all the time. He painted, that is to say, with bright opaque pigments and with white mixed with transparent pigments, always bearing in mind that later he would apply general washes of coloured varnish and add positive notes with red lake and other transparent pigments. This means that cleaning a picture by Gainsborough is a most delicate and difficult business; because if, together with the

[1] Cf. below, p. 195.

dirt, any of the final transparent touches or general glazes be removed, the whole colour scheme becomes impaired; and when restorers attempt to make good the damage by repainting they are likely to injure the colour scheme still more. More than one fine picture by Gainsborough has been completely ruined in this way; and we sometimes underrate him as a colourist in consequence. This method of work, moreover, has other disadvantages. In a system where crudities and discords are set down to be resolved by the later process of transparent additions, there is always a risk, unless the painter is very scientific in his procedure —which Gainsborough was not—that the final glazes may not do their work quite perfectly. In certain pictures by Gainsborough—the *Madame Bacelli* and *Mrs. Siddons*, for example— the discord-resolution by the final glazes appears, to my personal colour sense, to be incomplete. But when the process has been evidently successful, as is generally the case in Gainsborough's work, he appears as a most attractive colourist, the English link in a chain consisting of Rubens, Watteau, Gainsborough, Renoir.

I have spoken of Gainsborough's susceptibility to impressions; and pointed out that we owe much that delights us in his pictures to his self-indulgence. But this does not mean that as a portrait painter he subordinated his will to that of his sitters. His receptivity made him conscious of their will and gave him contact with their spirit; but his self-indulgence, when he was painting a portrait, took the form, as I have said, of painting as he wanted to paint, frequently throughout the picture, and nearly always here and there. Reynolds was amazed at the resemblance of Gainsborough's portraits to the sitters—which was always much closer than he himself was able to achieve and which he could not explain in technical terms. He thought perhaps in a vague way that Gainsborough had 'a gift for catching a likeness'. But the truth is, of course, that Gainsborough had a romantic interest in the difference between one face and another; that he did not try to make a still-life copy of his sitter's face in servility to the sitter, as Zoffany did, but satisfied an instinct by taking an interest in each individual face. The modern student regrets this instinct in Gainsborough. There are portraits like the celebrated *Mrs. Moody and her Children* where the painter's interest in the lady's gawky features accompanies a record of his pleasure in the colour of a sash; and the two records, different in character, cancel one another out. We like him best when he is most subjective, concerning himself less with features than with an expression—an air—which, we suspect, he has not discovered but imposed.

This expression, this air, which Gainsborough gives to his sitters, is not the air of rather theatrical elegance given by Van Dyck, or the air of worldly consequence given by Reynolds, but an air which can only be described as an air of refinement and culture. Van Dyck made all his sitters look like participants in a great Court pageant; Reynolds made them all look prosperous and powerful *nouveaux riches* in expensive mansions and parks; but Gainsborough's sitters all seem frail inbred heirs of generations of refinement. Furthermore, all Gainsborough's sitters seem presented to us as seen by the eyes of love. It is thus we feel that a sensitive lover of this woman would see the oval of her face; it is thus that a sensitive woman in love with a man would see his expression (Pls. 40, 41, 42).

This air of inherited refinement does not reappear in English portraiture till we get to the work of Ambrose McEvoy (1878-1927). 'There are days', McEvoy once said to me, 'when I think Gainsborough the greatest artist that ever lived.' And Gainsborough, I fancy, would have accepted McEvoy as his descendant. For here we meet again the romantic approach which records a face in a way recognisable by the casual observer and at the same time imposes a sublimated expression.

For this reason both Gainsborough and McEvoy were defeated when the sitter was antipathetic. McEvoy in self-defence would refuse to listen to anything disagreeable about a man or woman while he was painting the portrait. And there are portraits by Gainsborough which are disagreeable because evidently he could not overcome his dislike of the sitter. He

59a. SIR JOSHUA REYNOLDS
The Duchess of Devonshire and Child
Private Collection, England

59b. ALFRED STEVENS
Mother and Child
National Gallery, Millbank, London

60. SIR JOSHUA REYNOLDS
Lavinia, Countess of Spencer, and Child
Private Collection, England

could do nothing, for example, with the flamboyant vulgarity of Madame Bacelli, who danced at the Opera in Paris wearing her protector's Garter ribbon as a garter on her leg; though he could impose his air of refinement on Mrs. Elliott and 'Perdita', Mrs. Robinson, who were likewise ladies of the *demi-monde* (Pls. 42 and 40).[1]

The delicate air imposed by Gainsborough and McEvoy was achieved in part by the power to draw emotive fragments of life with a sensitive perception unimaginable by Reynolds, Romney, Raeburn and their imitators, or by their equivalents in our own day. Judged by the scientific standard of the Italian Renaissance, or by a standard of still-life descriptive painting, Gainsborough and McEvoy were not less incompetent as draughtsmen than Reynolds, Romney, Raeburn and the rest. But as draughtsmen both must be judged by the romantic standard; and so judged both are seen to have achieved a part of their results by the quality of their drawing which ignores anatomy but captures here and there a tremor which spells life (Pls. 40, 43, 45.)

In one respect McEvoy excelled his ancestor. He could suggest a grace of attitude and stance (Pls. 43 and 45) which Gainsborough rarely achieved. Gainsborough—which was strange in a man so much affected by music—seems always to have found difficulty in suggesting graceful posture or movement. His attempt to symbolise a dance movement in his *Madame Bacelli* is

[1]The newspaper comments on these two pictures when they were exhibited make curious reading. The critics seem to have been quite impervious to the delicate sublimation achieved by the artist; and the freedom with which the sitters' characters were referred to would be impossible in the modern press, which many people to-day find so shockingly indelicate. Mrs. Elliott was first known as Grace Dalrymple and more familiarly as 'Dolly the Tall'. Commenting on Gainsborough's picture (Pl. 42) the 'Public Advertiser' described the eyes as 'characteristic of her vocation', and 'The London Courant' wrote: 'a wanton countenance, and such hair, good God!' Other papers complained of the proximity of such portraits to those of ladies of rank; and one referred to 'an unfortunate lady (Miss Da——ple) of whom we say with Pope:
"If to her share some female errors fall
Look on her face and you'll forget them all." '

unquestionably a failure; and compared with figures by Van Dyck or Reynolds or McEvoy, his figures at all periods have a doll-like *gaucherie* and sometimes they are actually awkward. We meet this doll-like *gaucherie* of posture in the early *Heneage Lloyd and his Sister* (Pl. 36b) and *Lady Innes* (Pl. 31) and *Miss Juliet Mott* (Pl. 39) painted later at Bath. It is conspicuous in the celebrated double portrait *Mrs. Sheridan and Mrs. Tickell* and in *Mrs. Graham* (Pl. 50); and if we examine the posture in '*Perdita*': *Mrs. Robinson* (Pl. 40) which seems so graceful at first glance we find that the grace and movement are really suggested by the fluent movement of the brush.[1]

This doll-like *gaucherie* in Gainsborough's portraits, which does not exclude a certain *chic*, derives in the first place, I fancy, from his early acquaintance, through Gravelot, with French eighteenth-century engravings. It has a certain charm of its own —a charm to which rhythmic grace of posture has been sacrificed.

It was the custom in Gainsborough's day, as it is now, to give unstinted praise to his landscapes—which nevertheless he always had difficulty in selling. The critics all seem to have looked on him as an innovator whose originality consisted in unusual naturalism. But the modern student, familiar with the naturalistic landscapes of the nineteenth century, and with photographic impressionism run to seed, is more likely to be struck by the artificiality in Gainsborough's landscapes than by their natural-

[1]Lest it be objected that Mrs. Robinson's illness may have been partly responsible for the rather stiff posture of this figure, I must add that I assume the portrait to have been painted before the fatal drive. Mrs. Robinson, it will be recalled, was an actress who played Perdita in 'A Winter's Tale' and became the mistress of the Prince of Wales. She was subsequently the mistress of a cavalry officer who became involved in debt and sent her a message late at night that he would have to leave the country unless she procured him £800. She succeeded in borrowing £300 and procured a promise of the rest in the morning; and then started to drive on a bitterly cold night to her lover (who was waiting to sail from a Channel port), forgetting in her agitation to take warm clothes or rugs. She fell asleep and was taken up in so frozen a condition that she remained more or less a cripple unable to walk or even stand normally for the rest of her life.

61. SIR JOSHUA REYNOLDS
The Brummell Children
Kenwood Museum, London

ism. We find, it is true, the still-life approach in his early land-scape backgrounds painted under the influence of Dutch pic-tures (Pls. 36a, 36b, 37). But the landscapes which he produced in Bath, and later in London, now seem conspicuously stylistic in handling and very artificial in their composition. Gains-borough, who discovered himself as a portrait painter after his contact with Van Dyck's portraits in the mansions round Bath, discovered himself as a landscape painter in the same period from contact with landscapes by Rubens. When he en-countered Rubens' landscape painting he found records of excited reactions to landscape rhythms which corresponded to his own delight in the lanes and fields. He had by this time abandoned the Dutch still-life approach to landscape and was working in the picturesque tradition which I have discussed in the last chapter. As a landscape painter he remained within the picturesque category; but like Rubens he painted trees which really grow and wave and flutter.

Gainsborough's landscapes were never painted out of doors. He walked and rode about the country, and sometimes, pos-sibly, he made chalk sketches on the spot. But all his landscape pictures, and, I fancy, most of his landscape drawings, were made in the studio. The degenerate picturesque landscape painters always worked in this way, as we have seen; but the procedure in itself was not evidence of degeneration; it had been employed by the original inventors of all the picturesque styles—by Claude le Lorrain and by Poussin himself.

Poussin, moreover, had used a species of box or model theatre as an aid in constructing his compositions; and Gains-borough worked with a similar contrivance of which an eye-witness has left us an account:

'I had the honour to be acquainted with that truly British genius at Bath, and have more than once sat by him of an even-ing and seen him make models—or rather thoughts—for the landscape scenery on a little old-fashioned folding oak table, which stood under his kitchen dresser. . . . This table, held sacred for the purpose, he would order to be brought to his parlour, and thereon compose his designs. He would place cork or coal for his foregrounds; make middle grounds of sand and clay, bushes of mosses and lichens, and set up distant woods of broccoli.'

Reynolds says much the same thing in the Obituary Discourse: 'He framed . . . a kind of model of landscapes on his table; composed of broken stones, dried herbs, and pieces of looking glass, which he magnified and improved into rocks, trees, and water.'

Gainsborough's letters also show how greatly his approach to landscape painting differed from the still-life procedure. 'One part of a picture', he wrote, 'ought to be like the first part of a tune, that you guess what follows, and that makes the second part of the tune.' Here we have an artist concerned with the architecture—which he would have called the music—of his landscapes. And when we look at his drawings we see him at work, disposing darks and lights, and balancing contrasted forms both for landscapes and for portrait compositions (Pls. 51 and 52).

He had not, of course, Poussin's strength or range of imagination or the majestic powers of synthesis revealed in the *Château de Steen* by Rubens. Even with the aid of his machinery—the bits of cork, wood, glass and so forth—he could not realise an elaborate scene with complex rhythms like Poussin's *Funeral of Phocion*[1] or even the relatively simple *Landscape with Two Nymphs* (Pl. 133b). But of this he was quite conscious. 'If [an artist]', he wrote to Jackson, 'cannot master a number of objects so as to introduce them in friendship, let him do but few'; and he added, with a wink, 'and that you know, my Boy, makes simplicity.'[2] He knew his range, was careful not to step outside it, and produced within it most gracious and delightful pictures. His trees have sometimes the romantic raggedness of the picturesque-romantic style and sometimes something of the rhythmic growth in trees by Rubens and sometimes the suave grace of

[1]Plate 35b in my 'French Painting'.
[2]Cf. below, p. 208.

63. SIR JOSHUA REYNOLDS
Battle Scene, or Horseman in Armour
Dulwich Gallery, Dulwich

trees by Watteau. When he introduces figures they generally exhibit much more grace and movement than the figures in his portraits; and they are often merged in the rhythm of the landscape; his *Crossing the Stream* (Pl. 46), for example, a picturesque-genre composition, seems to me almost completely unified in rhythm; and the same applies to a composition with nude figures called *Diana and her Nymphs surprised by Actaeon*.

We must observe, however, that the unity of rhythm in *Crossing the Stream* (Pl. 46) is purely formal. There is no psychological unity between the figures and the landscape. Some artists can so relate figures to a landscape that their pictures constitute a world which seems to us credible as an image of the world we know. Or to put it differently some artists in their landscapes with figures can create a microcosm which is not only formally but also psychologically convincing. Poussin could always do this; Watteau could always do it; Le Douanier Rousseau could do it. But Gainsborough could do it, if at all, only by accident and on rare occasions. He has done it, I think, in *Diana and her Nymphs surprised by Actaeon*. Technically speaking, the thing seems to me to depend on the relation of the scale of the figures to the scale of the landscape; it depends on the artist's power to invent scales which have psychological significance. Gainsborough's *Crossing the Stream* is charming as a decoration, as a piece of picturesque-genre, and in formal rhythm. But it has not the psychological unity of Poussin's *Landscape with Two Nymphs* (Pl. 133b) or of the *Amusements Champêtres* by Watteau.[1]

The same applies, in my judgement, to Gainsborough's most ambitious and celebrated landscape with figures, *The Mall*, (Pls. 47, 48 and 49). The figures here, psychologically speaking, do not move in a world of their own until a third of the picture is cut away from the top. Moreover, in this picture there is also no formal union between the rhythm of the figures and the rhythm of the trees. The figures appear to be dressed-up dolls round whom a landscape conceived on another scale has been artificially disposed.

[1]Pl. 48 in my 'French Painting'.

And this in fact is what actually happened. There is a tradition that the figures represent members of the Royal Family walking in The Mall. But this is an error. The picture was not intended to represent The Mall; and the figures are not portraits. We know from the artist's friend Jackson that the figures were painted from dolls which Gainsborough dressed up for the purpose; and that the whole picture was a composition, for which he used presumably his bits of wood, cork, broccoli, etc., for constructing the landscape.

Nevertheless *The Mall* is an attractive picture. I saw it years ago when it was still in the English collection from which it passed to the United States; and I recall its silvery colour with delight. It was painted in 1783 and, strange as it sounds to-day, the artist was never able to sell it.

It is impossible to resist the temptation to wonder what Gainsborough might have produced had he lived in a happier environment and not been a victim of the English system of art patronage which seduces so many English artists into portraiture: Would he have developed on the same lines as Renoir to whom in many ways he stands so close? Renoir was financed for the greater part of his life by an art dealer who allowed him to paint whatever he chose and never required him to make money by portraiture. What would Gainsborough have done if he had worked in these conditions? Would he have been content to concentrate on formal creation, to create pictures containing thirty figures all with the same face such as Renoir produced in the classical spirit? I think not. Gainsborough at bottom was always a romantic. He was really interested in the difference between faces. He hated portrait painting as a profession. But he enjoyed painting portraits. If a Durand-Ruel had financed him he would, I fancy, have painted portraits all the same.

CHAPTER VIII

REYNOLDS
1723-1792

★

1. REYNOLDS' LIFE

JOSHUA REYNOLDS was born at Plympton Earl in Devon in the year that Kneller died. He was one of a family of eleven, the son of a parson who was a Fellow of Balliol College, Oxford, and headmaster of the Plympton Grammar School. He drew on his exercise books, impressed his parents with his talent and ambition, and induced them when he was seventeen to apprentice him for four years to the portrait painter Thomas Hudson whom we have already encountered as a friend of Hogarth. The premium and fees of the apprenticeship, £120 a year, were provided partly by his father and partly by a married sister and his brother-in-law.

Impatient to test his powers and to make money he left Hudson before the end of the third year; returning to Devon he started as a portrait painter among the local gentry and the naval officers from Plymouth. When he was twenty-three his father died; he then set up an establishment at Devonport with his two unmarried sisters Frances and Elizabeth.

An unsuccessful visit to London about eighteen months before had convinced him that he had small chance of ever capturing material success among the London dilettanti until he had been to Italy and learned to talk of Raphael and Michelangelo and other Italians with 'hard names'. But funds were not available till a chance meeting with Commodore Keppel gave him the opportunity of a free journey. Keppel was in command of a ship ordered to the Mediterranean and he offered the young artist a cabin.

Reynolds reached Rome in 1749, at the age of twenty-six,

and remained there for three years. He was helped financially by his two married sisters and he made some money at portrait painting in Minorca on the way out. Thereafter he added to his resources, as students in Rome habitually did, by occasional copying of old pictures, by portrait commissions from the English visitors, and also by caricature portrait groups in the manner of one Thomas Patch (1700-1782) who was then living in Italy and had started a vogue for pictures of this kind (Pl. 55). On the homeward journey in 1752 he visited Arezzo, Florence, Parma, Bologna and Venice; and he stayed for a month in Paris.

On his return he established himself in London with his sister Frances as housekeeper and hostess. He lived first in St. Martin's Lane and then in Great Newport Street where his success was so rapid that at the age of thirty-two, in the year 1755, when he had still been only two years in London, he had a hundred and twenty sitters for portraits.

Thus encouraged he made a bold bid for the position of successor to Kneller. He bought an imposing house in Leicester Fields, where he had large studios, a gallery open to the public, and accommodation for pupils and assistants. Like Van Dyck, Lely and Kneller he entertained continually, collected pictures by the Old Masters, and drove abroad in an elegant coach. Like his predecessors he gave his sitters the minimum of trouble, demanding only two or three sittings for the head.[1] He continually increased his prices, and as he increased them more and more commissions poured in. In 1764 he made £6000—equivalent perhaps to £30,000 in present values. In 1777 he was charging seventy guineas for a half-length and a hundred and fifty for a full length, prices which again, to get present equivalents, must certainly be multiplied by five. In that year he painted the large *Marlborough Group* and had about seventy-five sitters. For 'fancy subjects' or 'history pictures', always sold from the easel or commissioned in advance, he charged still larger sums. Alderman Boydell paid him the equivalent of £2500 as a first advance on a picture for his Shakespeare Gallery before he

[1]Cf. below, p. 139.

134

65. HENRY FUSELI
The Nightmare
Private Collection, Switzerland
From J. H. Füssli: Dichter und Maler, by Arnold Federmann

66. WILLIAM ETTY
Youth on the Prow and Pleasure at the Helm
National Gallery, London

would undertake to begin it. The Empress of Russia paid him the equivalent of £7500 for a 'history picture' of any subject he might choose. It was his custom to stop work at four o'clock and devote the remainder of the day to social intercourse as relaxation and for the benefit of his career. His diaries, which survive, record his daily engagements for dinner and so forth, and the names of his sitters who included most of the fashionable and successful men and women of the time. When, in 1768, the Royal Academy was founded, he was so conspicuous, both as a painter and as a social figure, that he was inevitably elected President.

Soon after this election he was knighted; and on December 10, 1768, at the age of forty-five, he delivered his Opening Discourse to the students of the Academy, as Sir Joshua Reynolds, P.R.A. Thereafter he ruled the Academy for twenty years, maintaining his position as the most conspicuous artist against all comers—Gainsborough himself not excepted.

In 1782 at the age of fifty-nine he had a paralytic stroke. From this illness he never completely recovered. But he resumed work after some months and continued to produce pictures for the next six years. Then his sight failed him. Suddenly, without warning, his left eye clouded and soon became completely blind; then the other eye became to some extent affected; and in 1789 he painted his last picture.

The cause of this distressing end to his labours has not, I believe, been ascertained. It was possibly a chronic malady of long standing, which was also perhaps the cause of his well-known deafness from the age of twenty-seven and of the paralytic stroke of 1782. He lived for less than three years after the failure of his eyesight and died at the age of sixty-eight before suffering the complete blindness that he continuously feared.

He was buried in St. Paul's Cathedral. The funeral was an imposing ceremony. The pall-bearers were nine noblemen, including two marquesses and three dukes.

2. REYNOLDS' CHARACTER

'A Sly Dog!' WILLIAM BLAKE.

'I consider Reynold's "Discourses" . . . as the Simulations of the Hypocrite who smiles particularly where he means to Betray. His Praise of Rafael is like the Hysteric Smile of Revenge. His Softness and Candour, the hidden trap and the poisoned feast. He praises Michel Angelo for Qualities which Michel Angelo abhorr'd and He blames Rafael for the only Qualities which Rafael Valued. . . . I always consider'd True Art and True Artists to be particularly Insulted and Degraded by the Reputation of these Discourses.' WILLIAM BLAKE.

'I certainly do Thank God that I am not like Reynolds.'
WILLIAM BLAKE.

So much has been written about Reynolds by his contemporaries and subsequently by well-equipped biographers, and so many of his letters survive, that his character presents no mystery to the unprejudiced student.

He was clearly a man of exceptional strength of will, determined from the outset to make himself not only a successful artist but also a great one. He was also quite clearly an arrivist, a humbug, and a snob; a man who exploited everyone he met in one way or another, and never relaxed in the steady pursuit of his two aims.

No English artist of his eminence is so unattractive as a personality. We watch the progress of this pompous, astute, urbane, discreet, industrious bachelor from J. Reynolds to Reynolds and from Reynolds to Sir Joshua Reynolds, P.R.A., and though we pay a formal tribute, we have no desire to grasp him by the hand. 'I consider Reynolds's "Discourses" ', wrote Blake, 'as the simulations of the hypocrite who smiles particularly where he means to betray.' And it seems to me impossible to avoid the conclusion that Blake veritably unmasked Reynolds, and that the 'Discourses' are truly the symbol of this careful, calculating, civilised, polished and deliberately successful life. When we close the standard biographies we are left with a host of im-

67b. GEORGE ROMNEY
Lady Hamilton
Private Collection, U.S.A.

67a. SIR HENRY RAEBURN
Mrs. Hill
Private Collection, U.S.A.

pressions of countless small smooth contacts between this little man and hundreds of his contemporaries; but we can recall no spontaneous act of disinterested service, no engaging gesture, not even an attractive failing, on his part.

The method he pursued for his advancement was the usual method of the successful woman climber in Society. He worked unceasingly to increase the circle of his acquaintance among the nobility and gentry and among people in authority in all walks of life. He dined out and he entertained. That he might not appear only one of the crowd in this society he built up at the same time and with equal patience another circle of a mildly Bohemian character in which he himself was the most powerful figure. As other painters could be of no use to him, and might become inconvenient as rivals, he excluded them all from this *soi-disant* Bohemian circle, which consisted of literary and theatrical people with discreet additions from the *demi-monde*. This circle soon became a mutual admiration society, which still seems important largely because the members wrote and talked so much about themselves and one another. When Reynolds dined in the mansions of the great he would talk of his friends in this exclusive *intelligentsia*; if a duke was mentioned with whom he was not acquainted, he would politely offer to introduce the speaker to Goldsmith or Dr. Johnson. On the following night if a member of his own circle became unruly he would dispose of him with a 'When I was last at Blenheim', or 'As His Majesty said to me last night'. He stage-managed contacts between his attendant *intelligentsia* and his acquaintance in the great world so that the contacts might serve his own designs. Like the successful climbing hostess he paraded his eccentrics—Johnson and Goldsmith—before the gentry, the bishops, and the politicians; and if the eccentrics protested, as Johnson protested from time to time that they 'would not be made a show of' he paraded before them some duchesses and bishops in exchange. He drew sustenance from everyone and gave to each enough only to secure the service he required.

He was at all times tactful and discreet—Johnson called him

'the most invulnerable man I know; the man with whom if you should quarrel you would find the most difficulty how to abuse'. Northcote, his pupil and biographer who lived in his house for years and watched him with an envious eye, has also stressed this trait: 'Sir Joshua', he tells us, 'was always cautious to preserve an unblemished character, and careful not to make any man his enemy.' And Northcote also relates an occasion when Reynolds, hearing of some very indiscreet speech or action of Goldsmith, said 'quickly': 'What a fool he is thus to commit himself'—and then tried to cover it with, 'He has so much more cause to be careful of his reputation than I have of mine.'

His terrible urbanity was very skilfully gradated. Like the only kind of climbing society hostess who really succeeds he always preserved his dignity while he bowed and flattered, and he saw to it that on proper occasions he was bowed to and flattered in his turn.

His letters—which make a striking contrast with those of Gainsborough—show the gradations of his urbanity in relation to conditions and the relative importance of the addressees. Thus in 1769, when he had just been made President of the Academy, he writes to the Hon. William Hamilton, then Ambassador in Naples and later the friend of Nelson and husband of the celebrated Lady Hamilton:

'I hope you never will think that this delay [in answering a letter] proceeds from any want of proper attention or that I should be so different from other Artists as not to be allways proud of the honour of being remember'd by so great a Patron and judge of Arts as Mr. Hamilton. I hope you have been able to pick up some Capital Pictures as well as Etruscan vases. I have the pleasure to acquaint you that the Arts flourish here with great vigour. We have as good Artists in every branch of the Art as any other nation can boast. And the King has very seriously taken them under his protection. He has established an Academy which opened the first of January. It is composed of forty and cannot exceed that number, out of which are chosen all the Officers. To the surprise of every body I have the honour

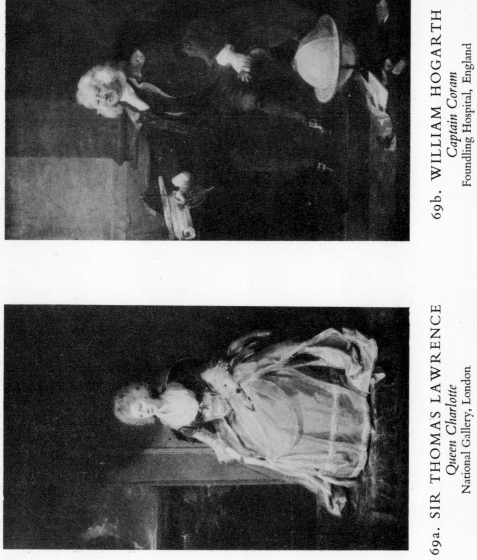

69a. SIR THOMAS LAWRENCE
Queen Charlotte
National Gallery, London

69b. WILLIAM HOGARTH
Captain Coram
Foundling Hospital, England

70. JOHN OPIE
Anne, Charlotte and John Gillett
Private Collection, New York

of being President, and it is only honour for there is no salary to this dignity. . . . If you should think it proper to mention to the King of Naples the establishment of a Royal Academy he would probably make a present of the Antiquities of Herculaneum. . . .'

Hamilton replied by sending some casts to the Academy; and Sir Joshua rewarded him as follows:

'I must acquaint you that in speaking to His Majesty some time ago of the Present you had made and mentioning some other particulars in the Letter He asked If I had the Letter about me and if he might see it. I had it in my pocket and put it in his hands. You have no reason to be displeased on any account but there was one circumstance rather fortunate, your having mentioned His Majesty in it with great affection and certainly without any expectation of his seeing it.'

He knew just how to place a man under obligation to himself and how to avoid servile gratitude to others. Half his surviving letters are notes of introduction, exhibitions of power disguised as kindnesses. Johnson knew him for a formidable fellow the first time they met. At this celebrated encounter two ladies present were regretting the death of a friend to whom they owed great obligations, and Reynolds said to them, 'You have, however, the comfort of being relieved from the burden of gratitude.'

He was an excellent man of business and knew how to impress his opponent at the beginning of the proceedings. When Alderman Boydell asked him to paint a picture for his Shakespeare Gallery Sir Joshua began by reminding him that it was beneath the dignity of the President of the Academy to work for a printseller. To a provincial gentleman who wrote asking his fees for portraits and if he had any 'subject pictures' for sale he replied as follows:

'I am just returnd from Blenheim consequently did not see your Letter till yesterday as they neglected sending it to me— My prizes—for a head is thirty five Guineas—As far as the Knees seventy—and for a whole-length one hundred and fifty.

'It requires in general three sittings about an hour and half each time but if the sitter chooses it the face could be begun and finished in one day. It is divided into separate times for the convenience and ease of the person who sits. When the face is finished the rest is done without troubling the sitter.

'I have no picture of the kind you mention by me. When I paint any picture of invention it is allways engaged before it is half finished.'

When the occasion seemed to him to call for it he could be superbly crushing. To a man who had called him a liar in circumstances where he undoubtedly appeared one (though in fact he had spoken the truth) he enclosed a document proving his veracity in a letter which began:

'You have the pleasure, if it is any pleasure to you, of reducing me to a mortifying situation: I must either treat your hard accusations of being a liar, with the contempt of silence (which you and your friends may think implies guilt) or I must submit to vindicate myself, like a criminal from this heavy charge. . . . When I assert anything I have the happiness of knowing that my friends believe what I say without being put to the blush, as I am at present, by being forced to produce proofs.'

The matter in dispute here was an alleged promise by Reynolds that the complainant, an engraver, should do a plate from *Mrs. Siddons as the Tragic Muse*, and the letter concludes as follows: 'You have been so good as to recommend to me to give for the future unequivocal answers. I shall immediately follow your advice, and do now in the most unequivocal manner inform you, that you shall NOT do the print. I am Sir, with all humility, and due acknowledgement of your dignity, your most humble Servant.'

The time came when he quarrelled with his sister Frances, who, as noted, had managed his house and acted as hostess in the early stages of his career in Great Newport Street and Leicester Fields. He dismissed her with a modest allowance, which she described as sufficient to keep her 'within the sphere of gentility' without the necessity of 'pecuniary schemes to raise it higher'. Her place was taken by one of his nieces Theophila Palmer and subsequently by her sister Mary. He had, as noted, a small house at Richmond, and some years after the quarrel Frances seems to have suggested that he should make over to her the freehold of this house, reserving the use of it for himself when the spirit moved him. As he had then been making the equivalent of £30,000 a year or more for fifteen years past he could well have afforded to transfer this security. But he replied as follows:

'Dear Sister—I am very much obliged to you for your kind and generous offer in regard to the house at Richmond not only in giving me leave to use it occasionally but even as long as I live provided I will give it to you, but as I have no such thoughts at present I can only thank you for your kindness—tho' I am much older than you I hope I am not yet arrived to dotage as you seem to think I am, voluntarily to put myself in the situation of receiving the favour of living in my own house instead of conferring the favour of letting you live in it. I am, your most affectionate Brother, J. Reynolds. I have enclosed a Bank Bill of ten Pounds.'

In 1784, when he had made still more money he succeeded the Scottish portrait painter Allan Ramsay as Principal Painter to the King, and he writes in several letters complaining of the salary. Here is one of these laments addressed to a bishop:

'Your Lordships congratulation on my succeeding Mr. Ramsay I take very kindly, but it is a most miserable office, it is reduced from two hundred, to thirty eight pounds per annum, the Kings Rat catcher I believe is a better place, and I am to be paid for the Pictures only a fourth part of what I have from other people, so that the Portraits of their Majesties are not likely to be better done now, than they used to be, I should be ruined if I was to paint them myself.'

In reading the last sentence we must however remember that numerous versions of the Royal portraits were habitually ordered. Ramsay, for example, had to provide ninety copies of his full-length portraits of the King and Queen.[1] Reynolds would thus have really made a great sacrifice in income if he had done all the work entailed by the office himself. But we cannot acquit him of greed for money. The small salary of this office

[1]Cf. below, p. 161.

141

really rankled; and he set on foot the following intrigue in a letter to the Duke of Rutland:

'May I now beg your Grace's indulgence and sollicit your interest in a matter which relates to myself. I believe I mentioned to your Grace the reduction of the salary of the King's Painter from two hundred to fifty pounds per annum. As there is great difficulty of having the old salary restored, as it would open the door to such numerous sollicitations, I thought there was an oppertunity of giving me a very honourable compensation in making me secretary and register to the Order of the Bath. Upon this ground, by means of Mr. Elliot, I asked for it, but it was too late; Mr. Pitt had already promised it to Mr. Lake, a gentleman who has some office in the Treasury. Since this negociation, Mr. Lake has been appointed one of the Commissioners of Accounts, a place of a thousand a year for life, and is supposed to be incompatible with his holding this place of secretary, etc.; at the same time, this latter is only three hundred a year, so that there can be no doubt, if he can hold only one, which he will keep. I have therefore to entreat your Grace to procure from Mr. Pitt that in case Mr. Lake relinquishes it, I may be the next. . . . If your Grace had been in London when Mr. Whithead dyed, I should not have despaired of having had the first promise. I have very little confidence in Mr. Elliot's interest, and therefore have not made a second application to him.'

The intrigue was not successful, and Reynolds had to content himself with watching his assistants paint the Royal portraits and pocketing the rat-catcher's wage.

Hogarth, in a passage already quoted, said that for avaricious portrait painters 'to commence dealers in pictures is natural. They collect under pretence of a love for the arts; but sell knowing the reputation they have stamped on the commodity, in the opinion of the ignorant; a despicable, damaged and repaired old canvas, sanctioned by their praise shall be purchased at any price and find a place in the noblest collections.'[1] This dictum comes irresistibly to mind as we watch Reynolds advising noble

[1] Cf. above, pp. 71 and 72.

71. GEORGE STUBBS
Warren Hastings on his Arab Horse
Private Collection

72a. GEORGE STUBBS
Reaping
Private Collection, England

72b. GEORGE STUBBS
Phaeton and Pair
National Gallery, London

lords on their purchases of 'Old Masters', buying on their behalf, and for himself, training his assistants to restore old pictures and to give an old appearance to new paint, and instructing his agents how to handle the owners of old pictures which he wanted to get hold of. It seems clear that as a rule he advised well the collectors who trusted him; as agent and dealer, he seems to have been quite honest; but he certainly exploited to the full the reputation which his own reputation stamped on the commodity, and when he bought things for himself as speculations he knew how to sell them at a profit.

All this is evidenced by his letters. For example:

'I set out for Brussels the day after I wrote to your Grace. . . . I was much disappointed in the pictures of the suppressed religious houses; they are the saddest trash that ever were collected together. . . . Though I was disappointed in the object of my journey, I have made some considerable purchases from private collections. I have bought a very capital picture of Rubens of Hercules and Omphale, a composition of seven or eight figures, perfectly preserved, and as bright as colouring can be carried. The figures are rather less than life; the height of the picture, I believe, is not above seven feet. I have likewise a Holy Family, a Silenus and Baccanalians, and two portraits, all by Rubens. I have a Virgin and Infant Christ and two portraits by Vandyck, and two of the best huntings of wild beasts, by Snyders and De Vos, that I ever saw. I begin now to be impatient for their arrival, which I expect every day. The banker, Mr. Danoot, was very ill when we were at Brussels, supposed to be dying; if that should happen his pictures will be sold. There are no pictures of Mieris either at Antwerp or Brussels. All the pictures in those two places which were worth bringing home I have bought—I mean of those which were upon sale—except indeed one, the Rape of Sabines, for which they asked £3500; excepting this, I have swept the country, and for this I would not exchange my Hercules and Omphale. If your Grace should choose to send any commision for the altarpiece of Rubens, or for the Vandyck, the sale begins the twelvth of September.'

It was thus that he wrote to the Duke of Rutland, a potential purchaser of the pictures bought. Here is a letter written to one of his agents about the procedure of buying:

'I return you a thousand thanks for your kind attention to my wishes about the two pictures of Rubens at the Capuchins, and you give me some hopes of a possibility of coming at them. I believe what I have offer'd, £300 for the two Pictures, is their full value, they have been much damaged and ill mended. As they are at present they appear to be worth little or nothing. I go upon speculation that I can mend them, and restore them to their original beauty, which if I can accomplish, I shall have got a prize, if they will not clean it will be so much mony thrown away. This is exactly the state of the Case. In regard to the copies to be made, I will be at that additional expence. I would send over a young Artist who formerly lived with me, for that purpose, and will give him proper directions how to give the copy an old appearance, so that few, even amongst the Connoiseurs shall distinguish the difference. If it is represented to the family by whom the Picture was given, that they are allmost destroyed and will soon be totally lost, they may reasonably think that putting copies in their place, is the best means of preserving the remembrance of the gift of their family. . I calculate the Copies to cost me about £100. When a man is about an object that will upon the whole cost £400 it is not worth while to bogle at small things, if making the principal of the family a compliment of a present of a Gold watch or any English trinket of the value of about twenty Pounds, I should be glad to do it.'

He acted for the Duke of Rutland in the purchase of eight pictures, *The Sacraments*, by Poussin. In this case also copies were put in the Italian Palace from which they were acquired. When the purchase had been completed Reynolds wrote to the Duke:

'I calculate that those pictures will cost your Grace 250 guineas each. I think they are worth double the money. . I think Mr. Beyers managed very well to get them out of Rome. The Boccapaduli Palace was visited by all foreigners, merely for the sake of those pictures by Poussine. Wellbore Ellis Agar told

73 · GEORGE STUBBS
The Melbourne Group
Private Collection, England

74. GEORGE STUBBS
The Princess Royal in Kensington Gardens

me they were offered to him some years ago for £1500, but he declined the purchase by the advice of Hamilton, the painter, on account, as he said, of their being in bad condition. It is very extraordinary that a man so conversant in pictures should not distinguish between mere dirtyness and what is defaced or damaged. Mr. Agar dined with me a few days since, with a party of connoiseurs; but the admiration of the company, and particularly of the good preservation of those pictures, so mortified him at having missed them, that he was for the whole day very much what the vulgar call *down in the mouth*, for he made very little use of it either for eating or talking. Lord Spencer tells me that he stood next, and was to have had them if your Grace had declined the purchase. One of the articles, he says, between Beyers and the Marquis was that he should bring the strangers as usual to see the copies, and which he says he is obliged to do, and, I suppose, swear they are originals; and it is very probable those copies will be sold again, and other copies put in their place. This trick has been played, to my knowledge, with pictures of Salvator Rosa by some of his descendants, who are now living at Rome, who pretend that the pictures have been in the family ever since their ancestor's death.'[1]

On another occasion he offered to exchange Gainsborough's *Girl with Pigs*, which he owned, for a damaged version of Titian's *Venus and Adonis* which belonged to Lord Ossory. But Lord Ossory did not trust the bargain and kept the Titian. 'What I proposed', Reynolds wrote when he learned of this

[1]The Hamilton mentioned in this letter was not, of course, Sir William, but one Gavin Hamilton associated in Rome with a swindling dealer named Jenkins in the planting of so-called Graeco-Roman statues, now in the British Museum and elsewhere, on Townley, Lord Lansdowne, and other dilettanti. (Cf. 'The Meaning of Modern Sculpture', pp. 56-72.) Reynolds had dealings with Jenkins and bought as he said 'upon speculation' a piece of sculpture from him for seven hundred guineas which, he wrote to the Duke of Rutland, he hoped to sell for a thousand. But he was too clever to buy for himself an 'antique' statue from Jenkins. The piece he bought was a group by Bernini (1598-1680), a pedigree work which had been made as a fountain for a Roman villa and had always been known there.

decision, 'I am still confident was a good bargain on both sides; however it is now over.'

A feature in all his letters is the careful avoidance of any obvious blowing of his own trumpet. When James Beattie was admitted to his circle he repaid the service by ranking Reynolds with Raphael and Titian in an essay on Beauty. He sent a proof before publication and Reynolds replied:

'I am much obliged to you for the honourable place you have given me cheek by jowl with Raphael and Titian, but I seriously think these names are too great to be associated with any modern name whatever; even if that modern was equal to either of them it would oppose too strongly our prejudices. I am far from wishing to decline the honour of having my name inserted, but I should think it will do better by itself—supposing it were thus: "but we do not find this affectation in the pictures of Reynolds, and in his discourses he has particularly cautioned the student against it"; and in the second place where I am mentioned, leaving out Titian, I shall make a respectable figure. Sometimes by endeavouring to do too much the effect of the whole is lost.'

How much more effective is this than Whistler's celebrated 'Why drag in Velasquez?'

There can be no doubt about it. Reynolds, as Blake put it, was 'a Sly Dog' indeed.

3. REYNOLDS' ART

'This Man was Hired to Depress Art. This is the Opinion of Will Blake. .
'Such Artists as Reynolds are at all times Hired by the Satans for the Depression of Art—a Pretence to Art to destroy Art.' WILLIAM BLAKE.

'Study consists in learning to see nature, and may be called the art of using other men's minds. . Our minds should be habituated to the contemplation of excellence . . we should to the last moment of our lives continue a settled intercourse with all the true examples of grandeur. Their inventions are not only the food of our infancy, but the substance which supplies the fullest maturity of our vigour.' SIR JOSHUA REYNOLDS.

75a. SAMUEL ALKEN
Duck Shooting
Private Collection, New York

75b. BEN MARSHALL
On the Moor
Private Collection, New York

76a. HENRY ALKEN
Steeple Chase—One of Four Pictures
Messrs. Knoedler's Galleries, London

76b. SIR EDWIN LANDSEER
Hunting Scene
Private Collection, U.S.A.

'[Reynolds] *endeavours to prove That there is No such thing as Inspiration and that any Man of a plain Understanding may by Thieving from Others become a Mich. Angelo. .*

'*Reynolds Thinks that Man Learns all he Knows. I say on the Contrary that Man Brings All That he has or can have Into the World with him. Man is Born like a garden ready Planted and Sown. The World is too poor to produce one Seed.*' WILLIAM BLAKE.

'*The mind is but a barren soil; a soil which is soon exhausted and will produce no crop—*' SIR JOSHUA REYNOLDS.

'*The mind that could have produced this Sentence must have been a Pitiful, a Pitiable Imbecility. I always thought that the Human Mind was the most Prolific of All Things and Inexhaustible...*' WILLIAM BLAKE.

'*—or only one, unless it be continually fertilised and enriched with foreign matter.*' SIR JOSHUA REYNOLDS.

'*Nonsense!*' WILLIAM BLAKE.

'*Reynolds n'a pas su voir chez Rembrandt qu'il pille, chez les Vénitiens qu'il traite de haut dans ses discours, autre chose qu'une pâte crémeuse et triturée, des tons fondus, des lumières et des ombres chaudes où l'or roussi joue dans les blancs épais. . . . Reynolds pourrait passer pour un grand peintre—grâce à ces portraits d'hommes surtout, parfois assez rudes et larges pour donner une idée vivante du soldat, du marin, du despote de lettres de ce temps-là—n'était son âme de grisette, affadie de songes niais. Ce sont des chats et des chiens enrubannés, des fillettes potelées avec des cerises aux oreilles, ce sont des regards noyés, des mains jointes, des visages roses de honte cachés sous de jolis bras ronds. Une peinture qui fait pleurer les vieilles dames et soupirer les jeunes filles, impuissante, équivoque, perverse, traînant dans des ruisseaux de parfums et de caramels le manteau de Rembrandt.*' ELIE FAURE.

'*Imitate not the composition but the man.*' EDWARD YOUNG (Author of 'Night Thoughts').[1]

REYNOLDS in his 'Discourses' continually urged the study of the Old Masters from whose works, he told his audience, a composite style of excellence could be extracted. Blake annotating a copy of the 'Discourses' expressed his disagreement in the vigorous terms I have quoted above. 'There is

[1]In 'Conjectures on Original Composition', 1759.

no such thing as a Composite Style,' Blake wrote elsewhere in these annotations. 'When a man talks of acquiring Invention and of learning how to produce Original Conception he must expect to be called a Fool by Men of Understanding.'

On the surface we have here a purely academic discussion. We seem at first glance to be present at a debate where Reynolds argues with urbanity that contact with the great art of the past can provide a student of average talent and average creative power with material that may make him a great artist. And Blake replies, with much less urbanity, that the student of average talent and average creative power is but an average fool, who is not less but more of a fool when he thinks that he can make good his deficiencies by theft; that the true artist, i.e. the 'inspired' creative artist, is born complete, so that contact with the art of the past can contribute nothing to his mind and spirit but only at best bring to the surface intuitions, powers, and knowledge already within them.

But we really have here something more than two rival academic theories. Considered purely as theories they are not indeed so very far apart—for if we understand Reynolds to maintain no more than that contact with other artists' minds, and not merely contact with their technical procedures, may or even must be useful in *some* way—it is arguable theoretically that we have here a formula on which both the debaters would agree. But the difference between these disputants is not really susceptible to any polite adjustment of this kind. There is here a clash of opposed attitudes and intentions, a veritable conflict between souls.

When artists with a long array of works to their credit, or discredit, make pronouncements about the history or principles of art, they are always really speaking of themselves and their own productions. Reynolds' 'Discourses' and Blake's annotations upon them, are both autobiographical. Reynolds is really talking about Reynolds; Blake about Blake.

To Blake's attitude I shall return later.[1] Here we are concerned with the art of Reynolds. And I have begun with this point in his 'Discourses' because, for Reynolds, it was a psychological necessity to believe that a man of average talents with no exceptional creative power could make himself a great artist by stealing from the work of other men. At the beginning, he had determined, with the full force of his exceptional will, to make himself not only a successful artist but also a great one. When he delivered his 'Discourses' he had made himself unquestionably a successful artist by procedures which he knew to be those most likely to bring material success in any field. But had he made himself a great artist? Of that he was not so sure. He was all his life quite genuinely modest as an artist. In his early years he believed that he had only average powers and that he was especially deficient in invention. 'It appeared to me too late', he wrote, 'when I went to Italy and began to feel my own deficiencies, to endeavour to acquire that readiness of invention which I observed others to possess'; and he had decided then and there to acquire the art which later he recommended in his 'Discourses'—'the art of using other men's minds'. He believed that the analysis of old pictures could make a man of average powers great artist because he *had* to believe it before he could believe that he himself had become a master by this means. He believed that 'nothing is denied to well-directed industry' because he had to believe it before he could believe that he who had relied so much on industry had reached the rank of the truly great.

When he went to Italy he doubtless knew that he was a heavy-handed painter and that his perception of form was approximate. But he also knew that art is not the neat mechanical recording of still-life experience; and that a man may become a great artist though his perception of form is approximate and his hand heavy. He knew, too, exactly the kind of picture that he wanted to paint. He wanted to paint portraits which would be arresting, decorative, and impressive. And he assumed that by stealing procedures from the Old Masters he would learn how this could be done. When he found himself arrested or impressed by an Old Master he looked for the source of the impression in some technical formula—in this or that quality of pigment, or blending of colours, or disposition of light and shade. He made copies and took measurements, he noted effects of chiaroscuro 'without any attention to the subject or drawing of the figures'. In particular he made an effort to extract secrets from Rembrandt, Titian, and Correggio because he thought he saw in these artists' procedures a heavy-handedness and an approximate perception of the same character as his own.

And so it went on. Not only in Italy but also in Paris where he stayed for a month on his way home. There he must have seen pictures by Rigaud (1659-1743), Nattier (1685-1766) and Raoux (1677-1734) who had all pilfered from the Rembrandt store, and pictures by Aved (1702-1766), Pesne (1683-1757), Charles-Antoine Coypel (1694-1752), Chardin (1699-1779) and La Tour (1704-1788)—contemporaries or near contemporaries whose names he never breathed. From each and all he learned tricks and procedures—but nothing more.[1]

On his return he sorted and assembled the spoil in his kitbag. He arranged and rearranged; put two and two, and three and five, together; he combined and separated; he believed that thus, and by intelligent industry, he would become a first-rate artist in spite of his conviction that his own powers were not first-rate.

But all the stolen elements—the pseudo-Rembrandtian chiaroscuro and texture, the 'Correggiosities of Correggio', the Titianesque drawing, the tricks picked up from here and there—all this is mere dead lumber in his work. The stolen procedures were of no use to him because stolen procedures are of no use to anyone—except to derivative hacks. Reynolds in his own work showed once and for all the absurdity of the eclectic doctrine that he preached. He painted pictures which have life and often grandeur—in spite of the kitbag in which he so confidently believed, not because of it.

He always underrated his personal creative power as an

[1]Cf. my 'French Painting', pp. 94 and 95, 127-142, and accompanying plates.

77. JULIA MAVROGORDATO
On the Downs—Lino-cut

78. JAMES WARD
Bulls Fighting

artist; and to compensate for his supposed deficiency he made a creative effort in almost every picture that he painted. He was not content, when he had made a first successful combination from the kitbag, to repeat the trick again and again. 'Damn him,' said Gainsborough, 'how various he is'; and the appreciation was a just one. Reynolds as a creative artist is marvellously various. He painted far fewer pot-boilers than Gainsborough himself. He had his studio assistants, as noted, but we know from Northcote that he would take his brush and repaint their work and transform it beyond recognition. In his enormous *œuvre* there are remarkably few hack pictures. Again and again he gives us pictorial invention. I can recall no picture from his easel that is solely or fundamentally a combination of the kitbag procedures—no picture, that is to say, which is essentially derivative and born, for that reason, dead. Reynolds in his mistrust of his own creative power may have believed that such merit as there is in his *Battle Scene* (Pl. 63) arrived there from the bronze by Leonardo da Vinci on which the central group is evidently based. But, in fact, the whole life of the picture, which is its only merit, comes from the painter.

I have quoted from a number of letters which exhibit the unattractive features of Reynolds as a man. Here is a letter written at the end of his life, when he had ceased painting owing to his blindness, a letter which shows him not only as a man but as an artist. It is addressed to Sheridan who had asked him the price of his wife's picture, *Mrs. Sheridan as St. Cecilia*, which had been painted fifteen years earlier and which hitherto Sheridan had not been able to buy. Reynolds answers:

'You will easily believe I have been often solicited to part with that picture and to fix a price on it, but to those solicitations I have always turned my deafest ear, well knowing that you would never give your consent, and without it I certainly should never part with it. I really value that picture at five hundred guineas. In the common course of business (exclusive of its being Mrs. Sheridan's picture) the price of a whole-length with two children would be three hundred; if therefore, from the

151

consideration of your exclusive right to the picture, I charge one hundred and fifty guineas, I should hope you will think me a reasonable man. It is with great regret I part with the best picture I ever painted, for tho' I have every year hoped to paint better and better, and may truly say, *Nil actum reputans dum quid superesset agendum*, it has not been always the case. However, there is now an end of the pursuit; the race is over whether it is won or lost.'

The race in fact had been won, because of that unceasing creative effort, because of that *nil actum reputans dum quid superesset agendum*. Reynolds has left us scores of portraits which live by their suggestion of expression related to circumstance, by an air of authority in men who wielded it (Pl. 56), of affection in young mothers with their children (Pls. 58, 59a and 60), of puppydom and kittenishness in very young children (Pls. 61 and 62) and of imitation grown-up-ness in children a little older—like *Prince William Frederick of Gloucester*. But that is not the full extent of his contribution. In spite of his study of old pictures he never learned to handle pigments scientifically and, as everyone knows, his pictures cracked and faded in his lifetime; many are now in deplorable ruin and many others have been unskilfully or too much restored. For this reason it is hard to judge him as a colourist. But as a designer of form against form, and a creator of pictorial rhythms, he is extremely various and impressive. Portrait after portrait is an original composition, not only as a two-dimensional decorative pattern, but also as an organisation of form in light and space. In his portraits—as distinguished from his 'subject pictures'—he is really first-rate in his power to suggest a movement that is never restless, and a grace that never seems affected or too sweet. We have but to compare his celebrated *Duchess of Devonshire and Child* (Pl. 59a) with the *Mother and Child* (Pl. 59b) by Alfred Stevens (1817-1875) to see where Reynolds stands. Stevens, a pasticheur who passed most of his life making drawings and sculpture in imitation of Michelangelo, is seen by the comparison to have no plastic invention, no sense of form, no feeling for rhythm, movement, or grace.

79a. GEORGE MORLAND
Hunting Mishap
Victoria and Albert Museum, London

79b. JAMES WARD
Horses Fighting

80. THOMAS ROWLANDSON
Smiling Man
Private Collection, London

The character of the grace and movement in portraits by Reynolds derives from his power on the one hand to control sensual and sexual reactions and his power on the other to avoid the still-life approach which Stevens had to fall back on when he tried to work with his own resources. In portraits by Reynolds the movement is not too exciting and the grace is not too sweet because both the movement and grace are integral parts of the rhythmic architecture of the picture. When he painted these women moving so gracefully in the parks round their country homes or in the saloons of their town mansions he was not recording sensual impressions of their appearance in his studio; he was using this grand lady or that *demi-mondaine* as material from which pictorial rhythm could be extracted. We can support the grace and movement in his portraits because it is classical and pictorial, not sexual and romantic, in kind.

But this applies only to his portraits. In his pictures with nude figures, painted in the solitude of his studio, pictures that he was driven to produce by a dual need to reveal and conceal secrets, we meet the characters set down by Elie Faure.[1] There is undeniably a detestable coyness in the sexual appeal which works through the pictorial rhythm in *The Snake in the Grass, or Love unbinding the Zone of Beauty* (Pl. 57). It is hardly too harsh to call this concept, which is the more intolerable by reason of the kitbag procedures in the actual painting, the *songe niais* of a *grisette*. It is indeed, as Faure says, a dragging of Rembrandt's cloak through gutters of caramel and perfume. The bachelor Reynolds who took out his pocket book and made a naughty sketch of a young person's thigh (Pl. 53) might pass for a good fellow in a suburban smoking room. But when we look at *The Death of Dido* (Pl. 64) we know why Elie Faure used the adjective 'perverse'. And the well-known sentimental pictures of children can surely be left to the sighs and tears of Elie Faure's maidens and *vieilles dames*.

It is usual to describe his windows in New College Oxford as failures; and it is true that the procedures adopted are not

[1] Cf. above, p. 147.

153

suitable for glass. But the cartoons nevertheless are far superior to his 'subject pictures'. As designs they are on a level with the portraits, genuine creations of abstract grace and rhythm, original contributions to pictorial style.

Encouraged by the incitements to thieving in his 'Discourses', the contemporaries and followers of Reynolds stole freely from his pictures.

JOHN HOPPNER (1758-1810), who had nothing of his own to contribute, stole the heavy touch and the pseudo-Rembrand-tian thick paint. GEORGE ROMNEY (1734-1802) a neurotic with weak will, who longed to make the imaginative contribution which was actually made by Blake, took the line of least resistance and painted hack portraits all his life. Falling in love with Lady Hamilton, he told the world that she was a graceful creature with wet red lips and lustrous eyes (Pl. 67b) and he painted her time and again with pictorial effects stolen from Reynolds. In his drawings he sometimes imitated Reynolds, capturing a little of the grace and dignity of the figures in the cartoons for the New College windows; and at other times he tried to imitate Blake and achieved nothing but purely rhetorical compositions.

TILLY KETTLE (1740-1786) who—like the REV. MATTHEW WILLIAM PETERS (1740?-1814)—imitated alternately both Gainsborough and Reynolds—had an eye for patterning (Pl. 54). JOHN OPIE (1761-1807), a Cornishman who had a spell of success as a portrait painter in the Reynolds tradition about 1780, also had this sense of patterning in a marked degree; and he had also the power of suggesting a significant expression (Pl. 70).

SIR THOMAS LAWRENCE (1769-1830) imitated the social air in the portraits by Reynolds. With great natural facility for painting he began on the level of Hogarth's *Captain Coram* (Pls. 69a and 69b), but eventually degenerated to the level of the popular romantic painters of our own day who produce large-eyed, red-mouthed images of luscious maidens on the covers of magazines.

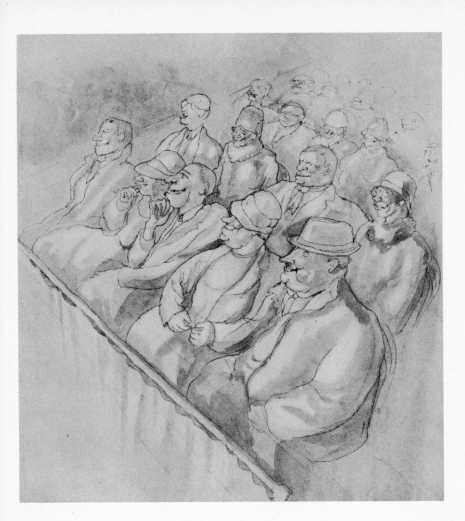

81. WILLIAM GAUNT
Music Hall Audience

82. E. F. BURNEY

Only two portrait painters stood out against the Reynolds influence: the Scotsman ALLAN RAMSAY (1713-1794) who remained resolutely a still-life portrait painter from start to finish, and another Scotsman SIR HENRY RAEBURN (1756-1823) who could record an air and an expression suggesting a type (Pl. 67a) and paint an arresting full-length life-size figure by the process of copying, like a camera, the shapes made by the lights and shadows which happened to fall upon it at the time (Pl. 68b).

Reynolds' 'subject pictures' were also extensively imitated. Peters on occasion carried the Reynolds' coyness to salacious indecency. H. Fuseli, to whom I refer later in several connections, imitated the painter of *The Death of Dido* (Pl. 64) in a celebrated piece of mumbo-jumbo called *The Nightmare* (Pl. 65). WILLIAM ETTY (1787-1849) captured here and there a little of the abstract rhythm and movement which Reynolds so frequently achieved (Pl. 66). But Etty's reactions were fundamentally sensual and romantic, and he was really more concerned to record these reactions than to create a picture. He saw naked girls as sinuous animals with silken skins; and he was primarily concerned to paint the sheen and the sinuosity. For this reason his pictures usually consist of nude figures with landscape disposed around them to fill up the canvas. And many of his pictures are just nude studies of the type which the French describe as 'académies'.

CHAPTER IX
PAINTINGS OF OUTDOOR LIFE

★

The English addiction to organised outdoor sports and games is too well known to call for comment; and a discussion of the ethics of adult ball-playing would be outside the subject of this book. Here we are concerned with these addictions only in so far as they have influenced English art.

The outdoor games played at the present time have been relatively rarely portrayed in English painting because their popularity did not become widespread until after the camera had proved itself a more efficient recorder in this field than the painter. But hunting, shooting, coaching, horse-racing, etc., engaged the attention of a number of able painters at the end of the eighteenth, and in the nineteenth century before the camera appeared and while its resources were still in process of development. The artists who specialised in this field were popular descriptive painters of figures in action, of animals, and of landscapes; many of them were connoisseurs of the activities, experts on the 'points' of the animals, and able to produce a portrait not only of a horse or dog but also of its owner.

One of the earliest English painters of such subjects whose works have survived is JOHN WOOTTON (1678?-1765). He painted hunting and racing scenes, portraits of dogs, portraits of racers at Newmarket, and also, it is said, picturesque landscape compositions. In London he had a handsome studio in Cavendish Square where he produced a state portrait of *George II on Horseback*—the face being painted by the Irishman, Charles Jervas, to whom Pope went for lessons when he took up painting about 1713.

JAMES SEYMOUR (1702-1752) had at one time a reputation as the ablest horse painter of the day—though prints after his pictures hardly suggest that he deserved it. He is described as a spendthrift and gambler who ruined his father, a wealthy banker, amateur artist and collector of pictures.

GEORGE STUBBS (1724-1806) at any rate was Seymour's superior as an artist; and indeed, judged by modern standards, he holds high rank not only among the horse painters but in the English School as a whole.

Born in Liverpool, the son of a currier of means, he was apprenticed to Henry Winstanley, an engraver occupied at the time in Lord Derby's gallery at Knowsley Hall. When he was twenty he established himself as a portrait painter in Leeds. Later he studied anatomy under a surgeon in York and lectured on the subject to students in the hospital. At the age of thirty he went to Italy. On his return he began an intensive study of the anatomy of horses which he continued for many years; at one time he lived in a lonely house in Lincolnshire where he was continually dissecting. Eventually he came to London and published a work on the Anatomy of the Horse, illustrated by his own engravings (1760-1766). This was a great success and won for him a European reputation and a large practice as a painter of horses. One critic in 1766 referred to him as follows:

> 'The wide Creation waits upon his call,
> He paints each species and excels in all,
> Whilst wondering Nature asks with jealous Tone
> Which Stubbs's labours are and which her own.'

In 1780 he was elected an A.R.A. and full membership was offered the next year. But as he refused to deposit a Diploma Picture, which, then as now, was obligatory, the election was not ratified.

At one time he took an interest in the technique of painting in enamel on earthenware; and he produced a number of panels which were fired by Wedgwood. I reproduce one: *Warren Hastings on his Arab Horse* (Pl. 71).

In his old age he began an illustrated work called 'A

Comparative Anatomical Exposition of the Structure of the Human Body with that of a Tiger and Common Fowls'. But he died before this was completed.

Stubbs was thus in the first place a horse painter with exceptional scientific knowledge of the subject. He was also an artist with real feeling for form. The spacial organisation in his portrait of *The Princess Royal in Kensington Gardens* (Pl. 74), and the deliberate, and dignified design in *The Melbourne Group* (Pl. 73) and *Phaeton and Pair* (Pl. 72b) make a strong appeal to the student of to-day. We get another aspect of his powers in *Reaping* (Pl. 72a) where he appears as a genre painter of English rural life.

SAWREY GILPIN (1733-1807) was much employed in painting portraits of racehorses at Newmarket. He also aimed at distinction in 'history' painting and produced compositions entitled *The Election of Darius* and *The Triumph of Camillus*. He was urged to apply for election as a Foundation Member of the Royal Academy but apparently he did not do so or he was not elected. He became, however, A.R.A. in 1795 and R.A. two years later.

Benjamin Marshall, known as BEN MARSHALL (1767-1835) was an able follower of Stubbs. He began as a portrait painter and was responsible for a portrait—well known in an engraving —of the celebrated pugilist John Jackson. He eventually established himself at Newmarket where he produced numerous pictures of horses often with trainer, jockey or groom. He had a sense of the dramatic in the disposition of light and shade and there is often a suggestion of weather in his skies (Pl. 75b).

DEAN WOLSTENHOLME, SENIOR (1757-1837), a Yorkshireman of means, began life as a sportsman and amateur artist. But having lost most of his money in lawsuits, he became a professional painter of hunting, shooting and coursing subjects which were engraved and very popular. His son, DEAN WOLSTENHOLME, JUNIOR (1798-1882), engraved his father's pictures and also sporting pictures of his own. Dean Wolstenholme, Junior, was also a connoisseur and fancier of pigeons which he drew and aquatinted with skill. In the history of that fancy his name lives as the perfecter of 'The Almond Tumbler'.

83. HENRY FUSELI
La Débutante
National Gallery, Millbank, London

84. JOHN BROWN
Woman and Duenna
Private Collection, London

There were other families of sporting artists besides the Wolstenholmes. For popular art, in all its forms, is a trade like any other; and a wise son always continues his father's business unless circumstances or an inner compulsion lead him to some other method of earning his living. We find this in the history of Dutch popular genre painting in the seventeenth century; we find it in French popular painting in the 'Grand Manner' at the end of the seventeenth and all through the eighteenth century, and in English art we find it in the sporting paintings and in the land-scape painting of the Norwich School. Sometimes the first members of the family were the only considerable artists; sometimes a son lifted his father's business to a higher level. In the case of the Norwich School the foundation members were only imitated by their successors. In the case of the sporting artists the second and third generations often made contributions of their own.

One of these families of sporting painters was named Sar-torius. The founder was JOHN SARTORIUS who seems to have come from Nuremberg. His son, Francis Sartorius, born in 1734, was the father of JOHN N. SARTORIUS (c.1755 - c.1828) and he in turn was the father of JOHN F. SARTORIUS (c.1775 - c.1830). A lady, Miss M. Sartorius, who also painted, seems to have confined herself to flowers.

We then get a family called Alken, of Scandinavian origin, established here in the middle of the eighteenth century. SAMUEL ALKEN (1750-1815) was the father of HENRY ALKEN (1785-1851) and of SAMUEL ALKEN, JUNIOR (1784-1825). HENRY GORDON ALKEN (1810-1892) was the son of Henry Alken. Samuel Alken seems to have been influenced by Stubbs (Pl. 75a). Henry Alken, who signed his early work 'Ben Tally O', excelled at representing the life and movement of the hunting field; he also had talent as a landscape painter, and was able to suggest typical aspects of the English country in the hunting season. Prints after his paintings were very popular in his lifetime and remain so to this day (Pl. 76a).

The history of English sporting painting cannot be dis-sociated from the history of the English sporting print. Stubbs himself was an engraver as well as painter; so were many of the others; and those who could not engrave employed professional engravers to reproduce their work. The printsellers always found it easy to sell sporting prints, especially those which were merrily coloured; and many of these prints are coloured aquatints. Prints which constitute a series have always been especially popular. One such set, *The Life and Death of a Racehorse*, by THOMAS GOOCH (*c.*1750 - *c.*1803) was aquatinted by the artist, and another *The High Mettled Racer* was designed by Rowlandson. A well-known series after Henry Alken, known as *The Night Riders of Nacton*, represents a steeplechase by moonlight—the riders wearing nightcaps and shirts over military trousers. Other very popular prints emanated from engravers employed by Robert Pollard. Among these engravers JOHN SCOTT (1774-1828) was especially skilful. ROBERT POLLARD (1758-1838) himself came to London from Newcastle, and took painting lessons from Richard Wilson before establishing his firm of printsellers, publishers and engravers specialising in sporting subjects. His son, JAMES POLLARD, painted lively pictures of coaching, racing, steeplechasing and so forth, some of which he engraved himself.

We meet a family tradition again in the Herrings. There was first John F. Herring, and then his son Benjamin Herring who worked in the same field. JOHN F. HERRING (1795-1865) started life as a stage-coach driver and painted inn-signs in his spare time; he was then taken up and trained by Abraham Cooper (1787-1868) who painted horses and other animals, and also battle pictures including (in 1816) a *Battle of Waterloo*. Herring soon began to paint portraits of racehorses as a business, and as he had an excellent eye for the 'points' he won immediate and well-deserved success. His work is of abiding interest to those concerned with the breeding of racehorses because he painted highly individualised portraits of all the St. Leger winners for thirty-five years.

PHILIP REINAGLE (1749-1833) who produced *The Sportsman's Cabinet*—a celebrated series of pictures of sporting dogs—

85. JOHN BROWN
The Three Graces
Private Collection, London

86a. JOHN BROWN
Women Promenading
Private Collection, London

86b. HENRY FUSELI
Woman's Head
Private Collection, London

and who collaborated with George Morland in a large picture of a *Dorset Meet*, began life as a pupil-assistant to Allan Ramsay. Reinagle's son related that Ramsay was ordered to produce ninety whole-length portraits of the King and Queen and that Reinagle painted them for fifty guineas a pair—Ramsay, who signed them, receiving two hundred.[1] Reinagle was also an expert in imitating the Dutch animal-painters and many pictures ascribed to Paul Potter, Berchem, etc., are said to be his work. He was made A.R.A. in 1787 and R.A. in 1812. His son, RAMSAY RICHARD REINAGLE, who painted landscapes, was associated with Constable, painted his portrait, and claimed him as a pupil. He was made an A.R.A. in 1814, R.A. in 1823, and in 1826 he was employed by the Academy to restore Leonardo da Vinci's cartoon of *The Holy Family and St. Anne*, which had come into the Academy's possession no one knows when or how, and had already been restored by John Inigo Richards, R.A., in 1791. In 1848 he was forced to retire from the Academy for having exhibited as his own work a picture which he had bought and not painted.

Philip Reinagle was associated with ROBERT BARKER (1739-1806) who started the fashion for large panoramic views which became so popular in the eighteenth century and eventually culminated in de Loutherbourg's 'Eidophusikon'.[2]

SAMUEL HOWITT (1765-1822) who painted hunting and shooting pictures was a member of a Quaker family well known in Nottinghamshire, and the brother-in-law of Rowlandson. He contributed to publications called *Orme's Collection of British Field Sports* and *Oriental Field Sports*. Others who won reputations as animal and sporting painters were GEORGE GARRARD (1760-1826), a pupil of Sawrey Gilpin; JOHN FERNELEY (1781-1860), a pupil of Ben Marshall, who painted hunting pictures and equestrian portrait groups; WILLIAM BARRAUD (1810-1850) who painted an attractive equestrian group of *Queen Victoria as a Child with her Mother, the Duchess of Kent*; JAMES BARENGER (1780-1831); R. B. DAVIS (1782-1854); H. B.

[1]Cf. above, p. 141.   [2]Cf. above, p. 100.

CHALON (1770-1849); and M. EGERTON who suggested the movements of horses in sprightly and engaging symbols which will be readily understood by those who enjoy modern work like *Horses on the Downs* by Julia Mavrogordato (Pl. 77). Egerton's racing and coaching pictures are mainly known from the pretty coloured aquatints produced from them by George Hunt in 1825.

This branch of art can also claim one President of the Royal Academy, Sir Francis Grant, and one artist who was offered the Presidency and refused it—Sir Edwin Landseer.

FRANCIS GRANT (1810-1878) came from a Scottish family and was educated at Harrow. He began his career by exhibiting pictures of hunting meets and other sporting subjects. His *Breakfast at Melton* was painted when he was twenty-four and his *Meeting of H.M. Staghounds at Ascot Heath* when he was twenty-seven. A few years later he abandoned this field and devoted himself to portraiture, and it was as a successful portrait painter that he was elected to the Presidency.

EDWIN LANDSEER (1802-1873) was a pupil of his father, an engraver, and of Benjamin Haydon, who made him dissect animals and draw the Elgin Marbles. He was a very precocious artist who exhibited paintings of dogs in the Royal Academy at the age of thirteen. At the age of sixteen he produced a picture called *Fighting Dogs getting Wind* and at eighteen the *Hunting Scene* which I reproduce (Pl. 76b). The French horse painter Théodore Géricault, who was in England in 1820, was greatly impressed with Landseer's talent at this age. But Landseer soon developed an attitude in animal painting which appealed to the public at large rather than to artists like Géricault or to spectators especially concerned with outdoor life. He humanised the animals and invested them with sentimental attributes to tell a sentimental tale. He painted for fifty years after the period admired by Géricault but produced little of interest to students of to-day. When he was approaching seventy he modelled the lions at the base of the Nelson Monument in Trafalgar Square.

87. AUBREY BEARDSLEY
Messalina
National Gallery, Millbank, London

88. EDWARD BURRA
Marseilles Bar

James Ward (1769-1859), another painter much admired by Géricault on his London visit, painted numerous pictures of animals including *Bull Baiting, Horses Fighting* (Pl. 79b), *Bulls Fighting* (Pl. 78) and *The Descent of the Swan.* He also made engravings representing animals in combat. He specialised to some extent in the study of prize cattle and painted many prize animals for their owners. His *Landscape with Cattle*, now in the National Gallery, London, painted about 1820 and thus probably seen by Géricault, was a deliberate challenge to Paul Potter's *The Bull*; and the cattle shown were prize animals of the time. His *Bulls Fighting* (Pl. 78) was painted about 1804 after he had seen Rubens' landscape *Le Château de Steen*, in the studio of Benjamin West.[1] *Bulls Fighting* was sent to the Royal Academy with other works including a large picture called *The Serpent of Ceylon* which the Hanging Committee rejected. Ward, in a rage at the rejection, withdrew all his pictures and exhibited them as a one-man show in a gallery where *The Serpent of Ceylon* was bought by a Mr. Earle of Philadelphia who then toured it in America.

Ward was an able craftsman who drew with intensity and gave his pictures an air of solidity by heavy impasto. He was, I fancy, a neurotic and a species of poet, very conscious of the life-force and receptive of dramatic impressions. The National Gallery of British Art (Millbank) has his huge picture *Gordale Scar, Yorkshire,* (c. 1815)—a chasm between limestone cliffs, which was also drawn by Turner, and which impressed both Wordsworth and Gray. Wordsworth wrote of the place:

'Gordale chasm, terrific as the lair
Where the young lions crouch.'

Gray wrote of it: 'I saw it not without shuddering'; and Ward evidently reacted in a similar way to this phenomenon which in his day would still have been referred to as 'sublime'.[2] In Ward's *Regent's Park: Cattle Piece*, painted in 1807, we get a dramatic effect of light which heralds Turner's *Petworth Park* (Pl. 102) and a handling of impasto which must remind the modern

[1]Cf. below, p. 197.   [2]Cf. above, p. 92.

163

student of Van Gogh. This picture really represents Marylebone Park Fields which were pasture transformed into the Regent's Park about five years after the picture was painted.

Ward married the sister of George Morland, and Morland married his; and till apparently about 1800 Ward painted rural, genre, and anecdotic pictures, influenced by Morland, which were engraved as popular prints. In 1794 he was appointed 'painter and mezzotinter' to the Prince of Wales. *The Strayed Child* and *The Strayed Child restored* belong to this phase of his activity which also includes a picture called *The Haymakers* (*The Sleeping Child*).

Ward disappeared from the London art world in 1830 at the age of sixty-one, and lived in retirement in the country till his death at the age of ninety-one. He is said to have painted four hundred pictures. If this be so, the vast majority have disappeared.

The English sporting pictures just discussed were out of the limelight in the last years of the nineteenth century and the first decade of our own when Whistler's Art for Art's Sake slogan was the order of the day. Since then a renewal of interest in this branch of art has been brought about by the talents of A. J. Munnings who has applied Impressionist formulae to the painting of these subjects and to other aspects of outdoor life. Whistler's influence found expression in the drawings of animals by Joseph Crawhall (1861-1913); and we get the influence of the Modern Movement in Julia Mavrogordato's *Horses on the Downs* (Pl. 77).

CHAPTER X

CARICATURE AND COMMENT

*

In discussing Hogarth's social subjects I have pointed out that the historian and the archaeologist cannot look to him for categoric records; that he was not, in his own phrase, a 'still-life painter' but a commentator, making caricatures in the original sense of charged or stressed (*caricata*) presentations. Caricature-comments of this and other kinds have at all times been made by English artists, whose attitudes and procedures are worth examination, if only because they stand much closer to the attitudes and procedures of other types of artist than is commonly supposed.

In caricature, as in other forms of art, we must distinguish between the procedures of original caricaturists which have meaning, and those of hack derivative practitioners which have none. Quite apart from differences between the mental powers and psychological approaches in original and hack caricaturists, which are apparent to all intelligent and sensitive spectators, there are technical procedures which differentiate the one type from the other. The difference is always that, in the one case the procedure has special significance in the particular drawing, whereas in the other it is used because other caricaturists have already used it. In the distortion of proportions, for example, the original caricature-commentator will put a very large head on a small body, or vice versa, when this departure from the normal is observable in some degree in the character of the man or in his appearance; but the hack practitioner will draw a large head on a small body or vice versa as a general procedure because he has observed the distortion in drawings by admired caricaturists.

Furthermore, the original caricaturist-commentator achieves an affective result—a comic effect—by witty form in these distortions; the character of the lines and the relations of forms will in themselves be funny, and the drawing will thus look funny to those who do not know the object of the comment. But the hack derivative practitioner, who imitates such drawings, degrades the witty lines and forms to stereotyped conventions which cannot be funny because they are born dead.

I have pointed out elsewhere that there is a close connection between original romantic art and caricature; the distortion in both cases being a means of calling attention to deviations from the normal.[1] The original romantic artist—Rossetti, for example—becomes emotional at the unusual length of some woman's neck and makes a distorted representation to stress this peculiarity which he finds emotive (Pl. 122b). The original caricaturist observes in much the same manner; but the search in his case is not for romantically emotive abnormalities, but for abnormalities which he can use to stress some social or psychological idea or which strike him as funny in themselves. When painting a scene with action, the original romantic selects or invents a dramatic moment, an emotive fragment of time; and the original caricaturist gives us a comic moment, or a moment which reveals the social or psychological character of the principal figure or figures or the social or psychological character of an episode.

The original caricaturist also stands close to the original portrait painter who can give us a portrait of artistic value by suggesting an expression. In the drawing *Smiling Man* (Pl. 80), Rowlandson, for example, joins hands with the portrait painters whose portraits survive as works of art. Like the portrait painter the caricaturist can suggest expression not only in the face but in the whole body. And he has advantages over the portrait painter. He can relate the expressions without difficulty to a number of different circumstances and show a Mr. Pickwick or a Dr. Syntax or a Don Quixote in fifty situations. Or he can show a

[1] 'The Modern Movement in Art', pp. 30, 150, 151.

166

89. RICHARD WALTER SICKERT
The Old Bedford

number of expressions, as it were, in the abstract, related to the same circumstance; thus Hogarth in the well-known print called *The Laughing Audience* exhibits the laugh as he observed it on a number of faces; and we get this procedure, with the addition of satirical comment, in the drawing called *A Music Hall Audience* (Pl. 81) by the living English artist, William Gaunt.

For there is, of course, a close connection between caricature and satire. The caricaturist-commentator normally calls attention to follies by exaggerating the comic element in some selected fool. But he may also get his effect by the multiplication of comic situations exhibiting the folly. Thus Hogarth accumulated absurdities in the scenes in *A Rake's Progress* and *Marriage A-la-Mode*, which show Tom Rakewell and the Countess exploited by the ministers to fashionable fads; and he accumulated old pictures and 'exotick' bric-à-brac in the saloon scene of *Marriage A-la-Mode* (Pl. 18b). We find this procedure a hundred years later in *An Elegant Establishment for Young Ladies* (Pl. 82) by EDWARD FRANCIS BURNEY (1760-1848)—a relation of Frances Burney whose 'Evelina' he illustrated by some drawings; and we may note in passing how freely Burney, a second-rate derivative caricaturist, has stolen from Hogarth.

As a satirist the caricaturist-commentator may dispense with the comic altogether and join forces with those who use the pencil to record their contempts and hatreds of social aspects or particular people. We have already encountered this in Hogarth's attacks on Bridewell and Bedlam (Pls. 16a, 16b and 17) and in his *Four Stages of Cruelty*. It was a caricaturist of this sort and one who would go further and not shrink from defamatory abuse that Sarah Duchess of Marlborough was seeking when she said on one occasion, 'Young man, you come from Italy. They tell me of a new invention there called caricatura drawing. Can you find me somebody that will make me a caricatura of Lady Masham, describing her covered with running sores and ulcers, that I may send it to the Queen to give her a slight idea of her favourite?'[1]

[1] Quoted in 'A History of Caricature' by Bohun Lynch (Faber and Faber).

On the opposite side there are caricaturist-commentators who record appreciation—not the romantic's emotional appreciation, but intellectual appreciation or philosophic comprehension. Here, if physical characters are stressed, their purpose is to remind the spectator that the exceptionally fine man, or the man of exceptional performance, is nevertheless not immune from the thousand natural shocks which flesh is heir to. If the comic appears in this type of caricature the laugh raised is not derision but a mark of sympathy. A caricaturist of this type may show, for example, the long-haired conductor of an orchestra extracting delicately a silken thread of melody from the first violins and exhibiting to the public behind him the bald patch which comes eventually even to musicians with the most exuberant growth. Or he may show a man who has just achieved a feat of signal daring reduced to timidity by some occurrence that has the same effect on the ordinary man.

An interesting form of caricature-comment consists in the suggestion of a charged or stressed atmosphere without specific representation of its physical causes or accompaniments. The artist has experienced an atmosphere caused by or accompanied by physical experience. He records the atmosphere but changes the physical causes or accompaniments. These transmutations of time and place are analogous, I think, to transmutations in imaginative art to which I refer later. In the field of caricature-comment we meet this type of transmutation in *La Débutante* (Pl. 83) by Henry Fuseli to whom I have already referred in relation to Reynolds (Pls. 64 and 65) and to whom I refer again in connection with Blake. It also occurs in John Brown's *Woman and Duenna* (Pl. 84), *The Three Graces* (Pl. 85) and *Women Promenading* (Pl. 86a) as anyone who compares them with drawings of similar subjects by Constantin Guys (1805-1892) will realise at once.

This JOHN BROWN (1752-1787) was the son of an Edinburgh goldsmith and watchmaker. He had his first instruction in drawing at the Edinburgh School of Art under a French teacher, William Delacour, who drew his portrait. At the age of nine-

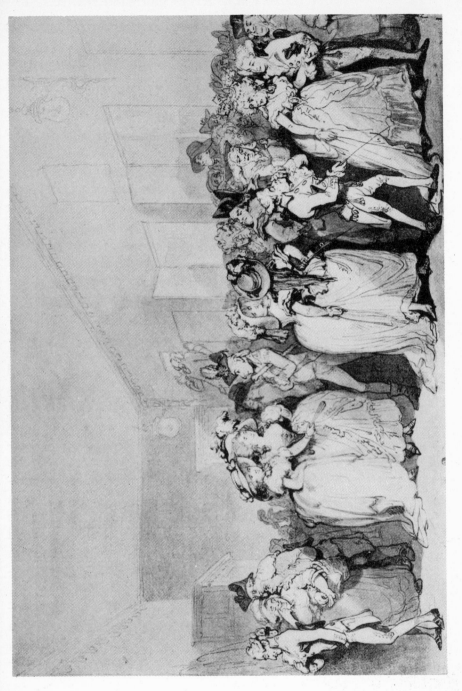

91. THOMAS ROWLANDSON
Box Lobby Loungers
Private Collection

teen he went to Rome and he remained in Italy for a number of years consorting with dilettanti, especially with Townley, famous for his collection of the so-called Graeco-Roman concoctions known as the Townley Marbles in the British Museum.[1] He specialised as a draughtsman and was employed to make drawings of 'antiques'. Returning to Edinburgh he made a reputation with portraits in pencil and drew many members of the Scottish Society of Antiquaries. He is also said to have drawn Mrs. Siddons. In 1786 he went to London. He died the year after at the age of thirty-five.

Brown was a man of parts who mastered the Italian language and was cultivated in music; he wrote verse and published an essay called 'Letters upon the Poetry and Music of the Italian Opera'. He was for many years a friend of the eccentric Scottish judge James Burnett, Lord Monboddo, who entertained Dr. Johnson and shocked him by calling himself Farmer Burnett, and 'going about with a little round hat', and who in other moods gave suppers where 'odours as well as light were diffused from the lamps' and 'flowers of all hues' adorned the chamber.

Several of his drawings are in the National Gallery of Scotland. These include portraits and a drawing of a *Seated Girl* which would not have looked out of place in 'The Yellow Book' just over a hundred years later.

When Brown was in Italy he probably met Fuseli who was there at that time. The drawings which I reproduce (Pls. 83, 84, 85, 86a, 86b) evidence a connection between the two men. I am not sure whether Brown imitated Fuseli or Fuseli Brown; no help in the problem comes from the story told by J. T. Smith in 'Nollekens and his Times' that when Brown was praised in Fuseli's presence Fuseli exclaimed, 'Well Brown, Brown, we have had enough of Brown; let us now talk of Cipriani who is in hell', because such irritation is characteristic both of artists who are robbers and of artists who have been robbed. We know, however, that Nollekens said Fuseli copied a print in his studio

[1]Cf. above, p. 145.

and used it for a figure in one of his drawings, and that Fuseli imitated both Reynolds (Pls. 64 and 65) and Blake.[1]

A type of transmutation analogous to these drawings by Brown and Fuseli also occurs in the caricature-comments by AUBREY BEARDSLEY (1872-1898), whose *Messalina* I reproduce (Pl. 87). Beardsley had recourse to transmutation as a means of escape from the life around him which he was not robust enough to accept and feel at home with. Experience of surrounding life brought upon him a species of panic; and he had to transmute it and make it part of an imagined world where he could move at ease before he could visualise it clearly and without fear. The technique which he invented for this purpose was a means not only of effecting the transmutation but also a means of suggesting a subtly charged atmosphere. In itself, when not used to effect a transmutation and suggest an atmosphere, his technical procedure is nothing more than exquisitely refined decoration—as the student who compares his illustrations to Pope's 'Rape of the Lock' with his illustrations to Wilde's 'Salome' will see; and it is mainly this minor decorative aspect of his contribution that has been picked up by his imitators.

Beardsley's attitude must be carefully distinguished from that of the living English artist Edward Burra who has made some clever contributions to caricature-comment. Beardsley would secretly have experienced panic in the scene which Burra has depicted in *Marseilles Bar* (Pl. 88). But Burra was not affected in that way. He was so little afraid of the scene that it seemed to him unreal and fantastic, a grotesque parody of life, already in itself not so much an actual scene as a distorted caricature-comment. Standing outside his subject, intensely fascinated, but quite detached from it, he made his observations; and when the time came to draw he recorded truthfully his vivid impression of a grotesque puppet-show. Because he was able on the one hand to accept the scene without panic, and because he refused on the other to identify himself with or to have intimate emotional contact with it, he felt no need to transmute it in time or place.

[1]Cf. below, pp. 234-236.

93. THOMAS ROWLANDSON
Light Horse Barracks
Messrs. Frank Sabin Galleries, London

94a. THOMAS ROWLANDSON
Fairlop Fair
Messrs. Frank Sabin Galleries, London

94b. THOMAS ROWLANDSON
Bagshot Heath
Private Collection

He was able to suggest the·charged atmosphere by means of presentations which are caricatured in the sense of charged or loaded; and he uses both affective distortions and the Hogarthian procedure of accumulation. His drawing is thus quite different in character from the transmuted drawings by Brown, Fuseli and Beardsley.

Original caricaturists are always capable of work in other fields and almost invariably produce it. Their caricatures are often only one aspect of their work as a whole, and they are often also an aspect of contemporary culture and a contribution to it. Conversely many original artists of all kinds produce occasional caricature-comments or works which approximate to them. Many of the social comments of the French nineteenth-century Romantics, Degas (1834-1917), and Toulouse-Lautrec (1864-1901), for example, are on the borderland of caricature-comment, and we find the same thing in their modern English descendant, Richard Walter Sickert, whose *Portrait in the rue Aguardo* (Pl. 68a) is brilliant romantic portraiture, brilliant Impressionism, and caricature-comment at one and the same time.

When an original artist joins hands with the caricaturists in this way we get *ipso facto* a contribution to the technique of caricature. An artist of the stature of Sickert does not imitate existing caricature procedures in his caricature-comments. Sickert's vision is fundamentally impressionist; like all the original Impressionists of the nineteenth century he is primarily a painter of effects of light; but he is also a modern artist concerned with architectural form. If we compare his picture *The Old Bedford* (Pl. 89) with Hogarth's *Laughing Audience* or with William Gaunt's *Music Hall Audience* (Pl. 81) all these characters are obvious. Sickert remains Sickert when he contributes to social comment.

The drawing called *Pole Jump* (Pl. 90) by Wyndham Lewis is another illustration of this point. This was done at a time when Lewis was a pioneer of Cubism in England and was himself experimenting in distortions for architectural ends. In this drawing he steps into the field of caricature-comment and enriches its history by so doing. Since this drawing was made, about fifteen years ago, we have seen numerous caricatures in pseudo-Cubist technique from hack practitioners incapable alike of caricature-comment and of understanding the Cubist-Classical revival of interest in form. The student will find it useful to compare some of these addle-pated derivative productions with the *Pole Jump*, where witty comments are expressed in distortions of form which are equally witty.

Some caricaturists are independent commentators, others are propagandists for some group attitude of their environment. The drawings of the first class of caricaturists survive as works of art; those of the second survive only as objects of interest to historians and archaeologists. Thus the work of political cartoonists which is usually of the second class rarely interests the student of art because its intention, in the large sense in which I use the word throughout this book, is rarely original. Some caricaturists have worked both as independent commentators and servants of prevailing attitudes at different times of their careers. In such cases the student of art can capture contact with the first aspect of their production but not with the second. The lowest form of caricature—the only kind which can properly be described as base and degraded—is the caricature which serves some mass hysteria or persecuting sadistic tyranny of the moment and contributes to the dissemination of its propaganda. The most trivial form of caricature is the caricature which serves prevailing snobbisms.

THOMAS ROWLANDSON (1756-1827) was the greatest of English caricaturist-commentators. His immense production is a kind of English equivalent to Balzac's *Comédie Humaine*. In the history of European painting it is the connecting link between the French eighteenth-century *tableaux de modes* and *estampes galantes* and the social comments of Daumier (1808-1879) and Guys (1805-1892).

He was born in London, the son of a well-to-do tradesman, who encouraged his obvious talent for drawing and procured his admission to the Academy schools. When he was sixteen he was sent to Paris to a French aunt who developed a great affection for him and kept him with her for three years. In Paris he worked in the Ecole de l'Académie Royale and doubtless became familiar with the new movement in French art of the period—the paintings and drawings by Fragonard, and the *gouaches* and engravings of *tableaux de modes* by Baudouin (1723-1769), Lavreince (1737-1807), and Augustin St. Aubin (1737-1807). He certainly knew Janinet (1752-1814)—who was of his own age and a student at the same time in the Ecole de l'Académie Royale; and probably Vien's pupil Debucourt (1755-1832). Vien (1716-1809) then at the height of his reputation was much discussed as the painter who carried out the decorations at Louveciennes for Mme du Barry when Fragonard's panels had been rejected.[1]

In 1775 when he was nineteen he returned to London and the Academy schools where his skill in drawing impressed the students and professors; and he began to send drawings to the Academy exhibitions.

About this time he found himself without funds because his father, who was a gambler and a speculator, had lost all his money. But the aunt in Paris seems to have come to the rescue; and when she died, soon after, she left him the equivalent in present values of some £35,000.[2] Rowlandson, however, was not of a thrifty disposition and he had inherited his father's taste for gambling. He soon squandered and lost this capital and had to settle down about 1782, when he was twenty-six, to make money by his work.

He began as a caricaturist-commentator on abuses of the moment, and a humorous commentator on social life; he drew and published prints of duchesses kissing butchers to secure votes, a gouty parson receiving a tithe pig from a half-starved yokel, naval officers taking grog on board with one type of female companion and tea on shore with another type, sleek army officers drinking wine outside an inn and giving alms to a

[1]Cf. my 'French Painting', pp. 157, 165, 181 and 183.
[2]£7000 and a good deal of valuable silver and other property.

beggar woman who has one child on her back and is about to give birth to another, and so on and so forth. At the same time he resolved to attract attention by an ambitious *tableau de modes*, and he drew *Vauxhall Gardens*, an elaborate composition with numerous figures including portraits of celebrities, which he exhibited in the Academy in 1784. This promenade scene was a great success in the exhibition and also when engraved; and it is probable that Debucourt's celebrated *Promenade de la Galerie du Palais Royal* (1787) and *La Promenade Publique* (1792) were influenced by it.

He followed this success with other drawings exhibited in the Academy in the next three years, one of which, *Box Lobby Loungers* (Pl. 91) I reproduce. In this drawing we see the whole *dramatis personae* of one aspect of his *Comédie Humaine*. The types here represented, distorted more and more for emphasis as time went on (Pl. 92), occur again and again in his drawings, and etchings, and in the colour prints from his designs. We have here as it were the cast of one of his repertory theatres assembled on the stage. With this material he produced a complete comedy of public and private manners in his day. We see the same crowd taking mud baths and drinking the waters at Bath, we see them at a military review, we see them discomfited by a squall of wind in Hyde Park, thrown into confusion by the fall of a fat man as they mount a staircase at a reception, and attitudinising at a Royal Drawing Room or at Boodle's Club. On the other occasions he shows us gentlemen carried to bed by yawning servants after emptying scores of bottles at a hunt supper; he takes us to military headquarters where the officers make their toilettes assisted by *soubrettes*; and into the *Light Horse Barracks* where all is geniality while the horses neigh and the hussars take the lassies on their knee (Pl. 93). In smaller scenes we see two or three of his actors engaged in domestic felicities or wrangles, nursing their ailments, fired to rage by jealousy, or scolding the housemaid because the sheets are damp; and all the time young people kiss behind the backs of their parents and girls escape from windows when the doors are barred (Pl. 95).

95. THOMAS ROWLANDSON
The Elopement
Leicester Galleries, London

96. THOMAS GIRTIN
Kirkstall Abbey

But this repertory theatre, and this set of actors, were not the only material in Rowlandson's art. He travelled all over England and also in France, Germany, Holland and Belgium, making drawings and sketches and storing up impressions wherever he went. A close friend of George Morland, he sometimes drew rural picturesque-genre scenes in the Morland manner, and drew them with so spirited a touch that David Wilkie (1785–1841) in *Pitlessie Fair* could do nothing but translate them, with less verve and spirit, to the clumsier medium of oil paint.

Rowlandson had also an individual vision of landscape. He could suggest open country and luxuriant verdure and set before us an outdoor scene with numerous figures all brilliantly distorted for emphasis and all marvellously true (Pl. 94a). At times he joins hands with the painters of sporting pictures and gives us coaching scenes where the horses really gallop in the open country and the gipsy children tumble for pennies as the coach rattles by (Pl. 94b).

But even so we have not summarised his whole contribution. If all the drawings and prints of the categories I have mentioned had perished, his name would still survive on the strength of others. All this represents his visual equipment as an artist, his habitually broad sympathy with the life around him which he could usually accept and comment on without transmutation, his power to charm us with his delicate handling of the reed pen and watercolour washes of pretty pale colours. But there was another aspect to his temperament. Owing to his habit of gambling and his thriftless manner of life he was often short of money, though money was always coming in. The attractive drawings I have been discussing were bought by collectors and he always had arrangements with printsellers, notably with two named Fores and Ackermann, for whom he produced illustrations—the well-known drawings called the *Comforts of Bath* (1798) being done for Fores, those reproduced in *The Miseries of Life* (1808) and *The Tours of Dr. Syntax* (1812–1820) being done for Ackermann. But these publishers would not reproduce another type of drawing—his most personal and original productions—in which we find a concept of mankind as *la bête humaine*—a gross beast intent on purely animal pleasures and suffering purely animal pains, a persecuting beast leering at bull-baiting and delighting in torture; and at the same time a persecuted beast maddened by bed bugs, the sport of Death who hands the punchbowl and mocks at the antics of his victims.

In these drawings, of which *The Cobbler's Cure for a Scolding Wife* is a well-known example, Rowlandson's distortions suggest a monstrous fatness or leanness, and create diabolic expressions recalling Japanese drawings (with which he was certainly familiar). The distortions here are not the distortions for emphasis which occur in Rowlandson's drawings of the types here reproduced. Nor are they the distortions of modern architectural art. They are the distortions of a nightmare where mankind is all shrivelled and decayed or swollen to bursting. They are morbid distortions amounting to transmutation born, I imagine, of some secret obsession.

Many of Rowlandson's drawings of this type were engraved or etched, crudely coloured, and published by a printseller called Tegg. The prints as published often bear, I fancy, but scant resemblance to the original drawings which had probably to be 'toned down' and modified even though Tegg addressed himself to a public with gross tastes and little or no sensibility. At the same time the brilliance of the original drawing, as drawing, was destroyed in the reproduction, the contours and modelling being falsified in coarse copying and by clumsy application of colour.

It is generally assumed that the drawings of this type represent a later activity, and they are taken as evidence that Rowlandson degenerated as an artist and a man. I cannot endorse this assumption. The chronology of much of his work is uncertain. But we find this aspect of his temperament in drawings and prints which can be dated before 1800. There would seem, it is true, to be an intensification of the obsessional distortions as time goes on, but the attitude, I think, was present intermittently at all periods.

97. J. S. COTMAN
Landscape with Cows
Victoria and Albert Museum, London

J. M. W. TURNER

There would also seem to be no support for the notion that the so-called later style was a species of pot-boiling to which he was condemned by poverty in his later years. He probably made money, and spent it, and lost it, as fast and in the same ways, at all times of his life; he could, of course, and did make pretty easily sold attractive drawings in his later years; there is no evidence that his later work was all in the nature of hurried hack work for Tegg or others who catered for crude tastes; and when he died he left about £3000, equivalent to something like £12,000 in values of to-day.

There was surely some latent recurring morbidity in Rowlandson which he relieved by this terrible concept of *la bête humaine*; and it is perhaps significant that at the end of his life he is said to have made many drawings of bestialised human heads by the side of heads of animals.

CHAPTER XI

TOPOGRAPHICAL LANDSCAPE

★

Many of the English picturesque-classical landscapes, which I have discussed in an earlier chapter, contained a topographical element and were based on views of actual Italian villas or Roman remains. This tradition of topographical descriptive art went back in England to Tudor times when the English gentry established themselves in country houses surrounded with gardens and parks. It is still often possible to find in neglected corners of country houses a sixteenth-century painting of the original house that stood upon the site. Such pictures were the work of itinerant artists who knocked at the door, appealed to the owner's sense of property, and provided, for a small sum, a portrait of his house and its surroundings. This practice continued into and throughout the eighteenth century. The artists often engraved these productions; and collections of such topographical records were published in portfolios and as books, till, eventually, all the country seats of England, the cathedrals, and churches had been recorded in this way. Owing to the influence of the picturesque tradition, drawings and engravings of ruins—ruined abbeys, ruined castles and so forth—were especially popular in the eighteenth and at the beginning of the nineteenth century. There was also a market then, as there is to-day, and as there has always been, for topographical paintings, drawings and engravings of London.

At the end of the eighteenth century most of the English topographical artists worked in watercolour; some worked in aquatint; a few painted in oils. I have already mentioned the

178

99. J. M. W. TURNER
Hero and Leander
National Gallery, Millbank, London

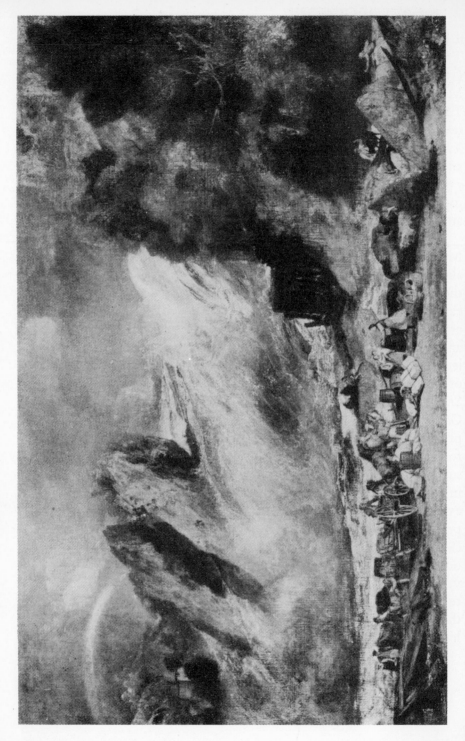

names of Paul Sandby[1] and Samuel Scott.[2] I must now add THOMAS HEARNE (1744-1817), MICHAEL ANGELO ROOKER (1740-1813), WILLIAM MARLOW (1740-1812), THOMAS MALTON (1748-1782), and EDWARD DAYES (1763-1804). These men were skilful practitioners and their work appears respectable even when contrasted with the brilliant topographical drawings produced at the present day by Muirhead Bone and his follower Henry Rushbury.

At the turn of the eighteenth to the nineteenth century this topographical tradition was attacked by the new Romantic attitude. It was attacked, that is to say, by Girtin and Turner.

The attack took place in the London parlour of Dr. Thomas Monro, who had treated J. R. Cozens in his last illness, as already noted,[3] and who chanced to play an important role in the history of English art. Monro was a specialist in mental disease and one of George III's doctors; he was also an amateur artist who made drawings in the picturesque-classical tradition, and collected paintings, drawings, and watercolours. His collection was large and varied; he had an *Esther and Haman* by or ascribed to Rembrandt, and pictures by Salvator Rosa, Snyders and Zuccarelli; he had drawings by Canaletto, Wilson, Gainsborough and the leading topographical and picturesque practitioners—de Loutherbourg, Sandby, Dayes, Hearne and so forth; and he had a great many drawings of Swiss and Italian subjects by J. R. Cozens. He kept this miscellaneous collection in his handsome house in Adelphi Terrace and there, in the evenings, he entertained young artists, gave them oyster suppers, and set them to copy drawings by Cozens and others as an excuse for providing them with odd half-crowns—equivalent to odd guineas at the present day. The young artists included, at various times, Louis Francia, a Frenchman who made picturesque drawings, including a *Moonlight Composition* (now in the Victoria and Albert Museum), and afterwards gave drawing lessons to Bonington[4]; John Varley, of whom I shall speak again

---

[1]Cf. above, p. 65. [2]Cf. above, p. 73.
[3]Cf. above, p. 99. [4]Cf. below, p. 211.

in connection with Blake; Peter de Wint; Cotman, whose work I discuss later;[1] and, at one moment, about 1795, both Girtin and Turner.

THOMAS GIRTIN (1775-1802) was born at Southwark, the son of a brushmaker (or a rope and cordage contractor—the biographers differ). His elder brother was an engraver. He himself was early apprenticed to a drawing master named Fisher and afterwards to Dayes; and at eighteen he was already an efficient topographical draughtsman. About this time he met one James Moore, a city merchant and amateur draughtsman with antiquarian tastes. Moore was then preparing an illustrated publication called 'Monastic Remains and Ancient Castles in England and Wales' and another with views of places in Scotland; he employed Girtin, Dayes and others to work up his sketches as illustrations, and he may have taken Girtin with him on a tour to the North in 1792.

It was a couple of years later that Girtin met Dr. Monro and began to attend the evenings in Adelphi Terrace. He worked side by side with Turner, copying drawings by Cozens and others; and the two young men, who were then both about twenty, became friends. As the half-crowns and oysters provided by Monro—whom Turner always referred to later as 'the good doctor'—could not solve all their financial problems, both Girtin and Turner produced topographical drawings for the market; and at this time they seem to have travelled about together, making drawings sometimes of the same places.

A year or two later each was launched as an independent draughtsman. Girtin drew all over the country and went to Paris in 1801. In 1802 he painted and exhibited a Panorama of London in oil colours. But his health was seriously undermined —the result, according to his old master Dayes, of 'suffering the passions to overpower reason and to hurry . . . into acts of excess'—which probably means that he burned the candle at both ends. Before the end of 1802, at the age of twenty-seven, he died of some affection of the lungs.

[1]Cf. below, pp. 208-211.

As a watercolour draughtsman he was an innovator who enlarged watercolour technique in what proved, after a time, a disastrous direction. In his early days he worked in the traditional manner; his watercolours, that is to say, were literally *drawings*—line drawings 'shadowed' with monochrome washes, colours being subsequently added to suggest colour alone. In his later work he tried to make his watercolours *paintings* and to use colour in a naturalistic way. He thus opened the door to the watercolours of the nineteenth century, which were in no sense drawings, but fundamentally imitations of naturalistic paintings in oils.

It is difficult for the modern student to appreciate Girtin's particular achievement. Most of his drawings fall into the topographical class: he drew castles and cathedrals, churches, houses, villages, streets and views. But in his later work topography gives place to a record of communion between the artist and the scene contemplated; the drawing records not so much the place or the monument as some emotive quality extracted from the scene.

Girtin breaks right away from topography in drawings like *Tynemouth*, *View on the Wharf*, and *Kirkstall Abbey* (Pl. 96). Here he records moods suggested by effects, and thus appears as one of the earliest English painters of romantic landscape.

He was followed by Turner and Constable—romantics of such stature that his work, cut short by his early death, is entirely dwarfed. It is further dwarfed, when the modern student views it in the shadow not only of Turner and Constable but also of Cézanne and the landscape painters of our own age. Nevertheless in his day, and within his limits, Girtin was truly an original artist; and Turner himself had a high opinion of his gifts.

CHAPTER XII

TURNER
1775-1851

★

1. TURNER'S LIFE

JOSEPH MALLORD WILLIAM TURNER was born in Maiden Lane, Covent Garden. His father was a barber. His mother went mad and died in an asylum. He went to school at Brentford and Margate and showed precocious talent for drawing. Early in his teens he was already making money by colouring prints for the engraver John Raphael Smith. He took perspective lessons from the topographical draughtsman Thomas Malton, who advised his father to make him a tinker or a cobbler since he showed no aptitude for topographical drawing. He seems then to have obtained permission to make some copies in Reynolds' studio and to have been admitted to the Academy Schools. When he was about eighteen he had a studio of his own in Hand Court, Maiden Lane; and it was soon after this that he was taken up by Dr. Monro.

When he started to tour the country with Girtin, making topographical drawings, his subjects included picturesque buildings, ruins, views, and scenes of shipping at the South Coast ports. He seems to have had no difficulty in selling these drawings, which, before he was twenty, had already been discovered by printsellers who began to buy them for reproduction in their publications. Artistically he advanced rapidly and when he was twenty-four, in 1799, he had produced the drawing of *Norham Castle* which he regarded as the beginning of his career as an artist properly so called.

From the age of fifteen he had exhibited in the Royal Academy. His contributions were both in watercolours and in oils, the oil paintings included *Fishermen at Sea: off the Needles*

101. J. M. W. TURNER
Ulysses deriding Polyphemus
National Gallery, London

102. J. M. W. TURNER
Petworth Park
National Gallery, Millbank, London

(1796), *Moonlight at Millbank* (1798), *Buttermere Lake* (1798) and *Coniston Fells* (1798); and in 1799 at the age of twenty-four he was made an A.R.A.

In the next three years he began to challenge the Dutch sea-painters on the one hand, and, on the other, with *Aeneas with the Sibyl* (c. 1800), *The Tenth Plague of Egypt* (1802), *Jason in Search of the Golden Fleece* (1802), to win a reputation as a painter of picturesque-classical landscapes with figures.

In 1800 his father had given up the barber's shop and attached himself to his money-making son; he lived in his son's house and acted as informal assistant in the studio till he died in 1830. There is a legend that Turner at this time suffered a severe disappointment in a love affair. But no details are recorded.

In 1802, when he was twenty-seven, he was elected a full R.A. and he then made his first foreign tour—visiting Paris and travelling through France and Switzerland to Strasbourg. The drawings *The Devil's Bridge, St. Gothard's Pass* and *Chamonix: Mer de Glace*, and the oil paintings *Bonneville* (Pl. 105), *Calais Pier* and *The Vintage at Mâcon* (all three in the Royal Academy in 1803) record these first Continental impressions.

Meanwhile he was still working for engravers. He had drawn Beckford's fantastic Gothic Fonthill Abbey while it was being built in 1800; and he contributed drawings for 'The Oxford Almanac', 'Angus' Seats', and other publications between 1800 and 1808. In 1806 he began the famous *Liber Studiorum*—a series of landscape compositions (in emulation of Claude's *Liber Veritatis*) engraved under his own supervision. He published seventy plates of this *Liber Studiorum* between 1807 and 1819 in addition to other work for engravers.

His oil paintings between 1804 and 1808 include *The Shipwreck* (1805), *The Destruction of Sodom* (c. 1805), *The Deluge* (1805), *The Death of Nelson* (1806), *The 'Victory' returning from Trafalgar* (c. 1806), *The Goddess of Discord in the Garden of the Hesperides* (1806), the picturesque-romantic *Falls of the Rhine at Schaffhausen* (1806) (Pl. 100), the *Sun rising through Vapour* (1807) (Pl. 111b), *Spithead: Boats recovering an Anchor* (1808) and some genre pictures in the Dutch tradition—*The Black-smith's Shop* (1807) and *The Cobbler's Home* (1808). In 1807, when he was thirty-two, he was made Professor of Perspective at the Academy.

In the following year he took a house in Upper Mall, Hammersmith. There as in his previous house (which had been in Norton Street, Portland Road), he had a studio-gallery in which he exhibited his pictures—his *Shipwreck*, *Death of Nelson*, and the *Sun rising through Vapour* (Pl. 111b), being first shown to the public in this way. He found buyers for many of his pictures—especially the marine subjects—and was able to make good terms with publishers and printsellers. The early buyers of his pictures included Lord de Tabley, first owner of the *Sun rising through Vapour*, Lord Harewood, Hawksworth Fawkes, in whose house at Farnley he often stayed from 1802 onwards, and Lord Egremont, whom he visited for the first time at Petworth in 1809.

By 1812 he was able to buy, and practically rebuild, a house in Queen Anne Street, with a larger gallery for exhibiting his pictures; and this house he retained as his London headquarters till his death. From about 1805 onwards he had acquired the habit of making oil sketches of Thames scenery near London. He now also bought, and rebuilt, a small house on the river at Twickenham, and some of his pictures of the period 1810-1814, —*The Thames at Kingston Bank* (1813) and *Frosty Morning*: *Sunrise* (1813), for example—record rural impressions. In this period he also painted ever more and more ambitious compositions in the picturesque-classical tradition—*Dido and Aeneas: The Morning of the Chase* (1814) (Pl. 25), *Appulia and Appulus* (1814); and the storm scene called *Snowstorm: Hannibal crossing the Alps* where we get a forecast of his later manner.

In 1812 he was in Devonshire, where he went out fishing in rough weather in order to study effects of sea and sky. There, it is recorded, he was always armed with small sketchbooks in which he both drew and wrote his impressions at all times and places; he would camp anywhere and everywhere for a night,

103a. J. M. W. TURNER
Dawn: After the Wreck
Private Collection, London

103b. J. M. W. TURNER
The Snowstorm
National Gallery, Millbank, London

104. J. M. W. TURNER
Rembrandt's Daughter
Private Collection, U.S.A.

supping off cheese and porter and sleeping, if need be, in a chair.

In the period 1814-1826 he made a great many drawings, some of which were engraved in Cooke's 'Picturesque views of the Southern Coast of England' (1814-1826), in 'Views in Sussex', 'Rivers of Devon', Whittaker's 'Richmondshire' (1818-1823), 'Rivers of England' (1823-1827), and 'Provincial and Picturesque Scenery of Scotland' (1826). These drawings were the fruit of many wanderings and systematic tours, including a visit to Scotland in 1818. But even so they represent only part of his output, part of his sketching, and part of his wanderings. In 1817 he was in Belgium, Holland, and on the Rhine where he produced fifty drawings; in 1819 he went to Italy through France and Savoy and made a great many notes and drawings. The oil pictures of this period include *Crossing the Brook* (1815), *Dido building Carthage* (1815), *The Field of Waterloo* (1818), *Rome from the Vatican, Raffaelle accompanied by La Fornarina preparing his Pictures for the Loggia* (1820), *The Bay of Baiae with Apollo and Sibyl* (1823), and *The Forum* (1826).

In 1827 at the age of fifty-two he was at the height of his success. He had profitable arrangements with publishers, from whom he demanded excellent terms and sometimes as many as a hundred proofs for himself; there were a number of collectors who specialised in his watercolours; and he was rich enough to ask large prices for his oil paintings, the more important of which he now refused to sell. Between 1827 and 1830 he made drawings for a collection of engravings called 'Ports of England' and for other publications including an illustrated edition of Rogers' 'Italy'. The oil paintings of these years include *Now for the Painter* (1827), *Port Ruysdael* (1827), *The Bird Cage* (1828), *Petworth Park* (1829) (Pl. 102), *Chichester Canal* (1829), *Ulysses deriding Polyphemus* (1829) (Pl. 101), *The Loretto Necklace* (1829), and *Pilate Washing his Hands* (1830).

When his father died in 1830 Turner was fifty-five. He had sold the Twickenham house, which was his father's headquarters, in 1826, and thereafter the old man had lived at Queen

Anne Street. At some time, not exactly known, Turner had introduced to Queen Anne Street a housekeeper, called Hannah Danby, and after his father's death this woman, whose face was rendered unsightly by some disease, was in sole charge of the Queen Anne Street premises. After 1830, and possibly for some time before that date, he employed as an agent a dealer named Griffith who kept in touch with collectors of his pictures and served him well in other ways.

Between 1830 and 1839 he seems to have been in a curious period of transition. There were times when he was content to ring the changes on old successes—as in *Caligula's Palace and Bridge*, *Apollo and Daphne* (1832) and *The Fighting Téméraire* (1839) and was apparently concerned with nothing so much as making money. And there were other times when he worked with disinterested concentration and advanced towards that last period where he strained the resources of both oil and water-colour for the expression of his experience. The unfinished *Fire at Sea* painted about 1834 and the *Hero and Leander* (Pl. 99), exhibited in 1837, mark the beginning of the splendid final phase in which he was completely personal and original. This phase culminates in *The Slave Ship* (Pl. 112) exhibited in 1840, *The Snowstorm* (1842) (Pl. 103b) and *Queen Mab's Cave* (1843), and in watercolours of the character of *The Splügen Pass* (Pl. 98).

It was within this period 1830-1839 that Turner was 'discovered' by Ruskin. I have discussed the relations between the two men in my study of Ruskin's life and work.[1] Here I need only mention the central dates.

Ruskin was given the edition of Rogers' 'Italy' with the engravings after Turner's drawings in 1832 when he was thirteen. When he was sixteen in 1835 he saw some Turner water-colours of various periods in a private collection and from that time his father began to collect them. In 1836, when he was seventeen and Turner was sixty-one, he wrote an essay protest-

[1] 'John Ruskin. An Introduction to further study of his Life and Work'. By R. H. Wilenski (Faber and Faber, 1933).

105. J. M. W. TURNER
Bonneville

106. J. S. COTMAN
The Drop Gate
National Gallery, Millbank, London

ing against hostile criticisms of Turner's pictures in the Academy of that year: *Juliet and her Nurse, Rome from Mount Aventine* and *Mercury and Argus*. His father sent the essay to Turner (who was personally unknown to him); Turner advised against publication; and the essay was not published. Ruskin met Turner in 1840 when he himself was twenty-one and Turner was sixty-five. He made a bad impression but, as he and his father were now important buyers, other meetings soon occurred. The first volume of *Modern Painters* was published in 1843. After that date Turner used to dine from time to time in the Ruskin mansion at Denmark Hill; and he was present at Ruskin's birthday parties from 1844 to 1850.

The common notion that Ruskin made Turner's reputation is thus entirely wrong. But Ruskin was nevertheless his only articulate champion in this particular period when the Academicians and the recognised critics were unable to follow the final development of his art. Ruskin alone saw the majestic intention of *The Slave Ship* (Pl. 112) which his father bought and gave him to celebrate the publication of the first volume of *Modern Painters*; and when, years later, a group of admirers gave him the drawing called *The Splügen Pass* (Pl. 98) to celebrate his recovery from his first attack of madness they paid a fitting tribute, because he had proclaimed the merits of the drawing at the time when it was done.

After 1840 Turner's pictures became steadily more and more abstract, and the artist himself became more and more of a recluse. He was rarely at Queen Anne Street; the house was occupied most of the time by Hannah Danby alone, and access to the gallery was difficult. The end came on December 19, 1851, when Turner was seventy-six. He was at the time in a house at Chelsea, where he had a secret establishment, and where he and the woman he lived with were known as Captain and Mrs. Booth. His estate was sworn at £140,000—equivalent to half a million sterling in present money.[1]

[1]Immediately after Turner's death Ruskin's father went round to Queen Anne Street in the hope of being able to earmark some pictures

2. TURNER'S CHARACTER

For our knowledge of Turner's private life and character we have to rely, for the most part, on fragmentary records of people who knew him at various periods. He was not afflicted with that morbid interest in his own character which drove Ruskin to write about himself in letters and diaries on almost every day of his long life. He seems to have written few letters and very few of them have been preserved.

Many stories are told of the neglected condition of the establishment at Queen Anne Street and the miserly characters of the father and son. We are told that Turner senior, who used to come up from the Twickenham house to open the gallery in Queen Anne Street every morning, fretted at the fares till he found a market gardener who would drive him up daily on top of the vegetables in return for a glass of gin; that everything in the house was dilapidated and covered with dust; that there was one broken decanter on Turner's sideboard from which a visitor would be given a single glass of sherry; and so forth.

We need not, I fancy, attach much importance to these accounts, some of which refer to experiences in the last period. The Turners were certainly misers; there were certainly no and drawings for the family collection. He wrote the following account of his visit in a letter to Ruskin who was then abroad:

'I have just been through Turner's house. . . . His labour is more astonishing than his genius. There are £80,000 of oil pictures, done and undone. Boxes half as big as your study table, filled with drawings and sketches. . . . Nothing since Pompeii so impressed me . . . the accumulated dust of forty years partially cleared off; daylight for the first time admitted by opening a window on the finest production of art buried for forty years. The drawing room has, it is reckoned, £25,000 worth of proofs, and sketches and drawings and prints. . . . The house must be as dry as a bone—the parcels were apparently quite uninjured. The very large pictures were spotted but not much. They stood leaning, one against another, in the large low rooms . . . no frames . . . The will desires all to be framed and repaired, and put into the best showing state; as if he could not release his money to do this till he was dead. The top of his gallery is one ruin of glass and patches of paper, now only just made weatherproof.'

elegant appointments in the Queen Anne Street house; but somehow, reading between the lines, I see the gallery, which was open to the public, kept reasonably clean in the middle period, and the private apartments and studio not much untidier or more dusty than the generality of studios inhabited by artists who are bachelors. Turner, in the middle period, it is recorded, was abstemious in drink; and he cared little what he ate. His old father was a peasant who had come originally from Devon, and he knew nothing of luxury; neither he nor his son looked on the London house as a home; they regarded it as a place of business where they occasionally slept. Their home at this period was the little house at Twickenham, where Turner kept a boat and a gig and took some interest in the garden and where he had a pool into which he put the fish he had caught in the river. We must also remember that Turner himself was continually away and so even the Twickenham house was little more than an occasional home for him. The two men, father and son, it is clear, quite understood one another. They looked upon the same things—Turner's paintings, amassing money, and avoiding interference—as essentials; and it never occurred to either to bother about anything else. Hannah Danby was doubtless taken in when the old man's health impeded his power to contribute to these essentials. The story of the broken decanter and the single glass of sherry is probably quite accurate. Ruskin himself had the experience. But this was in the last period—in 1844— at one in the morning. Ruskin says nothing about the decanter but mentions that there was a single tallow candle to illumine the ceremony and adds that the wine itself was first-rate—a judgement which we can accept without hesitation seeing that sherry was the wine in which Ruskin senior's business especially excelled. But we must not, I think, assume that Turner was mean and inhospitable at all periods in his relations with his friends. It is recorded that when he was in Devonshire in 1812 he 'stood' a picnic with cold meats, shellfish and wines to a company of nine, which included some ladies. He had many friends in all walks of life—from sailors and the women who frequented the port taverns, to the inhabitants of Petworth and other mansions; and when he made a friendship it endured.

It is true that he never gave away a picture or a drawing; that he hoarded thousands of drawings and pictures and prints from engravings of his drawings in the Queen Anne Street house. But that was another matter altogether. To Turner his life's work taken as a whole was all that really mattered. As we know from Ruskin he always became angry when anyone attempted to assess degrees of merit in his pictures or to discuss them one by one. He looked on his whole life's work as one gesture and in the last period his desire was concentrated on the foundation of a public gallery where his production could be envisaged as a whole.

Thus it came that in his later years he was unwilling to sell his pictures and did not care whether the Queen Anne Street gallery was dusted or not or whether visitors were admitted or refused admission by Hannah Danby; that in his will he left nineteen thousand drawings and some two hundred oil paintings to the nation, that he twice refused £100,000 for the pictures hoarded in his studio; and that, with a gesture of superb pride, he refused to sell *Dido building Carthage* to the National Gallery saying that it was waste of national money as he had already given it to the nation in his will.

He has often been spoken of, and was doubtless often referred to in his lifetime, as a misanthrope. But he left most of his fortune to found a charitable institution for poor artists; it was the fault of lawyers and not his fault that this provision in his will was never put into effect; and I suspect that there were many men and women in various places in England, and abroad, who thought of the man, whom they knew by some name that was not Turner, as a kindly eccentric and not as a misanthrope.

Of Turner's 'double life' much has been written and more circulated in gossip. He was always reticent about his private habits. He is reputed to have had several natural children. His will refers to two girls, cousins of Hannah Danby, who are assumed to have been his daughters. At Chelsea in the last

107a. JOHN NASH
The Wood
Victoria and Albert Museum, London

107b. JOHN CROME
Chapel Fields, Norwich
National Gallery, Millbank, London

108. JOHN CROME
Back of the New Mills, Norwich

period it was believed that 'Captain Booth' was a retired naval officer who had taken to drink; for it seems clear that in the later part of his life his consumption of stimulants considerably increased.

He was a man, evidently, who lived outside the 'art world' which he regarded purely as an organisation for making money. When it pleased him he would attend an Academy function, but he took no pleasure in the social aspect of his position as a member of that body. He never conceived the ambition to have dukes and marquesses for his pall-bearers. For Society he cared nothing. His friends in Society were the people who admired his work, who liked him personally, and who had the decency to respect his reticence about his manner of life when he was not in their company.

He was, if I read him rightly, not in the least neurotic or abnormal in any way. He was sane and simple. Born a peasant, he had, in his way of life, the peasant's attitude from the beginning to the end.

3. TURNER'S ART

This peasant was a great artist. And in his art he was the least peasant and the most cosmopolitan of all English painters.

Turner's ambition was to escape from the peasant by means of his art. This man who cared not a straw whether he was dining with an earl or a potman, who cared nothing for the applause of his brother Academicians, was determined to win a footing on Parnassus and have the right there to shake Rembrandt, Poussin and Watteau by the hand.

No artist of the English School had such wide and real contact with the masters of the past. Reynolds, as we have seen, analysed their pictures but never penetrated through the pictures to the men. Turner achieved that penetration. He could not analyse the procedures of his favourite Old Masters. When

191

he painted 'in the manner of' Rembrandt (Pl. 104) or of Poussin or Watteau or even 'in the manner of' Claude this inability is clear. But he discovered—or as Blake would have said he knew from birth—what Rembrandt, Poussin and Watteau thought important; he understood their scale of values; and they in their turn would have understood his scale. He knew that he was greater than Claude; that the things he thought more important really are more important. But he never claimed to be greater than Rembrandt or than Poussin; and he said that he had learned more from Watteau than from anyone else.

I used to think that Turner's globe-trotting revealed a weakness in his attitude; that he travelled all over England and the Continent, partly because publishers were willing to publish engravings of different places, and partly in the spirit of the addle-pated artist who imagines that pictures of ten different places are of necessity ten different pictures. And I used to think that his pictures 'in the manner of' various Old Masters could be classed with the acres of insignificant derivative art. Now I think that Turner travelled incessantly because nothing less than experience of the whole world would content him; and that his pictures 'in the manner of' various Old Masters were gestures proclaiming his sense of kinship with the masters of the past—gestures which never impeded his simultaneous effort in the creation of original art.

The whole universe in space and all history in time were Turner's oyster. There were no limits to the enlargements of experience that he desired. He tried to make his art a synthesis of all European painting and at the same time a synthesis of his own visual and spiritual experience. But he could never make any particular picture, or any one group of pictures, a microcosm in itself. Poussin had been able to determine, quite consciously, his own scale of values; and to assemble and organise, as consciously, the various aspects of his experience; he had known how to suggest a universe that was bounded by his picture's frame, and to give his pictures a top and bottom, a beginning, a middle and an end. Poussin could do this because

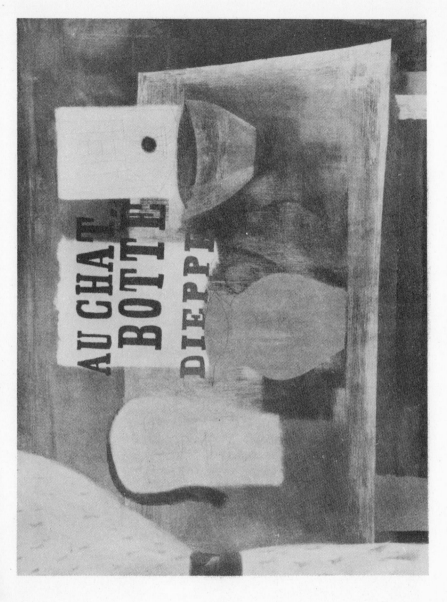

109. BEN NICHOLSON
Composition

110a. JOHN CROME
On the Yare
Private Collection, England

110b. RICHARD WILSON
River Scene
National Gallery, London

he was not only quite consciously a philosopher but also quite consciously an architect as well. Turner was not intellectual enough to achieve these processes. The range of his experience and the range of his activity were as wide as Poussin's. But he was not sufficiently an architect to organise his experience; he floundered within it—making as he floundered a titanic gesture that was great and inspiring though chaotic and almost without form.

It was thus a sure instinct that made him protest when attempts were made to assess any single work of his considered by itself. He knew that he had painted in a hundred different ways and that his pictures had a hundred different faults and a hundred different merits; and that his life's gesture could only be compassed when his life's work was looked at as a whole.

As Ruskin discovered to his consternation it is impossible to describe fully, explain in detail, and adequately assess Turner's vast and various production without describing, explaining and assessing half the pictures painted in Europe before and since his time. When we say that he was an individual master both in picturesque-classical and picturesque-romantic composition, and in naturalistic, romantic, and impressionist landscape and seascape—we have still omitted the noblest and most personal of his contributions. For he was the inventor of a new type of picture—the picture that symbolised the elements conceived as abstract forces. Poussin as an architect felt the need of finite symbols; he used the Nile to symbolise all waters, and a Roman statue to symbolise the Nile. Turner, who was no architect, had what Spengler calls the Faustian Sense of the Infinite, and he sought for abstract symbols to symbolise the elements—for symbols without form to symbolise forces without bounds in time or space.

It was towards this abstraction that he floundered so grandly all his life. From attempts at naturalistic painting of rough seas off Calais Pier he advanced to a picturesque-romantic work like the *Falls of the Rhine at Schaffhausen* (Pl. 100) which is the climax of that form of art; from that he advanced to *The Slave Ship* (Pl. 112); and finally to *The Snowstorm* (Pl. 103b) the climax of his own art.

The modern student finds it easier to see Turner's shortcomings than to appreciate his greatness. Turner was not an architect and he had no taste. These are serious shortcomings in the eyes of a generation which has witnessed a tremendous renaissance of architecture in every aspect of art, and which often fails to distinguish taste not only from culture but also from man's aesthetic reactions as such. Turner, it is true, cannot be acquitted of either shortcoming. But we must take him as we find him and recognise the influence of his own awareness of these characters upon his work. Turner the peasant knew that he had no taste; and he made great efforts to demonstrate that he was not a peasant in his art; he strove repeatedly to produce a perfect picturesque-classical picture—a furniture picture *de luxe*, an object of fine taste; and when he thought he had succeeded he made the one vulgar gesture that we know of—the instruction that his *Dido building Carthage* should always hang by Claude's *Embarkation of the Queen of Sheba*. He knew too that there was an architectural quality in Poussin's work and Watteau's, even in Rembrandt's, that eluded him; and by a normal rationalisation he strove to invent an art in which architecture had no role to play—an art concerned to symbolise forces without form.

It is impossible to deny that he played a pioneer part in the Romantic debacle of the nineteenth century. But by the same token he must be recognised as a spirit in tune with the masters of that age. It was not till Cézanne and Seurat came that art recovered from his influence. But Cézanne and Seurat could not have done what they did without Monet, Pissarro and Renoir, who all discovered themselves by contact with his mind and spirit.

Turner was no architect and he had no taste. It is good to remember both characteristics. But it is also good to remember that he painted not only *Bonneville* (Pl. 105) but also *The Snow-*

111a. JOHN CROME
Yarmouth Beach
Castle Museum, Norwich

111b. J. M. W. TURNER
Sun rising through Vapour
National Gallery, London

storm (Pl. 103b) and a little watercolour called *Dawn: After the Wreck* (Pl. 103a).

Technical procedures are always a matter of minor importance and interest. In Turner's art this is especially the case. He drew and painted in a hundred ways, using all kinds of mediums, painting with brushes and stumps, rubbing with his fingers, scratching with penknives, and so forth. He also drew and painted both on the spot and in the studio. It is recorded that when he had his house at Twickenham he sometimes painted large canvases in a punt, but that he never worked up these canvases into pictures and kept them rolled up in a bundle which he neglected. Several large unfinished paintings recently exhibited in the National Gallery (Millbank), London, including one called *Gipsy Camp*, belong presumably to this series. A number of small landscapes in oil, evidently painted at one sitting, are of the type which the French call *pochades*—rapid records in oil-paint of transitory effects in nature. Pochades or sketches of this kind, which were produced by the thousand in the nineteenth century, and are produced by the thousand to-day, must be distinguished from the so-called 'sketches' which are really pictures—Gainsborough's first *Perdita: Mrs. Robinson* (Pl. 40) or Constable's first *The Valley Farm* (Pl. 113), for example.[1] They must also be distinguished from sketches made as shorthand notes for a picture. The pochade is a record of a purely visual impression, almost automatically produced by eye and hand in rapid imitative action. The experienced *pochadier* can produce such records and carry on a conversation or think about the gas bill at the same time. As far as it goes the pochade is a complete and final object in itself with its own type of appeal; it is pleasant to see evidence of a swiftly moving hand and to be able to recognise the type of transitory visual effect recorded. But no picture of any value has ever been constructed with nothing but a pochade as the basis. Landscape painters accumulate scores of pochades in their studios but they can never use them. They can do nothing with them but sell them, or turn them upside down

[1]Cf. above, p. 124, and below, pp. 218, 219.

and paint other pochades on the top. Turner never attempted to use his pochades as bases for his pictures. He constructed his landscape compositions, both in oil and watercolour, entirely in his studio, using a quite different type of sketch—the drawing or watercolour intellectually produced as a shorthand note for a subsequent picture, a type of sketch in which visual impressions are reduced to an auxiliary role and consciously organised. He never explained the difference between his pochades and his first notes for pictures because he never explained anything to anyone, not even, probably, to himself. In the eyes of a man who saw him 'sketching' out of doors he was doing the same thing on the day when he made the pochades called *Windsor Castle from the Meadows* and *Walton Reach* as on the day when he made his first drawing for *The Splügen Pass*. But in fact he was doing two quite different things. And it is important to realise the difference at this point because chronologically we have now reached the landscape painting of the nineteenth century when the difference was very frequently forgotten.

CHAPTER XIII

NINETEENTH-CENTURY LANDSCAPE

★

Compared with Turner, who attempted to stride the globe and grapple with the elements, all the English landscape painters of the nineteenth century were provincial amateurs. Their art, born in the English countryside, had, at first, no connection with the official art in London—the portraits by Hoppner and Lawrence, the nude studies by Etty, and the 'history pictures' by the unsuccessful Englishmen James Barry (1741-1806) and Benjamin Haydon (1786-1846) and the successful Americans John Singleton Copley (1737-1815) and Benjamin West (1738-1806) who followed Reynolds as President of the Royal Academy. It also had no connection with the English art of the period which means most to the modern student—the art of William Blake. English landscape painting in the beginning was an art of rural landscape, a form of modest self-expression by provincials, a record by simple men of their own happiness in their fields and villages. The painters felt rooted in the countryside, they were content with the experience it provided, and their pictures record this satisfaction.

In a sense this art was born of the genius of the English people. Englishmen are always suspicious of 'Art' with a large 'A' because with their instinct for scenting a bluffer they have always recognised many of the most conspicuous official artists as really tradesmen in disguise. English landscape painting was born to some extent of this mistrust of the official art world, of this quiet reaction against the pretensions of the Knellers, the Lawrences and the Wests. It was a gesture of the kind made by a man who would rather pick out with one finger a tune of his own selection than listen to the official programme provided for him by the Musical Director of the Radio.

Then again it was connected with the English tendency to claustrophobia which must be distinguished from the English addiction to organised sports and outdoor games. The English are never completely happy within doors. They are only truly happy in the open air. Many, I fancy, become game-addicts in the first place from claustrophobia. Many will walk from one place to another merely for the satisfaction of being in the open air; and when they are tired they will sit down and rejoice that they are not in a city or a house, that they are far from walls and carpets, from tax collectors, from successful portrait painters— and art critics.

It is easy when thus seated beneath a tree to persuade ourselves that the pleasant sensation is in some way connected with an artistic impulse. Nine times out of ten we have selected the seat because we admire the prospect; and nine times out of ten we admire the prospect because it recalls a painted landscape seen in a gallery—or a hundred painted landscapes telescoped to one vague image. As we sit and admire we are apt to persuade ourselves that we have 'an eye for nature'; the next stage is to acquire the implements of the artist; and the next is to cover paper or canvas with an image which approximately resembles both the prospect and the memory of the pictures which led us to desire to paint it. A little applause from our friends, one such picture hung in a London exhibition, and we 'take up' landscape painting and hope to be hung again and again.

Conditions in the nineteenth century in England produced amateur landscape painters of this type by the thousand. They also produced two or three amateurs who were really artists.

Of these JOHN CROME (1768-1821) must be first considered.

Crome was the son of a journeyman weaver of Norwich. Except for occasional visits to London, one or two trips to the Lakes, and a brief visit to Paris, he spent his whole life in the region of his native town. As a boy he 'went on The Palace', i.e., he went to an open space in Norwich known as 'The Palace'

113. JOHN CONSTABLE
The Valley Farm—So-called 'Sketch'
Victoria and Albert Museum

114a. PHILIP WILSON STEER
Chepstow Castle
National Gallery, Millbank, London

114b. JOHN CONSTABLE
Dell in Helmingham Park
National Gallery, Millbank, London

where boys and girls of the people stood daily on the chance of finding some employment—just as to this day on the Ramblas of Barcelona house-painters stand with their whitewashing brushes, and as artists' models used to stand, and may still stand, in certain squares in Rome. Crome from 'The Palace' was engaged as an errand boy by a local doctor and he retained this employment for two years—though he afterwards related that he used to change the labels on the medicine bottles he delivered. When he left the doctor—perhaps as a result of this habit—he became an apprentice to a coach and sign painter. He thus acquired the habit of painting, and eventually produced some pictures. One of these pictures came, in some manner, to the notice of a Norwich citizen named Thomas Harvey, an amateur artist and collector who owned Gainsborough's *The Cottage Door* (Pl. 24) and landscapes by Richard Wilson and the Dutchmen including Hobbema and Cuyp. Crome, who copied in Harvey's collection, was greatly impressed by the pictures; Wilson and the Dutchman influenced his painting all his life; his last words are said to have been: 'Hobbema, my dear Hobbema, how I loved you.'

Harvey gave him some instruction in drawing and painting; and through Harvey he met Thomas Beechey (1753-1839), a successful London portrait painter who was then a resident of Norwich and not yet launched on his career. The meeting was of no importance to Crome, who was then eighteen, but it produced an account of him from Beechey which is worth recording: 'Crome when I first knew him', Beechey wrote, 'was an awkward, uninformed country lad, but extremely shrewd in all his remarks upon art, though he wanted words and terms to express his meaning.' Beechey also claims that he gave Crome some instruction. John Opie, painter of *Anne, Charlotte and John Gillett* (Pl. 70), whose talents I have already referred to,[1] certainly helped him about ten years later. Opie's widow has described this association: 'My husband', she wrote, 'was not acquainted with our friend John Crome before the year 1798

[1]Cf. above, p. 154.

when we first visited Norwich after our marriage. Crome used frequently to come to my husband in Norwich; and I have frequently seen him and Crome and Thomas Harvey in the painting room of the latter. I have also seen my husband painting for Crome; that is, the latter looking on, while the former painted a landscape or figures. And, occasionally, I have seen him at work on Crome's own canvas, while the latter amused us with droll stories and humorous conversations and observations. But this is, to the best of my belief, the extent of *assistance* he derived from my husband.'

Crome meanwhile had married a local girl whom he had been courting and who was about to have a child. He seems to have made the money he required by sign painting and by giving drawing lessons to the daughters of the local gentry. In the diary of one of his pupils in 1798 we read: 'I had a good drawing this morning, but in the course of it gave way to passion with both Crome and Betsy—Crome because he would attend to Betsy and not to me and Betsy because she was so provoking.'

By 1801 when he was thirty-three he was able to found an art school centred in his own house from which he took his pupils into the country to sketch; and soon after he was appointed drawing master at the Norwich Grammar School.

The trip to the Lake District already mentioned took place in 1802. Crome went as drawing master to the Betsy already mentioned and her five sisters. On a wet day, at Ambleside, another diary entry by one of the girls reads: 'Chenda, Cilla and Mr. Crome were comfortably seated in a romantic little summer-house, painting a beautiful waterfall.' This picture by Crome seems not to have survived. But it was presumably on this trip that he made the drawing, or oil sketch, for a large painting called *The Slate Quarries* (Pl. 27b).

Anxious to find a market for his oil pictures he organised, in 1803, 'The Norwich Society of Artists', an art club consisting of local painters, mostly drawing masters, who met at first in a tavern called 'The Hole in the Wall' and later in a house of their

115. JOHN CONSTABLE
Stoke-by-Nayland
Chicago Art Institute, U.S.A.

116a. JOHN CONSTABLE
Weymouth Bay
National Gallery, London

116b. JOHN CONSTABLE
On the Stour near Dedham
Victoria and Albert Museum, London

own where they held exhibitions of their works. He sent pictures from time to time to the Royal Academy, but most of his work, from 1805 till his death, was shown in the annual exhibitions of this Norwich Society.

Characteristic pictures probably painted between 1806 and 1814 are *View on the Solent*, *Moonrise on the Yare*, *On the Yare* (Pl. 110a), *Mousehold Heath: Boy keeping Sheep*, *Back of the New Mills, Norwich* (Pl. 108), *Yarmouth Beach* (Pl. 111a) and *Woody Landscape at Colney*.

In 1814 he went, apparently by way of Ostend, to Paris in order to see the Italian and other pictures looted by Napoleon which were then on exhibition. He was accompanied by two men-friends and wrote as follows from Paris to his wife:

'My Dear Wife—After one of the most pleasant journeys of one hundred and seventy miles over one of the most fertile countreys I ever saw we arrived in the capital of France. You may imagine how everything struck us with surprise; people of all nations going to and fro—Turks, Jews, etc. I shall not enter into ye particulars in this my letter, but suffice it to say we are all in good health, and in good lodgings—that in Paris is the one great difficulty. We have been at St. Cloud and Versailes; I cannot describe it on letter. We have seen three palaces the most magnificent in world. I shall not trouble you with a long letter this time as the post goes out in an hour that time will not allow me was I so disposed. This morning I am going to see the object of my journey, that is the Thuilleries. I am told here I shall find many English artists. . . . Pray let me know how you are going on, giving best respects to all friends. I believe the English may boast of having the start of these foreigners, but a happier race of people there cannot be. I shall make this journey pay. I shall be very careful how I lay out my money. I have seen some shops. They ask treble what they will take, so you may suppose what a set they are. . . . I am, etc., yours till death, John Crome.'

He seems to have come back by Boulogne; and pictures called *Paris: Boulevard des Italiens*, *Fishmarket on the Beach at*

Boulogne, and *Bruges River*: *Ostend in the Distance* record impressions of the trip.

By 1814 when he was forty-six he was thus able to afford this journey; and for the remaining seven years of his life he seems to have sold a certain number of paintings to local gentry, obtaining sometimes as much as £50—equivalent to something like £200 in present values—for his larger pictures. But he was never able to dispense with teaching or to give up his post as drawing master at the Grammar School.

His later pictures include *Mousehold Heath*, *The Poringland Oak*, *Chapel Fields*, *Norwich* (Pl. 107b), *The Burdock*, *The Water Vole*, *Cottage near Lakenham*, *Mill near Lakenham* and *Mousehold Mill*.

Crome, I believe, never painted his landscapes in the open air. He made watercolours and drawings on the spot and painted his oil pictures from them, with the aid probably of prints, etchings and old landscape drawings in his studio. He always collected prints and drawings and in 1812, when he sold some, the announcement of the sale included the name of Rembrandt. It is presumed that he owned some of the landscape etchings by Rembrandt which his own work, in one aspect, inevitably recalls.

As a landscape painter he represents, with Wilson, the transition from the picturesque traditions of the eighteenth century to the romantic attitude of the nineteenth. *The Slate Quarries* (Pl. 27b) is a translation into oil paint of the mountain drawings by J. R. Cozens. Like Wilson's *On the Wye* (Pl. 27a) it is the work of a man too fundamentally romantic to work happily within the worn-out mould of the picturesque. Neither Crome nor Wilson had the mental power of the great classical masters of landscape like Poussin and Rubens. In *The Slate Quarries* Crome was not able to analyse and then synthesise the scene before him by the classical procedure. The picture, by reason of its considerable size and the size of the formal units which compose it, by reason also of thick paint and opaque grey colouring, is impressive at first glance; but the longer we stand before it the

117. RICHARD PARKES BONINGTON
The Parterre d'eau at Versailles
Louvre Museum, Paris

118. J. S. COTMAN
The Normandy River
Private Collection, London

more woolly and approximate the artist's perception is seen to be. Woolliness appears also in Crome's work when he is imitating Hobbema as in *Chapel Fields, Norwich* (Pl. 107b). If we set this picture by the side of any drawing or painting by an intelligent artist in touch with the modern movement—*The Wood* (Pl. 107a), for example, by John Nash—we see the approximate character of Crome's perception in this case. Even in a picture like *The Poringland Oak*, Crome's perception is incomplete and approximate—though here, as in Hobbema's pictures, there is a pretence of realisation which may deceive the average layman who has never looked intently at the complex form of a tree.

This point is of cardinal importance for the student of landscape painting. Landscapes like *Chapel Fields, Norwich*, and the *Poringland Oak* are really still-life painting in Hogarth's sense.[1] They pretend to complete imitation of the appearance of specific forms. But the pretence is ridiculous, as Ruskin pointed out: 'We can paint a cat or a fiddle so that they look as if we could take them up, but we cannot imitate the ocean or the Alps. . . . We can imitate fruit, but not a tree; flowers but not a pasture.' The intelligent artist always recognises this limitation of his art. Only addle-pated artists attempt the impossible in this way, and suppose that they can record complex phenomena by the still-life procedure. Every intelligent artist knows that he can provide, if he wants to (which he usually does not), a detailed account of a lemon on his table, but that the moment he steps into the garden he has to paint a 'potted' account of his experience; and that the further afield he goes—the more majestic and complex the phenomena he contemplates—the more imperious the need of potting becomes. The masters in landscape, as in other fields of painting, are and always have been the men who can 'pot' in a way which preserves the essential flavour of their experience. Derivative artists are men who make potted versions of experience already potted. Assuming that Oxo is made from cattle and that it has the flavour of beef—we may say that the masters in landscape painting are makers of 'Oxo'; that their

[1]Cf. above, pp. 103, 109, 110.

imitators are men who make synthetic Oxo without recourse to cattle; and that the artists who apply the still-life procedure to landscape are makers of waxwork oxen and cows to amuse children and childish adults at Madame Tussaud's.

When Crome attempted the still-life procedure in landscapes with mountains or trees, he thus attempted the impossible and inevitably failed; and the artists of the Norwich Club who imitated his failures—James Stark (1794-1859), George Vincent (1798-1830), John Bernay Crome (1794-1842) and John Berney Ladbroke (1803-1879), for example—failed inevitably still more. It was only when Crome restricted himself to very simple phenomena that the still-life procedure could be convincing. *The Cottage near Lakenham* and *The Mill near Lakenham* are satisfactory because they both represent only objects sufficiently simple in form to be susceptible of still-life illusionist delineation—and they exhibit incidentally a charm of colour in the reds and a surface quality which doubtless resulted from Crome's contact in Paris with paintings by Titian. In *The Back of the New Mills, Norwich* (Pl. 108), the still-life procedure is already strained beyond its limits. Here the artist has tried to apply the procedure to half a village with boats, houses, trees and so forth, a collection of objects susceptible of illusionist delineation in different degrees. As a result there is no common denominator in the degree of still-life imitation; the specific forms of the easily copied objects, the houses, for example, are more completely copied than the specific forms of the trees which it is impossible to copy with the same degree of completeness.

The first problem in landscape painting is to get over this difficulty, to achieve a uniform realisation of everything depicted. The classical masters of landscape analyse specific forms, simplify them all to a common denominator, and then, as it were, build up their pictures with bricks which can be dovetailed one with another because they are all made of the same material; the modern classical-architectural painters proceed in the same manner—extreme Cubism being this procedure pushed to its logical conclusion; the Romantic masters selecting either some emotive fragment of life, or some emotive effect of several fragments in relation, make the emotive aspect the exclusive subject of their pictures and achieve a common denominator and unity in that way; and the Impressionists work with the action of light as the common denominator. No master of landscape, classical, romantic, impressionist or modern cubist-classical, has ever set out to paint a landscape as if it were a cherry which he wanted the birds to come down and peck at. The attempt has never been made by intelligent artists because they all know that though they can paint a cherry which birds may peck at they can never paint a tree which birds will try to roost in or a forest which a tiger will try to prowl in—even if the picture be on a life-size scale.

And here we must distinguish between still-life painting and the painting of still-life. The procedure of illusionist imitation, which, following Hogarth, I have called still-life painting all through this book, is the expression of an attitude. Hogarth called it the still-life attitude because in his day it was the usual attitude of painters of still-life subjects. There is, however, no reason why the painter of still-life subjects should adopt the still-life attitude; this was made clear by Chardin, one of Hogarth's contemporaries in France. Chardin in the second half of his life painted exclusively still-life subjects. But his attitude was not the still-life but the architectural attitude. He was concerned not with jugs and pots and pans but with form; not with apples and dead rabbits but with the problems which occupy the attention of architects—proportions, recessions, volumes, balance and so on. Modern painters of still-life subjects have adopted Chardin's attitude and carried it still further away from the cherry-to-be-pecked-by-the-bird ideal. The objects which they assemble before them are used primarily as a jumping-off point for a composition which is to have the emotional appeal of architecture. They regard the objects in themselves as of small importance because they are mainly concerned with their mutual formal relations or with formal rhythms to be extracted from them. They can extract the material for an affective picture from a dead plant and a window frame, as Paul Nash has done in the *Still Life* (Pl. 160); and they can suggest an affective quality of light, a mood, and an atmosphere, with scarcely any representational elements, as in the *Composition* (Pl. 109) by Ben Nicholson. The attitude of these modern painters of still-life subjects is really much closer to that of Poussin in *The Death of Phocion* and the *Landscape with Two Nymphs* (Pl. 133b) than to the still-life attitude. And Crome's attitude in *Back of the New Mills, Norwich*, is really much nearer to the cherry-to-be-pecked-at still-life approach than to Poussin's architectural approach or to the attitude of modern painters of still-life subjects. For *Back of the New Mills, Norwich*, is not an architectural construction. It has no top or bottom or sides or beginning or end. It is not a formal microcosm, an intellectually organised world within the frame. There is no reason for the presence of the trees in the particular place where they occur in the picture—except that they happened to be there at the time when the picture was painted. The picture does not grow inwards from its four boundaries, it just stops at the top and the bottom and at right and left when it gets to the edges of the canvas. It would serve equally well as two pictures if divided at the left of the small house. It is only luck that no avaricious dealer has not actually divided it as a dealer actually divided Crome's *Mousehold Heath*.[1]

But Crome was not always a still-life painter. He was fundamentally a romantic artist who was decoyed to the still-life attitude by Hobbema and the other Dutchmen whose works he happened to encounter at an impressionable age. At bottom he reacted to emotive effects in landscape, as Wilson had reacted to them in his *River Scene* (Pl. 110b) and as Girtin had reacted to them in *Tynemouth, View on the Wharf*, and *Kirkstall Abbey* (Pl. 96). We see Crome as a master of romantic landscape in *Moonrise on the Yare*, in *Bruges River: Ostend in the Distance*, in *On the Yare* (Pl. 110a), in *Yarmouth Harbour*. Here his procedure is the same as that of the portrait painters who paint not the

[1]This picture as we know it in the National Gallery, London, consists of the two pieces joined together and restored.

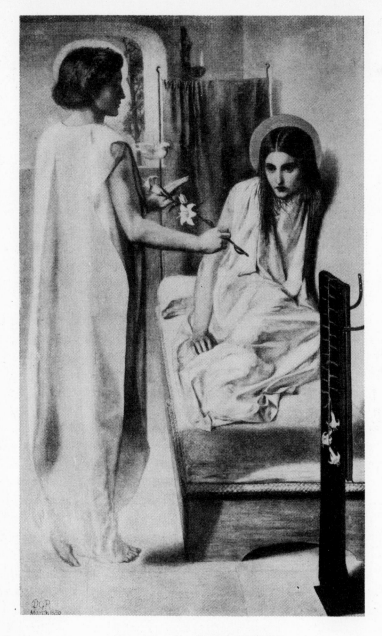

119. D. G. ROSSETTI
Ecce Ancilla Domini
National Gallery, London

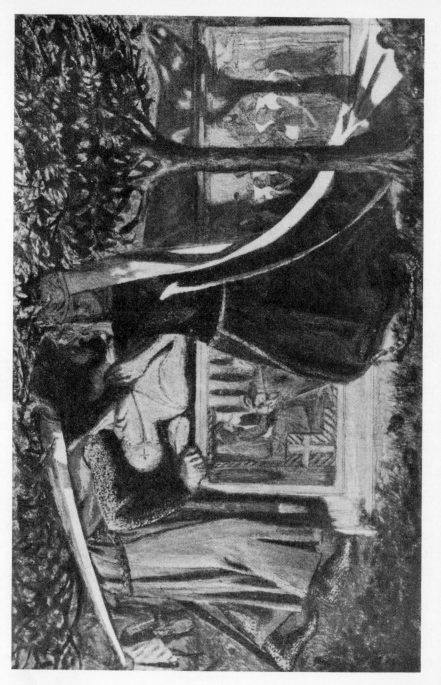

features of the sitter but an expression in relation to circumstance. Crome's romantic landscapes record his experience of expression on the face of a fragment of landscape. In such pictures he ceases to be a still-life painter attempting impossible imitations of tree forms and reveals himself as a romantic artist. And in his romantic pictures, by concerning himself exclusively with the emotivity of the phenomena depicted, he found a common denominator whereby he could unify his experience of form.

In *Yarmouth Beach* (Pl. 111a) we see him half-way to this achievement, providing an emotive element by stressing the light clouds in a way that was to be further exploited by Bonington (Pl. 117) and Constable (Pls. 116a and 116b). In *On the Yare* he has solved the problem. Here the emotive aspect is the common denominator throughout and completely unifies the picture.

It was to this kind of unification that Crome was referring when he gave the often-quoted advice to his pupil and imitator James Stark:

'In your letter you wish me to give you my opinion of your picture. I should have liked it better if you had made it more of a whole. . . . Breath must be attended to . . . if you paint but a muscle give it breath. . . . Trifles in nature must be overlooked that we may have our feelings raised by seeing the whole picture at a glance, not knowing how or why we are so charmed. . . . Do not distress us with accidental trifles in nature but keep the masses large and in good and beautiful lines, and give the sky, which plays so important a part in all landscape, and so supreme a one in our low level lines of distance, the prominence it deserves, and in the coming years the posterity you paint for shall admire your work.'

Crome's biographers habitually suggest that when he wrote 'breath' he intended to write 'breadth'. Probably he did; he was no better at spelling than Gainsborough and Reynolds. But what he meant, all the same, was nearer 'breath' than 'breadth'. He meant to recommend the unification of the picture to record an emotive aspect, the very breath of the scene romantically experienced.

His biographers also habitually suggest that the passages quoted represent a fundamental doctrine for landscape painting —the doctrine that landscape pictures built up with large units of form are *ipso facto* better than those built up with small ones. Such a rule cannot, of course, be maintained. Nor was Crome really trying thus to lay down as a rule or an aesthetic principle what Gainsborough had laid down as a counsel of expedience when he wrote: 'If [an artist] cannot master a number of objects so as to introduce them in friendship let him do but few, and that you know, my Boy, makes simplicity.'[1] Crome in his dictum, if he really meant breadth and not breath, was really doing exactly what Gainsborough was doing in his, and what all artists in their dicta about art always in fact do—he was defending his own practice and rationalising his own limitations. Poussin would not have said what Crome and Gainsborough said; Rubens would not have said it; Turner would not have said it; because all three could unify five hundred units 'in friendship' with no more effort than Crome and Gainsborough required to unify five.

JOHN SELL COTMAN (1782-1842), Vice-President of the Norwich Society of Artists when Crome was President, is the only other painter of the Norwich School whose work is of interest to the general student of our day.

The son of a well-to-do Norwich draper and silk merchant, he impressed his parents by his talent for drawing and was sent to London about the age of sixteen. He somehow made the acquaintance of Dr. Monro, copied drawings by Girtin and Turner in his house, and probably became acquainted with both artists. He seems to have been provided with enough money by his father to live comfortably in London, whence he toured the country making topographical drawings without apparently any pressing need to sell them. His tours between 1800 and 1806 took him to Devon, Yorkshire, Lincolnshire, Durham and

[1]Cf. above, p. 130.

121. D. G. ROSSETTI
How they met Themselves

122b. D. G. ROSSETTI
Mrs. Morris

122a. D. G. ROSSETTI
Elizabeth Siddal
National Gallery, Millbank, London

Wales. He occasionally paid flying visits to Norwich where he gave drawing lessons to young ladies and gentlemen at the high rate of half a guinea an hour—equivalent, we must remember, to at least two guineas to-day. He exhibited some of his drawings in the Royal Academy, where they attracted small attention if any. In 1806 when he was twenty-four he had an attack of melancholia and decided to leave London and exhibit no longer at the Academy.

Returning to his native town he married a farmer's daughter, played a prominent part in the activities of the Norwich Society of Artists, and exhibited many of his drawings at their exhibitions. He took pupils, painted portraits, continued to draw landscapes, and tried to launch a circulating library of drawings which subscribers could copy in their homes.

About 1811 he moved to Yarmouth, where he began to paint more frequently in oil than had hitherto been his habit, and also produced a number of etchings of architectural subjects which were published in series. Yarmouth remained his headquarters for the next twelve years. He made, however, frequent excursions to various parts of the country and visited Normandy in 1817, 1818 and 1820.

In 1823 he returned to Norwich. Two years later he was elected an Associate of the London Society of Painters in Water Colours. But in spite of this encouragement he seems to have had another severe attack of melancholia: 'My views in life', he wrote at this time, 'are so completely blasted, that I sink under the repeated and constant exertion of body and mind. Every effort has been tried, even without hope of success; hence that loss of spirits amounting almost to despair.'

Eventually Turner and other friends procured for him the post of drawing master at King's College, London, which he held till his death nine years later at the age of sixty.

Cotman in character was very different from Crome, who was his senior by fourteen years. Crome, a romantic peasant, muddle-headed, but quite sane, was easygoing and easy to get on with. Cotman seems to have been a neurotic bourgeois, introspective, subject to fits of hilarity as well as to fits of depression, who was doubtless difficult to get on with.

He was much more intelligent than Crome and always looked on landscape painting as the intellectual procedure of 'potting' his architectural experience. He thus stands closer than Crome both to the painters of picturesque-classical landscape and to modern landscape painters in our own day. His *Viaduct* (Pl. 29) is equivalent to a fragment of a landscape composition by Poussin—of *The Finding of Moses*, for example, where just such a viaduct, so reflected, actually occurs. His *Baggage Waggon* (Pl. 30) and *The Drop Gate* (Pl. 106) are equivalent to fragments of landscapes by Wilson and Turner when they were exploring the picturesque-classical tradition (Pls. 20 and 105). In the upper part of *The Normandy River* (Pl. 118) he leaps right across the nineteenth century to the landscape painting of our own time.

In his numerous topographical drawings Cotman knew how to escape the pitfall of the still-life procedure. Drawings like the well-known *Greta Bridge* and *Durham* exhibit a real grasp of the picturesque-classical approach. At other times—as in the celebrated oil painting *The Waterfall*—he gives us a picture which is more Chinese than European in its form. At other times again he has evidently been influenced by the romantic approach in certain drawings by Girtin (Pls. 96 and 97).

In the nineteenth century his drawings and paintings, hidden in the private houses of East Anglian families which had acquired them in his lifetime, remained relatively unknown. His name is not mentioned, for example, in the books or letters or diaries of Ruskin. But at the end of the century the patterning in his topographical drawings made an appeal to students educated to admire it by Japanese prints, Whistler's paintings, and the pioneer posters by Toulouse-Lautrec and the Beggarstaff Brothers—James Pryde and William Nicholson.

He was thus first picked out from oblivion by appreciation of one aspect of his contribution—the posterlike drawings which suggest recession by a series of 'flats' like the wings in a stage scene. Later when Cézanne's concept of landscape painting

123. GWEN JOHN
Lady reading
National Gallery, Millbank, London

124a. WILLIAM HOLMAN HUNT
The Scapegoat
Lady Lever Art Gallery, Port Sunlight, England

124b. WILLIAM HOLMAN HUNT
The Festival of St. Swithun
Ashmolean Museum, Oxford

began to be understood in England other aspects of Cotman's achievement began to be appreciated. And to-day his intentions in *The Normandy River* (Pl. 118) mean a lot to many artists because they bear resemblance to their own.[1]

RICHARD PARKES BONINGTON (1802-1828) can conveniently be mentioned at this point. Born at Arnold, near Nottingham, he might have passed his life, like Crome, as a provincial drawing master, if his father, who was Governor of Nottingham Gaol, had not been guilty of irregularities which caused a removal of the family to Calais when his son was about sixteen. The peccant Governor had a taste for drawing and portrait painting and at one time attempted to earn his living by his brush. Seeing that his son unquestionably had talent he arranged with Louis Francia to take him as a pupil. Francia (1772-1839), whom I have already mentioned as one of Dr. Monro's protégés, was a friend of Girtin and John Varley. He drew water-colour landscapes and coast scenes and made compositions in illustration of the poets. He was a pioneer in lithography, and published a number of copies of English landscape drawings by Gainsborough, Girtin, and A. W. Calcott (1779-1844), a landscape and marine painter ranked above Turner by the official art world as late as 1860. Francia had been born in Calais and had returned there shortly before the Boningtons arrived.

Bonington, under Francia's tuition, soon mastered the water-colour medium and the technique of lithography. In 1820 at the age of eighteen he entered the Ecole des Beaux Arts and then became one of the four hundred pupils of Baron Gros (1771-1835), who had been attached to Napoleon's staff, painted pictures of his triumphs, and had chosen for him the pictures looted from Italy which Crome went to Paris to see before they were returned by the Allies. Gros was a pioneer of the new Romantic Movement, with which Bonington thus had contact at once. Gros knew Delacroix (1798-1863), then about to score his first success with *Dante and Virgil* at the Salon; and Bonington met Delacroix at this time.

[1]Cf. Appendix IV, p. 275.

As a result of this contact with Delacroix, Bonington was infected with the *moyen-âge* virus then officially encouraged by the Bourbon regime;[1] and he began to produce oil pictures of *François I and Marguerite of Navarre, Henri III and the English Ambassador, Henri IV and the Spanish Ambassador*, and so forth. As a result of the same contact he was also infected with 'Orientalism' and painted various illustrations to the 'Arabian Nights'. At the same time he continued to paint oil and water colour landscapes and coast scenes in Normandy and elsewhere.

In 1824 when he was twenty-two he saw Constable's exhibits in the Salon; and the year after, when Delacroix went to England, he seems to have been one of the party and to have sought out pictures by Constable, whose Salon paintings both he and Delacroix had much admired. After this he came several times to England and never failed to seek pictures by Constable. As a result we find the influence of Constable's painting in his later work (Pls. 116a, 116b, 117).

At some time, probably before 1824, he went to Italy and painted some views of Venice. In Venice he is said to have contracted tuberculosis; in Paris he had sunstroke and a bad attack of brain fever; he died of tuberculosis in London at the age of twenty-six.

Bonington seems to have been able to make a living by his work—unless a lace-making business established by his father in Calais was able to provide him with funds; and he probably owed his success to Delacroix, who never tired of singing his praise. 'I knew Bonington,' Delacroix wrote, 'and was very fond of him. . . His English phlegm, which nothing could disturb, robbed him of some of the qualities which make life pleasant. As a lad he developed an astonishing dexterity in the use of watercolours, which were in 1817 an English novelty. Other artists were perhaps more powerful or more accurate than Bonington, but no one in the modern school, perhaps no earlier artist, possessed the lightness of execution which makes his works, in a certain sense, diamonds, by which the eye is

[1]Cf. below, p. 220.

enticed and charmed independently of the subject or of imitative appeal. The same is true of the costume pictures which he subsequently painted. Even here I could never grow weary of marvelling at the absence of effort and his great ease of execution . . . Not that he was quickly satisfied; on the contrary, he often began over again perfectly finished pieces which seemed wonderful to us. His dexterity was, however, so great that in a moment he produced with his brush new effects which were as charming as the first and more truthful.'

The modern student will endorse this judgement. In all the types of his production Bonington exhibits a formal vision expressed in pigment handled with the rapid spontaneous emotive touch which was an article of faith with the young Romantics whom he admired and with whom he was associated. Like his associates he sometimes experimented with the heavy impasto used by Rembrandt—as we see in his well-known portrait *La Gouvernante*; at other times in his use of impasto he follows Constable.

Some of his pictures—*The Parterre d'eau at Versailles* (Pl. 117), for example—were apparently painted rapidly on the spot. With Turner and Constable he must thus be regarded as partly responsible for the pochade fashion which continued all through the nineteenth century and survives among the followers of the Impressionists at the present day.[1]

JOHN CONSTABLE (1776-1837), though a much greater and more original artist than Crome or Cotman or Bonington, has nothing to offer to the student of to-day—except the warning furnished by his elaborated pictures. In the history of nineteenth-century painting he is quite as important as Turner himself. But the seed he sowed has already produced its harvest in French Romantic and Impressionist painting and that harvest has now been long consumed.

He was born at East Bergholt, Suffolk, the son of a prosperous miller who had inherited Flatford Mill. After an elementary education in local schools he began work in his father's

[1]Cf. above, p. 195, and below, p. 218.

mill. He showed talent for drawing and painting, and when he was about eighteen some of his work was brought to the notice of the Dowager Lady Beaumont. Her son, Sir George Beaumont, amateur artist and collector, showed him drawings by Girtin, allowed him to copy Claude's *Hagar and the Angel* then in his collection, and advised him to go to London to study.

Accordingly in 1795, at the age of nineteen, he went to London, worked under and received advice from Joseph Farington (1747-1821), artist and diarist, and J. T. Smith (1766-1833), artist, antiquary, 'copyist' of old paintings in Westminster, and author of 'Nollekens and his Times'.[1] After two years he felt that he had failed and his parents thought that they were wasting their money. He returned therefore to work in the paternal mill.

But he continued to sketch in his spare time, and by 1799, when he was twenty-three. he had made himself competent to produce some academic studies which gained him admission to the Royal Academy schools. For the next ten years he was in London with visits to Suffolk, Derbyshire and other places. In 1802 and 1803 he had pictures in the Royal Academy. In 1804 he probably saw, as James Ward saw, Rubens' *Le Château de Steen* in the studio of Benjamin West who had the picture (which then belonged to Sir George Beaumont) for restoration; and he may also have seen it again later, in 1815, when it was exhibited at the British Institution and made a great impression on many English artists.

West, who was then President of the Academy, seems to have taken an interest in Constable, and some specimens of his advice to him are recorded: 'Always remember', he said, 'that light and shadow never stand still. . . . Whatever object you are painting, keep in mind its prevailing character rather than its accidental appearance . . . and never be content till you have transferred that to canvas. In your skies, for instance, always aim at brightness . . . even in the darkest effects there should be brightness. Your darks should look like the darks of silver, not of lead or of

---

[1] Cf. below, p. 264.

125a. JOHN BRETT
The Stonebreaker
Walker Art Gallery, Liverpool

125b. W. S. BURTON
The Wounded Cavalier
Guildhall Museum, London

126. SIR JOHN E. MILLAIS
Ophelia

slate.' This was advice which Constable could take, because it formulated his own instincts and desires in landscape painting. He listened and remembered. All the rest of West's advice he doubtless instantly forgot.

Constable seems to have had no financial worries in these London years. He was presumably provided with funds from his father. He had not yet begun to sell his pictures, but he was able to live and travel about and to buy two landscapes by Gaspard Poussin.

In 1804 he obtained an order for an altarpiece, *Christ blessing Little Children*, for a church at Brantham. In 1808 he was employed by Lord Dysart to copy pictures by Reynolds and others in his collection. In 1809 he painted an altarpiece, *Christ blessing the Bread and Wine*, for Nayland Church.

Meanwhile he had decided that he wanted to marry Maria Bicknell, daughter of the Solicitor to the Admiralty, whom he had known since her childhood, as her grandfather, Dr. Rhudde, was the rector of Bergholt. He seems to have proposed to her about 1811 when he was thirty-five and she was twenty-four. Dr. Rhudde opposed the marriage; and as he was very rich, and the young lady's father was anxious not to jeopardise the inheritance, pressure was brought to bear upon her to refuse the proposal. Constable persisted, however, in his courtship; there were clandestine meetings and secret letters; and he made an effort to win an independent financial position by painting portraits.

In 1816 his father died, leaving him the equivalent of about £15,000 in present money.[1] He was now forty and took counsel with a friend, Archdeacon Fisher, about the problem of his protracted courtship. Fisher replied in the following letter: 'I am not a great letter writer, and, when I take pen in hand, I generally come to the point at once. I therefore write to tell you that I intend to be in London on Tuesday evening the 24th, and on Wednesday shall hold myself ready and happy to marry you. There, you see, I have used no roundabout phrases, but

[1] £4000.

said the thing at once in good plain English. So do you follow my example and get you to your lady, and instead of blundering out long sentences about "the hymeneal altar", etc., say that on Wednesday, September 25th, you are ready to marry her. If she replies like a sensible woman as I suspect she is, "Well, John, here is my hand, I'm ready," all well and good. If she says, "Yes, but another day will be more convenient," let her name it and I am at her service.' Here again the advice was acceptable. Constable took it. Maria, who was now twenty-nine, still hesitated and hinted that it might be better to wait for the death of the rich, implacable Dr. Rhudde. But Constable would wait no longer. The marriage took place; and Archdeacon Fisher carried them off to stay with him for their honeymoon.

Constable now had twelve happy and successful years. He had a house at Hampstead and a studio and gallery for showing his pictures in London. He had all the time been working out his personal attitude to landscape and he now devoted himself to his chosen field with enthusiastic delight. He had no financial difficulties—his wife inherited the equivalent of £15,000[1] from Dr. Rhudde in 1819, and he received the main inheritance, equivalent to about £70,000,[2] from her father some ten years later; and now at last when he was forty-three he was beginning to make money by his work.

In 1819 he was made an A.R.A. and sold his *View on the Stour* (1819) for a hundred guineas; *The Hay Wain* was sold in 1824 for £250 to a Frenchman and *The Lock* was sold the same year for a hundred and fifty guineas; in 1826 he had commissions to the value of £400 and published his scale of prices which ranged from twenty guineas for a twelve-inch pochade to a hundred and twenty guineas for pictures measuring fifty inches by forty, and to more for still larger pictures—prices which must, of course, be more than trebled to get equivalents in money of to-day.

To this period (1816-1827) belong a number of other well-known pictures, *A Cottage in a Cornfield* (1818), *Salisbury*

[1] £4000.   [2] £20,000.

127. FORD MADOX BROWN
Baa-lambs
Ashmolean Museum, Oxford

128a. STANLEY SPENCER
Kit Inspection
Burghclere Memorial Chapel, England

128b. STANLEY SPENCER
Tea in Hospital
Burghclere Memorial Chapel, England

Cathedral from the Bishop's Garden (1823), *The Leaping Horse* (1825), and *The Cornfield* (1826).

In 1827, when he was fifty-one, his life seemed in fact to have worked out in every way as he desired. He had a wife to whom he was devoted, and four children; he had been able to develop and practise his art without the necessity of compromise or prostitution for his daily bread; and he held a reputable place in his profession. Then suddenly his wife died; and from this bereavement he never recovered. His later years were marked by nervousness and despondencies; and he never ceased to wear mourning till he himself died in 1837.

The pictures of the last period 1827-1837 include *Dedham Vale* (1828), *Hampstead Heath* (1830), *Salisbury Cathedral: The Rainbow* (1831), *The Opening of Waterloo Bridge* (1832), *The Valley Farm* (1835), *The Cenotaph* (1836) and *Arundel Mill and Castle* (1837).

Constable's main contribution to art resides in his so-called 'sketches' which must be distinguished on the one hand from his pochades and on the other from his elaborated pictures. He developed late and wandered for years in a bypath. Though he never attempted to make painting do the impossible by concentrating on the still-life approach to landscape, he wasted a good deal of time toying with the picturesque tradition and imitating Gainsborough. When finally he found himself, and let himself go, he did something that had never been done in landscape painting before—except to some extent by Velasquez and Rubens. He symbolised in paint the flicker of light in the open air and the movement of clouds across the sky and conveyed in paint his excited delight in these phenomena. We see his contribution in things like the so-called *Sketch for the Hay Wain*, the so-called *Sketch for the Valley Farm* (Pl. 113), the *Dell in Helmingham Park* (Pl. 114b), *Weymouth Bay* (Pl. 116a), and *On the Stour near Dedham* (Pl. 116b).

Compared with any classical landscape—with Poussin's *Funeral of Phocion* or *Landscape with Two Nymphs* (Pl. 133b) or with Rubens' *Château de Steen* or *Sunset* or *Rainbow Landscape* or *Ulysses and Nausicaa*, or *Meleager and Atalante*—these works by Constable are inevitably called 'sketches' because they record only fragmentary and unorganised impressions. But they are not sketches in the sense of unfinished pictures or in the sense of shorthand notes for pictures (such as Turner made). Nor are they sketches in the sense of pochades—rapid mechanical notes of purely visual impressions—a type of sketch which Constable also produced in large numbers.[1] They are really *finished pictures* in the sense that they record a conscious experience and record it both completely and without any extraneous additions. Everything in these works—not least the rapid spontaneous deliberately emotive handling—contributes to the true expression of the experience.

But, perhaps as a result of his study of Rubens' *The Château de Steen*, Constable was constantly haunted by an ambition to paint pictures where specific form would be symbolised with a completeness which was not really part of his experience. In pursuit of this ambition he painted elaborated versions of some of these pictures and tried by passages of still-life painting to give them more completeness. These elaborated versions are untrue, not only because they represent in parts the still-life cherry-to-be-pecked-at approach applied to the impossible task of landscape, which we have already encountered in Crome's *Chapel Fields, Norwich* (Pl. 107b), but also because they are untrue to the artist's original experience which was romantic experience of emotive effects like Crome's experience in *On the Yare* (Pl. 110a). Occasionally Constable could recapture in memory some additional emotive element for the elaborated version. But as a rule, inevitably, he could not. Compared with the so-called sketches, which are the real original romantic pictures, the elaborated versions are failures which fail because they are partly fakes. But this, of course, is not obvious to a spectator who sees the elaborated version without knowledge of the picture proper, i.e. the 'sketch'. For most of the experience contained in the original picture has been transferred to the elaborated version

[1]Cf. above, pp. 195, 196.

129. STANLEY SPENCER
Drawing Water
Burghclere Memorial Chapel, England

130. STANLEY SPENCER
Resurrection
Burghclere Memorial Chapel, England

which thus contains an element of truth working through the untrue additions. It was thus that *The Hay Wain* seemed true in the Paris Salon of 1824; and it is thus that *Stoke-by-Nayland* (Pl. 115) and some of the other elaborated pictures by Constable exhibit elements of truth to-day.

His real contribution would be more obvious if the so-called sketches were labelled simply *The Hay Wain* or *The Valley Farm* and the so-called pictures painted from them were labelled *Elaborated Version of The Hay Wain* and *Elaborated Version of The Valley Farm*.

The French understood this. Confronted with Constable's elaborated pictures, they were able to extract the element that was real romantic art, the true record of excited experience, from the faked additional elements which were really still-life painting with no real function in this type of art. His real contribution thus had enormous influence on French Romantic painting and Impressionism. But the English landscape painters of the nineteenth century failed to make the distinction between Constable speaking truth and Constable speaking truth plus fake, or rather they made the distinction the wrong way round, assuming that the elaborated pictures would have been better if they had contained more of the still-life procedure, i.e. the fake, and less of what they called 'Constable's Snow', i.e. the true record of his emotional experience. Thus though Constable had hundreds of English imitators in the nineteenth century who produced countless pastiches of his elaborated second versions—his real contribution was not understood in England until the French Romantics and Impressionists had familiarised English spectators with this type of art. Then, and not till then, do we get *Chepstow Castle* (Pl. 114a) by Wilson Steer.

CHAPTER XIV

THE PRE-RAPHAELITE MOVEMENT

*

The Pre-Raphaelite Brotherhood was formed in 1848. As everyone knows, the Brethren were Rossetti, Holman Hunt, John Everett Millais (1829-1896), and some less conspicuous figures. An older artist Ford Madox Brown (1821-1893) was associated with the movement but was never a member of the Brotherhood.

In one aspect the movement was tainted at the start. It contained within itself the fatal element of 'mediaevalism'. Ruskin was the first to recognise this as a defect and a danger. 'If their sympathies with the early artists', he wrote, 'lead them into mediaevalism or Romanism, they will of course come to nothing.' I have discussed elsewhere the character and genesis of the *moyen-âge* motifs in nineteenth-century painting.[1] Here I need only remind the reader that in England they began with Alderman Boydell's Shakespeare Gallery (*c.* 1780-1802); that they were launched in France in 1816 as a propaganda gesture by the Bourbon regime which desired to put the clock back behind the Revolution and to encourage an interest in the hero-kings of the distant past; that they were also partly a studio reaction against the pseudo-classical paintings of David, and partly an aspect of the Romantic Movement as a whole; and that they were continued everywhere all through the nineteenth century in meaningless pictures by addle-pated derivative practitioners. To appreciate the Pre-Raphaelite Movement as a gesture, as an intention in the larger sense, we must substract all this Wardour-

[1]Cf. 'John Ruskin' pp. 245-51, 'French Painting' pp. 194-5, and 'The Modern Movement in Art' pp. 58-60.

Street mediaevalism which was of no real service to any of the artists except Rossetti, who used it, as we shall see, in a special and personal way.

In the eighteen-forties before the Brotherhood was founded the 'subject pictures' most admired in the Royal Academy were painted *tableaux vivants*, grouped and illuminated like stage scenes; and the most admired artist was Daniel Maclise (1810-1870) who, Frith tells us in his 'Autobiography' was then spoken of in Academic circles as 'out and away the greatest artist that ever lived'. The Pre-Raphaelites thought these pictures rhetorical nonsense and they looked on the records of specific form contained in them as pastiches of the approximate perception popularised by Reynolds whom they called 'Sir Sloshua'. Coming by chance upon engravings from frescoes by Benozzo Gozzoli (1420-1498) they decided that the painters before Raphael had been honest men and they resolved to emulate them. For the rest Rossetti and Hunt, the only really big figures in the movement, had nothing in common.

DANTE GABRIEL ROSSETTI (1828-1882) as a painter felt at the beginning a desire to make two-dimensional compositions. His first impulse was to design patterns with glowing colour. He spoke from the beginning of wishing to express himself 'in colour'. In some pictures exhibited by Madox Brown, who had studied on the Continent, he found colour used as a vehicle of emotion, and he accordingly wrote to Brown, in a celebrated letter, that he wished 'to obtain some knowledge of colour', and to become his pupil. Brown set him to paint bottles—which was not what he wanted. So he left Brown. Shortly after he met Holman Hunt and once more asked for instruction in colour. But Hunt also set him to still-life painting not only of bottles but of everything he could see—including the human figure. This also was not what he wanted. So he left Hunt—after painting *The Girlhood of the Virgin* under his direction.

He then painted *Ecce Ancilla Domini* (Pl. 119) as his first independent work. In this picture, where the Virgin's attitude and raiment recall no painting of the Virgin in Christian art, and the

Angel is a figure without wings, there is no Wardour-Street mediaevalism or archaeology. There is, however, a flavour of pre-Renaissance painting due simply to Rossetti's deliberate avoidance of the illusionist perspective which was, of course, a cardinal element in the *tableau-vivant* pictures applauded in the Academy. This *Ecce Ancilla Domini* is a truly original production; but I have the feeling nevertheless that, as it stands, it is not entirely a true picture—that it should be labelled *Elaborated Version of Ecce Ancilla Domini* and that the true picture was some first 'sketch'.[1]

Soon after this Rossetti met Elizabeth Siddal who subsequently became his wife; and between the painting of *Ecce Ancilla Domini* (1850) and his wife's death (1862) he produced a series of watercolours of great interest.

In some of these watercolours, *The Blue Closet*, for example —though the pattern is intriguing—there is a meaningless use of mediaevalism. But in *Arthur's Tomb* and *How they met Themselves* it is used with peculiar significance.

Arthur's Tomb (Pl. 120) symbolises a deeply felt experience in a pictorial language fashioned to express it. The experience was so compelling that every constituent in the picture springs directly from it. The intense, complex, and at the same time, harsh, arresting, and simple design, the rush of passion in the drama, the charged atmosphere—all these spring from the experience and collaborate in the exterioration.

And here mediaevalism had real work to do. The experience symbolised was one which the artist was impelled both to record and to disguise. The mediaevalism here serves to effect a concealment. Rossetti has transmuted time and place in order that two souls might not be carried on the picture's sleeve.

In *How they met Themselves* (Pl. 121), drawn on his honeymoon, we have again a secret confessed and disguised. This picture of a girl and her lover, who meet their own ghosts in the shade of a wood, is a symbol of a fear, of a dread con-

[1]Cf. above, pp. 124, 219, and 'The Modern Movement in Art', pp. 70, 179 and 180.

131. STANLEY SPENCER
Christ carrying the Cross
National Gallery, Millbank, London

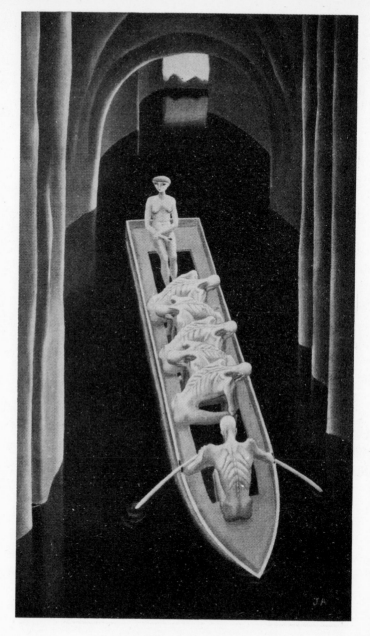

132. JOHN ARMSTRONG
The River of the Dead

quered for a while and exorcised by transmutation of time and place.

Elizabeth Siddal—'Guggum', as Rossetti called her—was at this period the central excitement of his life. She plagued him; and he plagued her; but he adored her appearance. Every attitude she took enchanted him. Just as Watteau drew every movement of the tall girl who frequented his studio for some years, so Rossetti drew every movement of 'Guggum'; he drew her laying the table, sitting idly in a rocking chair, standing for a moment by the window (Pl. 122a). He made scores of these drawings, all original, all emotional records of this excitement. In the years following her death he became a maker of pictures; and the women who sat to him, whatever his relations with them, were unable to excite him in this way. Then a day came when he found himself in love with Mrs. Morris, and believed that he had always loved her from the first glimpse of her long throat and dark hair and curling lips at the theatre in Oxford three years before he had married 'Guggum'. A new series of drawings and pictures resulted. He drew and painted Mrs. Morris scores of times with ever-increasingly romantic distortions (Pl. 122b). But the excitement here was hysterical. Middle age, remorse, a thousand self-indulgences, and too much chloral, all played parts in this experience. He had painted 'Guggum' just after her death as *Beata Beatrix*; that was the last time he had felt deeply enough to use mediaevalism as a species of disguise. When he painted Mrs. Morris as Beatrice in *Dante's Dream* the mediaevalism was an affectation without meaning or real purpose.

Rossetti's contribution was entirely personal. He took nothing from Hunt or Millais and hardly anything from Madox Brown. Though he was one of the Pre-Raphaelite Brethren he really played no part in the movement considered as an intention with a special creed. His pictures and drawings were very much imitated, and the imitations are often confused with the Pre-Raphaelite Movement or looked on as a Rossetti Movement assumed to have run parallel with it. To regard these imitations in either of these ways is of course an error. No Rossetti

Movement came or could come from Rossetti. All imitations of his contribution are imitations—derivative productions and no more.

The only name worth mentioning in this connection is SIR EDWARD BURNE-JONES (1833-1898) who began as an imitator of Rossetti, then became an imitator of Botticelli, and made in the end a personal contribution.

It is easier for us to appreciate Burne-Jones than it was for the generation that came between the time of his triumphs and our own day. In the 'nineties the art world in England was divided between those who delighted in Burne-Jones' 'subject pictures', and those who followed the doctrine of 'Art for Art's Sake' (which then meant 'Painting for Painting's Sake') imported from Paris in the 'seventies by the American, James McNeill Whistler (1834-1903). Whistler's doctrine, supported by Wilde, Pater, Moore, and W. E. Henley, won so complete a victory that it became as much as an artistic young person's social position was worth to refer to the 'subject' of a picture, and as much as a painter's reputation was worth to paint a subject more 'literary' than a young woman wearing a green necklace or to give the picture a title more 'literary' than *The Jade Note*. To-day we find Painting for Painting's Sake too superficial as a doctrine. Manet himself strikes us as a virtuoso. If we admire Whistler it is as an artist who went beyond his preaching and gave us much more—an atmosphere and architectural creations deliberately planned and considered. We now regard Whistler's premises, then so paradoxical, as obvious, and we give them wider and deeper application.

Burne-Jones, like Rossetti, used transmutations of time and place. But his procedure was much nearer to the transmutations in Fuseli's *La Débutante* (Pl. 83), Brown's *Woman and Duenna* and *The Three Graces* (Pls. 84 and 85), and Beardsley's *Messalina* (Pl. 87) than to the transmutations in Rossetti's *Arthur's Tomb* and *How they met Themselves* (Pls. 120 and 121). Burne-Jones used mediaevalism and Golden-Ageism as a means of escape from the world around him which he was not robust

133a. JOHN LINNELL
Contemplation
National Gallery, Millbank, London

133b. NICOLAS POUSSIN
Landscape with Two Nymphs
Condé Museum, Chantilly, France

134a. WILLIAM BLAKE
Illustration to Virgil's First Eclogue—Wood-engraving: actual size

134b. WILLIAM BLAKE
Illustration to Virgil's First Eclogue—Wood-engraving: actual size

134c. WILLIAM BLAKE
Illustration to Virgil's First Eclogue—Wood-engraving: actual size

enough to accept and conquer. His biographers describe his attitude, and doubtless he described it himself, as a revolt against the ugliness of industrialism. But it was really nothing less than a flight from life. Burne-Jones did not believe, as Blake believed, that the life around him was unreal and unimportant; he looked upon it as aggressively real and horribly inartistic. He turned his back upon it and transmuted his experience to a faint unaggressive unreality which he thought artistic. Blake said 'A spirit and a vision are not . . . a cloudy vapour or a nothing.' That, as I see things, is the *mot qui tue* applied to the intentions of Burne-Jones.

Nevertheless it is in his most unreal and most 'artistic' Golden-Age pictures and drawings that he made his real contribution. When he tried, after the transmutation, to imbue his picture with some substance by means of elaborate still-life painting he seems quite intolerable to the modern student. *King Cophetua and the Beggar Maid*, for example, has been elaborated into the silliest possible still-life record of two models posing in fancy dress on a heap of Wardour-Street bric-à-brac. But when Burne-Jones makes no such attempt at substance, when he is content to move in the faint unreal world of his own creation, to rejoice in its unreality—and, incidentally, to restrict himself to monochrome, for as a colourist he was always rudimentary—he does create an atmosphere; and within this atmosphere he sometimes makes his lines flow like the silvery melodies of Chopin.

The Rossetti Movement thus began with Rossetti and ended with Burne-Jones. The Pre-Raphaelite Movement properly so called was the creation of Hunt.

Ruskin had said to beginners—but to beginners only, as anyone can satisfy himself by referring to the context—'Go to nature, rejecting nothing, selecting nothing and scorning nothing'. W. HOLMAN HUNT (1827-1910) picked this up and made it the sum and substance of a theory of great art.

Hunt thought of painting as the still-life procedure and he tried by sheer force of will and energy to do the impossible and make it rival the daguerreotype. He painted *tableaux vivants* and launched the notion that a *tableau vivant* in bright daylight with much and minute imitation of specific details is admirable, though a *tableau vivant*, artificially illuminated like a scene in the theatre, with little approximate imitation of specific details, is abominable. He multiplied incident and minute delineations of specific forms in his pictures and laid it down as a rule that the amount of such incident and the number of specific forms minutely delineated must be held the measure of a picture's truth.

At the time this gesture was of value. The intense effort at observation in Hunt's pictures and his burning conscientiousness impressed and stimulated his contemporaries. His influence was irresistible. When he went to Palestine it remained behind. It kept Millais with his nose to the grindstone till he was released by the Royal Academy, which made him an Associate in 1853 five years after the Brotherhood began. We meet it in *The Stonebreaker* (Pl. 125a) by John Brett (1831-1902), in *The Wounded Cavalier* (Pl. 125b) by W. S. Burton (1824-1916), and in scores of other industriously painted still-life 'subject pictures' and landscapes of the period. Madox Brown—a truly imaginative artist capable of *Cordelia and Lear*, and *Elijah and the Widow's Son*, and capable also of the simplicity, the formal mastery and personal vision of *Baa-lambs* (Pl. 127)—was led by Hunt's gesture to accumulate a thousand records of specific forms in *Work*; W. P. Frith (1819-1909)—though he denied the influence of the Pre-Raphaelites and scoffed at them—was led by the same gesture to ten thousand such still-life records in *Ramsgate Sands*, *Derby Day* and *The Railway Station*.

But Hunt himself was by no means merely a categoric chronicler of minute specific forms. He was not a commonplace philistine, like Frith, pretentiously satisfied with commonplace experience. He had imagination and at moments a personal vision—witness *The Festival of St. Swithun* (Pl. 124b); there is originality in *The Hireling Shepherd*; and real drama in *The Scapegoat* (Pl. 124a). We cannot appreciate his gesture to-day

135a. EDWARD CALVERT
The Return Home—Wood-engraving: actual size

135b. EDWARD CALVERT
The Chamber Idyll—Wood-engraving: actual size

135c. EDWARD CALVERT
The Flood—Lithograph: actual size

136a. EDWARD CALVERT
The Bride—Engraving on copper

136b. EDWARD CALVERT
The Ploughman—Wood-engraving

because his failures, and most of his works are failures, are so aggressive. When he succeeds he succeeds by the force and intensity of his intention. When he fails the failure is likewise so forceful and insistent that we are driven to regard it not as failure but as offence. His failures, which are failures in sensibility and intelligence, are unredeemed by any minor charms. He was entirely without taste, and in his unfaltering devotion to his dogmas he scorned to acquire any graces of colour or linear design. The modern student has learned not only to look for linear significance but also, from his experience of paintings by Whistler, Renoir, Degas, and Cézanne, to look for simple harmonies, or complex subtleties, or rich sonorities, of colour. So high indeed is the esteem in which colour orchestration is now held that many students can delight in pictures where such orchestration is, properly speaking, the sole content. Spectators thus educated find the colour in all pictures by the Pre-Raphaelites—Rossetti himself not excepted—rudimentary and crude. And they find the colour in Hunt's pictures quite painfully unpleasant.

Hunt's technical procedures in picture-making, the method he adopted for his special ends, are of considerable interest to modern students and have a place in the history of art. For his system of accumulating incident, his demand that the spectator should take account of the sum of the parts in his picture and regard the sum as contributing to the product, his demand that his pictures should be read inch by inch and not merely regarded as an ensemble at a distance—brings him in line with the latest developments in European painting. And thus we get the paradox that Hunt's Pre-Raphaelism links Hogarth to Surrealism.[1]

Apart from Rossetti and Hunt there were no really considerable figures in the Pre-Raphaelite Movement. Millais under the dual inspiration of these two turned his natural gifts—his lynx eye and his sure hand—to good effect in *Jesus in the House of His Parents* and in *Ophelia* (Pl. 126). But he was fundamentally philistine—commonplace, conceited and sentimental. When the

[1]Cf. above, pp. 86-88, and below, pp. 283, 284.

Academy beckoned, he left Hunt, the Brotherhood, and effort behind. From time to time he painted a heap of autumn leaves or some other collection of small forms with great precision to show that he still could do it when he tried. From time to time he painted an upstanding still-life portrait. But these were incidents in a degeneration which could not be concealed by his fee of two thousand pounds for a portrait, a knighthood, and the Presidential Chair.

The aftermath of the Pre-Raphaelite Movement is still with us; the Wardour-Street mediaevalism of Madox Brown's *Chaucer at the Court of Edward III* and Millais' *Sir Isumbras at the Ford* still appears occasionally on the Royal Academy walls; Rossetti's drawings of Miss Siddal are prettily echoed, in the tones of Whistler's palette, by Gwen John (Pl. 123); and Holman Hunt at his best, the Hunt who painted *The Scapegoat* (Pl. 124a) and *The Festival of St. Swithun* (Pl. 124b) has at last found a real successor in Stanley Spencer whose recent paintings in The Burghclere Memorial Chapel I describe in Appendix V.[1]

[1]Cf. below, pp. 280-285.

CHAPTER XV

BLAKE
1757-1827

*

1. BLAKE'S LIFE

'I find on all hands great objections to my doing anything but the mere drudgery of business, and intimations that if I do not confine myself to this I shall not live. This has always pursued me. You will understand by this the source of all my uneasiness . . . For, that I cannot live without doing my duty to lay up treasures in heaven is Certain and Determined, and to this I have long made up my mind, and why this should be made an objection to Me, while Drunkenness, Lewdness, Gluttony and even Idleness itself does not hurt other men, let Satan himself Explain . . . I am not ashamed, afraid, or averse to tell you what Ought to be told: That I am under the direction of Messengers from Heaven, Daily and Nightly . . . I never obtrude such things on others unless question'd and then I never disguise the truth. If we fear to do the dictates of our Angels and tremble at the Tasks set before us; if we refuse to do Spiritual Acts because of Natural Fears or Natural Desires! Who can describe the dismal torments of such a state! . . . Though my path is difficult I have no fear of stumbling while I keep it.' WILLIAM BLAKE.

BLAKE lived more than half his life in the eighteenth century. He began to draw and engrave when Louis XV was still on the throne of France and Boucher was painting his last pictures and Fragonard was rising to fame with panels ordered by La Guimard and Madame du Barry. He was an almost exact contemporary of Louis David and Goya. He was thirty-one when Gainsborough died and thirty-five when the funeral of Sir Joshua Reynolds passed his door. He lived through the period of the French Revolution and the Napoleonic Wars. He was eighteen years older than Turner and twelve years older than Lawrence whom he lived to see President of the Royal Academy. I refer to him last because his work, though unknown and unregarded in his lifetime, and without influence on English nineteenth-century art, is much regarded by modern students and if I see things correctly it is about to be regarded more and more.

He was born in Broad Street, Golden Square, on November 28, 1757. His father, a hosier, was a dissenter who read Swedenborg. Nothing is known of his mother's turn of mind. He was a nervous child, extremely affected by punishment, and he was never sent to school. Years later his wife would relate that at the age of four he had seen God's head at the window, and that at the age of seven he had seen the prophet Ezekiel in the fields and angels among the trees 'their bright wings bespangling the boughs like stars'. We may assume, I think, that his parents took these statements with a grain of salt, but that he impressed them nevertheless as a prodigy. In any case, as he showed talent for drawing they sent him to a drawing class, bought casts for him to draw from at home, and gave him pocket money to spend on prints which he copied. When he was fourteen they apprenticed him to a competent engraver, James Basire, who had a school of engraving. Blake worked for seven years under Basire and learned a craft which at different periods of his lifetime brought him money. Basire, while Blake was with him, had a commission for some engravings of monuments in Westminster Abbey, and he sent the boy there to make drawings. And while he was with him Blake also had contact with Renaissance and Baroque art, as Basire had engraved the Raphael Cartoons at Hampton Court and a number of pictures by Guercino (1591-1666).

When he was twenty-one Blake left Basire and worked for a time in the Academy schools. In 1779, when he was twenty-two, he began to get employment as an engraver for booksellers; and he kept himself in this way for the next seven years, during which he also wrote poems, made water colour compositions, and got married. His wife was a peasant, a daughter of a market gardener. She signed the marriage register with a mark. Blake was twenty-four when he married her and she was twenty. Shortly after the marriage he started in business as printseller and

137. SAMUEL PALMER
The Lonely Tower—Etching

138. SAMUEL PALMER
In a Shoreham Garden
Victoria and Albert Museum, London

engraver with an old fellow apprentice named Parker. He continued to write poems, and began to experiment with colour printing. He planned a three-volume publication of his poems, with the text, as well as illustrations, engraved not printed; the edition was to be of two thousand copies which he proposed to sell at £100—say £400 in present values—apiece; when he told his wife of the plan she said: 'Whoever will not have them will be ignorant fools and not deserve to live.'

By this time he had met John Flaxman (1755-1826), a pseudo-classical illustrator, designer, and sculptor who worked for the potter Wedgwood and was highly regarded in his day. Flaxman was anxious to help him, and introduced him and his wife to literary and artistic gatherings at the house of a Rev. Henry and Mrs. Mathew, well-meaning dilettanti who expected their artist friends, as has been neatly said, 'to conform to the real, if scarcely visible, yoke of their polite patronage'. Mrs. Blake, who could still barely write her name, and Blake, who believed himself inspired, were not well adapted for this velvet yoke. But all went well till the Mathews provided the money for printing his poems. Blake took the money but despised himself for the contact to which he owed it; he quarrelled with the donors and squared accounts in his own mind by writing 'The Island in the Moon', a satire on the salon and its hosts who had placed him under obligation and thus infringed his integrity.

In 1787, when he was thirty, he ended his connection with the printselling and engraving business and decided to devote himself entirely to creative art. He took rooms in Poland Street and continued his experiments in colour engraving for the illustrated publication of his poems. The texts of 'The Songs of Innocence' and 'The Book of Thel' date from 1789; 'The Marriage of Heaven and Hell' and some paintings in glue tempera, including probably *Christ blessing Little Children* and *Bathsheba at the Bath* (Pl. 143) date from about 1790.

In this period he met some English sympathisers with the French Revolution, and was engaged to illustrate some of the writings of Mary Wollstonecraft; becoming fired with revolutionary enthusiasm, he walked abroad with the red cap of freedom on his head, and wrote 'The French Revolution' and 'A Song of Liberty' (1790-1792).

He kept himself and his wife in these years by making illustrations and engravings for other people's books and by engraving other people's drawings and pictures. In 1793 he moved to larger quarters in Lambeth and there at last he evolved a method of colour printing by means of which he was able to produce editions of his writings by his own process of 'illuminated printing' and also to print editions of his coloured drawings. While he was at Lambeth (1793-1800), from the age of thirty-six to forty-three, he printed the famous illuminated editions of *The Songs of Innocence*, *The Marriage of Heaven and Hell*, *The Book of Thel* and the colour-printed drawings *Satan exulting over Eve*, *The Elohim creating Adam* (Pl. 152b), *Glad Day* (from a very early drawing), *Elijah about to ascend in the Fiery Chariot*, *The Lazar House*, *Pity* (Pl. 146), *Newton*, *Nebuchadnezzar* and others. His process of reproduction was slow and involved much work by hand. He printed only a few copies of the drawings and soon abandoned the procedure altogether.

While he was working, literally day and night, at these productions, he was making money by giving drawing lessons at people's houses and by commissions from booksellers. In 1795, someone, nobody seems to know who, but presumably an influential pupil, procured him the offer of a post as Tutor in Drawing to the Royal Family. Once more he felt that his integrity was threatened. He declined the offer, and gave up all his pupils in a species of panic.

He was able to do this because he had just received an order from a bookseller for a series of drawings and engravings to illustrate Young's *Night Thoughts*. For this poem he made a hundred and thirty-seven watercolours and engraved forty-three plates. The publication was a financial failure and was discontinued after the first part. Blake later wrote his poem 'Vala' on the back of the unpublished sheets.

139. SAMUEL PALMER
Moonlight Landscape with Sheep
National Gallery, Millbank, London

140. PAUL NASH
Dyke by the Road—Woodcut

In 1799 when he was forty-two he found the first patron for his original pictures and drawings. This was Thomas Butts, a descendant of Henry VIII's physician, who recognised him as an interesting and unusual personality. Butts was intrigued by his genius and charmed with his simplicity and the simplicity of his wife. He called at the house one day and found them both naked in the summer-house reading 'Paradise Lost'—an episode which has caused terrible consternation among Blake's biographers, the latest of whom thinks that a 'nudist movement' in England at the time is necessary to explain it. Kind, sensible Butts needed no such explanation. He understood Blake, I fancy, better than most people understood him at the time and better than most people understand him to-day; he admired him as an artist, loved him as a man; and was tactfully kind to him for years. He wanted to help him and he knew how to do it. He arranged to take a picture or drawing from him every week for the price of a guinea—equivalent to making him an allowance of about £250 a year in present money—without any restriction on his freedom. Blake, over a number of years, sent him a series of remarkable paintings in tempera—*Eve tempted by the Serpent, The Nativity, The Infant Jesus riding on a Lamb, The Angel appearing to Zacharias, Abraham and Isaac, Satan smiting Job with Sore Boils* (Pl. 153)—and numerous water colours including *God answering Job out of the Whirlwind, The Body of Abel found by Adam and Eve, The Woman taken in Adultery, The Betrayal of Christ, Soldiers casting Lots for Christ's Garments,* and *The Entombment.*

In 1800 a well-to-do man of letters named William Hayley, then engaged on a life of the poet Cowper, was introduced to Blake by Flaxman, and commissioned him to draw and engrave a series of illustrations for this book and for his other literary productions, including poems. He also invited him to come and live near him at Felpham on the Sussex coast. Blake went there in September and remained three years. It was the first time that he had lived in the country or by the sea, and for a while he was very happy with his wife in a seaside cottage. He did the work required by Hayley and he also sent watercolours from time to time to Butts; he gave drawing lessons locally and painted, it is said, some miniature portraits of the gentry round about. Hayley was zealous in procuring him work and taught him some Latin, Hebrew and Greek.

At Felpham, Blake continued his poem called 'Vala' and re-named it with his new-found Greek 'The Four Zoas'. He also began there a poem in twelve books of which two parts—'Milton' and 'Jerusalem'—were eventually completed (1804).

Meanwhile Hayley's 'Life of Cowper' was finished and the employments which Hayley and Hayley's friends found for him became less and less worthy of the author of *Jerusalem* and the artist who had drawn the *Elohim creating Adam, Pity,* and *Satan smiting Job* (Pls. 152b, 146, and 153). Moreover the cottage was damp and both he and his wife had been ill with fever. When an order arrived from one of Hayley's friends for a set of decorated hand-screens for a lady's evening party, Blake had another revolt and panic. He said good-bye to Hayley and left Felpham.

Back in London in 1803 he again sought work from the booksellers and received an order to engrave some designs by Fuseli whom he had known for a number of years.

HENRY FUSELI (1741–1825) whose real name was Johann Heinrich Füssli was born and educated in Zurich. He became a close friend of his schoolfellow Lavater and the friendship continued in after life. Through Fuseli Blake became acquainted with Lavater's mystical speculations and his personal concept of Christianity, as well as with his celebrated book on physiognomy which Fuseli eventually had translated into English. Fuseli at twenty-one had become involved in a conflict with some of the Zurich authorities whom he charged with corruption; and although he apparently proved his case he thought it wise or was compelled to leave Switzerland. It was related in his lifetime that he had to leave Zurich because, with Lavater, he had terrified a young lady by 'attempting to produce the apparition of her deceased lover'; and the story is credible of the painter of *The Nightmare* (Pl. 65). From Switzerland in any

141. LEON UNDERWOOD
Tiger

142. WILLIAM BLAKE
The Spiritual Form of Nelson guiding Leviathan
National Gallery, Millbank, London

case he went to Berlin and then to England where he showed his work to Reynolds who was encouraging. He then went to Italy for eight years where, as already noted, he met John Brown.[1] He returned to England in 1778 at the age of thirty-seven and remained here for the remainder of his life. Four years later he painted *The Nightmare* (Pl. 65) to which I have already referred.[2] He was employed by Alderman Boydell in painting illustrations for his Shakespeare Gallery; and in 1779 he exhibited forty-seven paintings in illustration of Milton's poems. He was made an A.R.A. in 1788, R.A. in 1790, and then Professor of Painting and Keeper of the Academy. It is difficult to form any notion of his personality from the materials available. He was certainly regarded as an eccentric in his day. He was, it would seem, very attractive to a number of women. Mary Wollstonecraft was wildly in love with him for some years and tried in vain to detach him from his wife—who had been a model. For the rest he seems to have been an artist who never found himself or lacked some ingredient of the power to externalise experience. He wrote poems, he painted huge oil pictures, he made drawings—not only of the types reproduced (Pls. 83 and 86b) but also drawings imitating Blake and the Renaissance masters, especially Michelangelo. Everything that he did has vitality; but in everything there are elements which are factitious and derived. Lavater wrote of him: 'Nature intended him for a great poet, a great painter, a great orator; but to borrow his own words, "inexorable fate does not always proportion the will to our powers; it sometimes assigns a copious proportion of will to ordinary minds, whose faculties are very contracted; and frequently associates with the greatest faculties a will feeble and impotent". In a physiognomical account of him Lavater said, 'The nose seems to be the seat of an intrepid genius', in which connection it is interesting to note that Fuseli said in front of a self-portrait by Rembrandt: 'What a nose! why his nose is as big as his face! A fine fellow! I like to see a great man with a great nose.'[3] Fuseli's main significance in the history of English painting

[1]Cf. above, p. 169.   [2]Cf. above, p. 155.   [3]Cf. above, p. 109.

is the fact that he was kind to Blake and helped and encouraged him in many ways. He said of Blake that he was capital 'to steal from'. Blake admired his work and wrote in his annotations to Reynolds' 'Discourses': 'The Neglect of Fuseli's Milton in a Country pretending to the Encouragement of Art is a Sufficient Apology for My Vigorous Indignation, if indeed the Neglect of My own Powers had not been.' Blake also wrote in his pocket book:

'The only Man that e'er I knew
Who did not make me almost spue
Was Fuseli: he was both Turk and Jew—
And so, dear Christian Friends, how do you do?'

While Blake was engraving Fuseli's drawings for the book-sellers in 1803 he was also at work on illustrations for his own poem 'Jerusalem'; and he made a number of compositions in watercolour which include *The Death of the Virgin Mary*, *The Death of St. Joseph*, *The Angel of the Divine Presence clothing Adam and Eve with Skins* and *God blessing the Seventh Day*. It is probable that *Death on a White Horse* and *The River of Life* were also produced in this period. The composition called *Vala, Hyle, and Skofield*, a symbolic record of a summons served upon him in Felpham for turning a dragoon named Scholfield out of his garden, dates from 1804.

In 1805 he was commissioned to draw and engrave illustra-tions for Blair's *The Grave*. Soon after he had started work on them the publisher, one Cromek, decided to have the drawings engraved by another engraver whose style was less austere—for Blake disdained to work in the popular stipple and at this period still engraved in the older severe line which he had learnt with Basire. This breach of contract was a heavy blow to Blake who recorded his chagrin in a famous couplet:

'A petty sneaking knave I knew
Oh! Mr. Cromek how do ye do?'

Soon after this he produced the drawings called *Fire, Plague, Famine* and *Pestilence: The Death of the First-born* (Pl. 154a), and he began a series of drawings for 'Paradise Lost' including *Satan watching the Endearments of Adam and Eve, Adam and Eve Sleeping* (Pl. 149), *Adam and Eve and the Angel Raphael* (Pl. 148) and *The Temptation of Eve* (Pl. 150).

All this time he was a completely obscure artist. He was now over fifty but the general public had never heard his name. The only drawings which were at all known were the illustrations to *The Grave* which, as noted, were engraved by another artist who got all the credit. Fortune now seemed to turn still more relentlessly against him. He sent works at this period to the Royal Academy which had accepted drawings from time to time before; but now his drawings were rejected; and the same thing happened when he sent his work to the Royal Institution. Butts who had continuously bought his work and made him presents and advanced him money—though the first arrangement apparently ceased when the Felpham period began—now had more of his work than he could accommodate in his house, and from this time onward he bought gradually less. Moreover, Cromek now once more played the sneak at Blake's expense— for having seen the beginning of a design to illustrate Chaucer's Canterbury Pilgrims in his studio, he ordered a picture of the same subject from Thomas Stothard (1755-1834), a clever little academic pasticheur, and then took it round the country, selling engravings from it. Cromek did not reveal his treachery to Stothard, who had known Blake for years, given him things to engrave, and would not willingly have done him this injury. Blake, however, refused to believe that Stothard did not know of the existence of his own design for the *Canterbury Pilgrims*. He seems at this time to have fallen into a comprehensible mood of hostile depression. He quarrelled with Stothard; he also quarrelled with his old friend Flaxman; and he determined to force recognition from all parties by a public exhibition of his works.

The exhibition took place in 1809 in his brother's house in Broad Street. It contained sixteen works of various periods which for one reason or another he had not sold to Butts or otherwise disposed of. They included the *Canterbury Pilgrims* (with a prospectus inviting subscriptions to an engraving from it), the tempera paintings *Satan calling up his Legions*, *The Spiritual Form of Nelson guiding Leviathan* (Pl. 142); a large picture, seven feet by five, called *A Vision of the Last Judgement*, which has disappeared; and the drawings, *Soldiers casting Lots for Christ's Garments*, *The Body of Abel found by Adam and Eve*, and *The Whore of Babylon*. A 'Descriptive Catalogue' contained a partial statement of Blake's art-philosophy together with much redundancy and pugnacity.

The exhibition was a complete failure. Hardly anyone went. And a writer in 'The Examiner,' presumed to be Leigh Hunt, talked of the pictures as 'wretched', the artist as 'an unfortunate lunatic whose personal inoffensiveness secures him from confinement'; and of the catalogue as 'a farrago of nonsense, unintelligibility, and egregious vanity, the wild effusions of a distempered brain'. Butts bought the *Canterbury Pilgrims* and *The Whore of Babylon*.

After this Blake retired again into an obscurity which lasted for seven years. In this period he made a series of drawings from the *Life of Christ*, and a set of illustrations to Milton's 'Comus'. I reproduce *The Brothers plucking Grapes* (Pl. 144) and *The Return to the Parents* (Pl. 145), which seem to me among the finest of this *Comus* series. The *David and Goliath* (Pl. 154b) may also be a drawing of this time.

In 1817, when he was sixty, he was once more doing hack engraving for publishers. Flaxman, who had not allowed the quarrel to develop, and who was then seeking an engraver for his illustrations to Hesiod, arranged for the work to be given to Blake; and it was doubtless through Flaxman also that he obtained at this time an order to engrave a book of designs for Wedgwood. He was thus mechanically employed when a new friend appeared and a new phase in his life began.

The friend was JOHN LINNELL (1792-1882) a young artist then aged twenty-six. He met Blake in 1818 and began to do for him what Butts had done before. He made it clear to him that he believed in him and did not think him mad. He kept in touch with him and helped him in every way he could; he in-

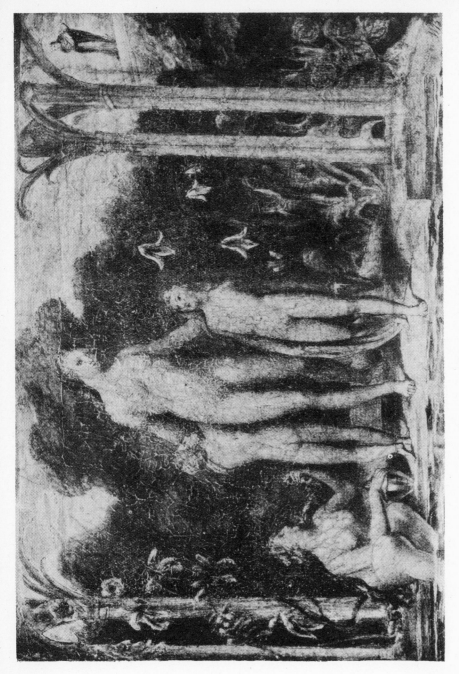

143. WILLIAM BLAKE
Bathsheba at the Bath
National Gallery, Millbank, London

144. WILLIAM BLAKE
Comus: The Brothers plucking Grapes
Boston Museum, Mass., U.S.A.

troduced other young artists to him, who revived his morale by treating him as a great and wise man and a great artist. He himself took lessons in engraving from him and in turn persuaded him to soften the austerity of his engraving technique; he encouraged him to take up wood engraving, and the result can be seen in the *Illustrations to Virgil's First Eclogue* three of which I reproduce (Pls. 134a, 134b, 134c); he encouraged him to print a complete copy of the illuminated *Jerusalem* with a hundred plates finished in colour; he urged him to write more poems —with the result that 'The Everlasting Gospel' and a new edition of an earlier book 'For Children: The Gates of Paradise' now called 'For the Sexes: The Gates of Paradise', were produced. He bought drawings which he had made for 'Paradise Regained' and gave him important commissions to which I refer later.

Linnell himself painted portraits and miniatures and illustrations to the scriptures. He also painted—and these are his most characteristic productions—a number of pastoral landscapes. In some of these, painted many years later, the contact with Blake and with his illustrations to Virgil's Eclogue is reflected. The design of a group of harvesters sleeping in the hollow of a cornsheaf lifts his *Noonday Rest* above the average level of rural genre; and I feel the memory of Blake behind his *Contemplation* (Pl. 133a). Blake said repeatedly that clarity of delineation, by line, as distinguished from approximate statement lurking in tones or indeterminate outlines, was essential in truthful imaginative art; and in *Contemplation* painted in 1872 we see Linnell interpreting this dictum of his master in terms of Holman Hunt's Pre-Raphaelite creed. In this ambitious picture —which, to modern taste, is as ugly in colour as Hunt's own pictures—Linnell has attempted to reproduce a whole vista of wooded country by industrious still-life procedures. The result, of course, as always, is not truth, but an approximation.[1] We see this at once if we compare this *Contemplation* with Poussin's *Landscape with two Nymphs* (Pl. 133b), which is a complete

[1]Cf. above, pp. 203-207.

organisation of the imagined space within the frame and of all the phenomena within it—not merely an approximate still-life painting of fortuitously adjacent fragments of life. Blake who praised Poussin as 'a particulariser' would have been the first, I think, to be impatient with Linnell's approximate records in this *Contemplation*. But Linnell nevertheless is an interesting figure in the history of English landscape because he joined hands on one side with Blake and vital Pre-Raphaelism, and on the other with degenerate Pre-Raphaelism as represented by the landscapes of Benjamin Leader (1831-1923).

The artists whom Linnell introduced to Blake included Varley, Calvert, Palmer and Richmond.

JOHN VARLEY (1778-1842) we have already met as one of the topographical watercolour draughtsman patronised by Dr. Monro.[1] His main occupation was the teaching of drawing. His pupils included Linnell and Palmer and also A. V. Copley Fielding (1787-1855), W. H. Hunt (1790-1864), Peter de Wint (1784-1849) and David Cox (1783-1859) who all produced watercolour landscapes admired in the nineteenth century. Varley pretended to be an astrologer, and his lady pupils, it is recorded, used to ask him to cast their nativities. Blake took him or pretended to take him seriously, and in his house he drew a number of *Visionary Heads* of historical personages whom he would 'call up' to sit for him as Varley named them. These heads, which have been much discussed, and have been held to be evidence of Blake's madness, are simply imaginary portraits; they tell us what Blake thought about *The Pharaoh who built the Pyramids* and other persons of the past. In Varley's house Blake also made the first drawing for the celebrated tempera painting *The Ghost of a Flea* to which I refer again later. Varley, whom we may set down, I think, as a bluffer, or at any rate as more than half a bluffer, doubtless made a good deal of capital out of Blake's apparent interest in his astrological pretensions; and in the year after Blake died he published a 'Treatise on Zodiacal Physiognomy'.

[1]Cf. above, p. 180.

EDWARD CALVERT (1799-1883) was born at Bideford in Devon, of a family which seems to have had some means. At fifteen he entered the Navy as a midshipman. His ship saw service, bombarded Algiers, and cruised among the islands of the Aegean. Adolescent, he wrote poetry, made drawings in his cabin, and read Virgil. At the age of twenty-one, in 1820, he retired from the Navy and went to the Academy schools where he had contact with Fuseli, who was then Keeper. In 1824 he met Blake who was then engaged on the wood-engravings *Illustrations to Virgil's First Eclogue* (Pls. 134a, 134b, 134c), and as a result of this meeting he began to engrave on wood and copper and to make lithographs. Calvert's wood engravings include the *The Return Home* (Pl. 135a), *The Chamber Idyll* (Pl. 135b), and *The Ploughman* (Pl. 136b); his lithographs include *The Flood* (Pl. 135c); his copper engravings include *The Bride* (Pl. 136a).

The first thing that must strike everyone about these engravings by Calvert is their very remarkable manual dexterity, seeing that the reproductions in Plates 135a, 135b, and 135c are the actual size of the prints. It may be that there are only two living artists in England who could surpass this manual delicacy and precision: Edward Dulac who, I am sorry to be obliged to add, was born and passed his early years in France, and Stephen Gooden. But Calvert's engravings are not only remarkable for their technical dexterity, they are also quite extraordinary as records of his grasp of Blake's instruction. We have here an understanding of Blake's dictum 'Grandeur of Ideas is Precision of Ideas' applied not only in the technical field but also in the field of imaginative realisation. In *The Return Home* (Pl 135a) for example we are given a double realisation—first a visual realisation of the rider returning to his cottage in the twilight, and then a mental realisation of the return to a companion who means so much to him that her figure burns like a bright light and fills the cottage door. A naturalistic representation with the figure silhouetted against the light within the cottage would not have been true in this picture because it was not part of the idea. *The Bride* (Pl. 136a) and *The Ploughman* (Pl. 136b) are the most obviously attractive of Calvert's engravings. But the other three I believe to be better—by which I mean more true to the artist's imaginative experience. *The Chamber Idyll*, *The Return Home* and *The Flood* are of all time and place because they have been completely realised.

After Blake's death Calvert's imaginative realisation grew ever weaker and he took more and more refuge in transmutation. He became sentimentally romantic and began to think and talk nonsense about 'The Golden Age' and the 'Glory that was Greece'. Eventually he went to Greece. And then he was destroyed.

His later works—where paintings in oil colours on paper predominate—are mainly transmutations of half-realised sentimental experience into Golden-Ageism and Pseudo-Hellenism. But he never quite forgot his master; he never deserted to what Blake called the 'vegetable' outlook. Such effort as he made in his later years was, as he himself said, an effort to 'transform physical truth into musical truth'. And though in regard to work so indeterminate it would be inaccurate to speak of 'melody', there is indeed a musical murmur, a faint formal harmony, in his later paintings which gives them considerable charm.

SAMUEL PALMER (1805-1881) was the son of a Newington bookseller who was a strict Baptist. It is recorded that he had an experience in childhood which made a deep impression. He found himself in a garden with a young nurse on a bright moonlight night and was awestruck by the shadows of the foliage of an elm cast on the wall by the moon; his nurse tried to restore him with the lines:

'Fond Man! The vision of a moment made,
Dream of a dream, and shadow of a shade.'

The child was destined to be no less unusual than the nurse. As Laurence Binyon says, ' "Vision", "dream" and "shadow", these were pregnant words, full of the very stuff out of which the young painter's art was to be made. And the light breaking in on the shadows . . . how often was this to be the main motive of his compositions'.

As he grew up Palmer read poetry, drew churches and cloisters, copied engravings and went to a drawing school. In 1819 when he was fourteen he had three landscape drawings in the Royal Academy. At this time he saw Turner's work and was affected by it. He was sixteen when he met Linnell, who introduced him to Blake four years later. The contact with Blake was a tremendous excitement for Palmer. Here was a man with whom he need have no shyness in confessing his secrets, a man to whom he could reveal the special aspects of experience which moved him. The result was a series of sepia drawings of moonlit landscapes which in their intensity are unique in the history of English landscape art. I reproduce one: *Moonlight Landscape with Sheep* (Pl. 139). Another called *The Crescent Moon* shows a sky blazing with a huge crescent moon and gigantic stars on a landscape with round black trees; a third called *The Harvest Moon* resembles in structure the drawing I reproduce except that the light breaks across the landscape, though the source of the light, the white moon, is facing the spectator. Nothing comparable with these drawings had appeared in English art before; and nothing comparable has since appeared till we get to Paul Nash's woodcut *Dyke by the Road* (Pl. 140) in our own day. Palmer suffered from ill health, and in 1826 he left London and retired to Shoreham. In 1833 he came back to London in order to be near Calvert to whom he was much attached. In 1837 when he was thirty-two he married Linnell's daughter. He then went to Italy for two years. In his case as in Linnell's and Calvert's the real significance of the Blake contact gradually wore out. He drew *Illustrations to Virgil's Eclogues*, and to Milton's *L'Allegro*; he drew portrait landscapes; and he made elaborate etchings. But the work of his later years does not reveal the intensity which we find in *Moonlight Landscape with Sheep* (Pl. 139) and *In a Shoreham Garden* (Pl. 138) and other drawings of his early days. Only in one or two of the etchings such as *The Bellman* and *The Lonely Tower* (Pl. 137) do we get a hint of it.

GEORGE RICHMOND (1809-1896) never had any spiritual contact with Blake at all. The contact here was social and what Blake would have described as 'vegetable'. Richmond imitated Blake's pastoral woodcuts and produced some etchings, notably one called *The Shepherd*, which on the surface have resemblance to Blake's 'style'. But he looked at Blake's works in the way that Reynolds looked at pictures in Italy—in order to steal from them. He never had what Gainsborough called 'genius in our sense of the word' or contact with the mind and spirit behind Blake's work. After Blake's death he went to Paris and came back to embark on a successful career as a fashionable portrait painter. We may also observe in passing that he repainted all the heads on the *Southwold Rood Screen*[1]; and that in 1843 he showed Ruskin a portfolio of drawings by Blake which Ruskin wanted to buy for £100, but did not do so because he was afraid that his father would not agree to provide the money.

Linnell, when he introduced these young artists to Blake, was not rich. But he was able to sell his own work and gradually to become helpful to Blake with money. This help was needed; for in 1821 Blake, who was then sixty-four, was in such financial difficulty that he had to sell to a dealer the portfolios of prints and engravings which he had continuously collected since his childhood. As I shall explain later it is in my judgement lamentable that he did not sell them many years before; but the occasion of the sale is none the less distressing. By 1823 Linnell was able to make a helpful arrangement. Blake had drawn a set of twenty-two illustrations to the *Book of Job* which his old friend Butts had bought. Linnell now proposed that he should do another set and engrave them for him. He arranged to pay £100 (equivalent we must remember to about £350 to-day) for twenty plates and offered to pay as much again out of the profits. In the event there were no profits; but he paid a further £50 in small instalments, representing them as profits coming in. In 1826 he made a similar arrangement for a set of illustrations to *The Divine Comedy*. In this case he gave the artist a folio volume

[1]Cf. below, pp. 250, 268.

of a hundred pages and arranged to pay him a weekly sum till the work was finished. Blake was sixty-nine when he started on this undertaking, and he began to learn Italian for the purpose. He made a hundred drawings and was still at work upon them when he died. I reproduce *Then a Spirit passed before my Face, the Hair of my Flesh stood up*, from the engravings to the *Book of Job* (Pl. 155) and seven of the drawings to *The Divine Comedy* (Pls. 156, 157a, 157b, 158a, 158b, 159a, 159b).

It was thus that Blake passed his last years, surrounded by these young disciples who formed themselves into a species of Brotherhood and called themselves 'The Ancients'. In his last illness he worked on the Dante drawings in bed. On the last day he was working on an impression of a colour print done many years earlier called *The Ancient of Days*. When he laid it down he called his wife to him, saying, 'Kate, you have been a good wife; I will draw your portrait.' She sat by the bed and he drew her for an hour. Then, as we know from her, 'he began to sing Hallelujahs and songs of joy and triumph, loudly and with ecstatic energy. His bursts of gladness made the walls resound.' And so he died at the age of seventy.

2. BLAKE'S CHARACTER

'*An unfortunate lunatic whose personal inoffensiveness secures him from confinement.*'   LEIGH HUNT (?) in 'The Examiner', 1809.

'*Kate, you have been a good wife; I will draw your portrait.*'
WILLIAM BLAKE.

There is an immense literature about Blake, a great deal of which revolves round the question 'Was he mad or was he not?' For my part, I confess, I do not see the problem in this way. In the case of Ruskin, whose mental processes I have discussed in my recent book, we have a man who had an attack of madness at the age of fifty-nine, and five or six more in the next few years, and who then for the remaining twenty years of his life was sane only for short intervals. But in the case of Blake the one plain fact of the whole story is that he never collapsed into permanent madness or had even a passing attack. All through his life he exhibited symptoms which from the pathological standpoint made such an attack possible at any minute. But that extra dislocation or extra pressure of false beliefs or false sense-impressions—or whatever it may be that causes these collapses—never, in fact, happened. And thus the question, as I see it, is not 'Was Blake mad or not?' but 'What kept him sane?'

The answer, I feel confident, can be briefly stated. He was saved by his wife. This simple peasant served him with devotion. She cooked his dinner and mended his socks; she helped him with the mechanical paraphernalia of his printing; she sat by his side hour after hour by day and often half through the night when he was writing and drawing; she obeyed him in every-thing; if he ordered her to go down on her knees and beg for-giveness from himself or anyone else she did it immediately without protest; in company at any rate she seems always to have addressed him as 'Mr. Blake'. But she was far more than an obedient and devoted wife, housekeeper and studio assistant. She was a spirit, living at the centre of his life, and never absent from it, who believed always and absolutely in his first postulate —the concept of the artist as an inspired spirit.

Blake's first postulate on which everything for him depend-ed, was his belief that art is a spiritual activity; and that the artist is a soul sent by God to fulfil this particular activity at the ex-pense, if need be, of all others. Had his wife been an unbeliever, had there been even moments when she failed in faith—Blake would surely have gone mad. He wrote:

'If the sun and moon should doubt,
They'd immediately go out.'

And by the sun and the moon he meant William and Kate.

He exhibited, as I have said, a whole series of symptoms of mental malady. These are outside my field in this book. Here I need only point out that the symptoms have nothing to do with his first postulate and also nothing to do with his second postulate, which I shall discuss in a minute. The symptoms have also nothing to do with the fact that Blake was an artist, a philosopher and a poet; we find them in personae of all types, in men who have never painted a picture, or written a line of verse. They do occur frequently, it is true, among artists and poets; but they are always pathological; they do not result from, or necessarily lead a man to, any specific vocation or occupation.

I assume that medical men in Blake's lifetime recognised the morbid symptoms as morbid. But no mental specialist who had contact with him has, as my knowledge goes, recorded his opinion. The people who knew him and recorded the opinion that he was mad were (a) Philistines who saw his drawings and read his writings and called him mad because his work was outside their familiar experience, (b) intelligent people who found his writings not only strange but so obscure as to be unintelligible, and (c) people who thought his first postulate in itself a delusion and so evidence of madness.

We are only concerned here with the third category of opinion. The opinion of the Philistines is philistine opinion and so of no importance. The character of his writings is outside my subject—though I must state in passing that recent students have elucidated a good deal in various ways and that the rest, I am confident, could be elucidated by collation with the events and pathological symptoms of the actual day when each page was written; the material for this further elucidation in Blake's case is not as copious as the material in the case of Ruskin, but there is sufficient to show, I think, that the kind of procedure which I have adopted in my study of Ruskin's writings would also clear up a good many obscurities and inconsequences in Blake's. The third category of opinion is the only one which is related to his work as a pictorial artist. And it is so closely related that we cannot evade the question, 'Was Blake's first postulate a delusion or not?'

Is it a delusion for an artist to assume that art is a spiritual activity, and that the artist is a soul sent by God to fulfil this particular activity at the expense, if need be, of all others? The question—unless we answer it by a profession of faith one way or the other—can only be answered by taking the line that, whether the postulate be a delusion or not, it is a postulate held, openly or secretly, in the present and the past, by all imaginative artists especially concerned with spiritual values. The art critic who in his heart denies the concept, can never get contact with this category of imaginative art because he can never get contact with the artist behind it. He may, of course, quarrel with the actual wording of the concept as I have put it down—he may quarrel with the words 'soul' and 'God' and substitute equivalents—without loss of power to achieve the contact. But he is and must always remain at sea when confronted with this type of art if in his heart he regards Blake's first postulate as a delusion.

Blake's wife accepted this postulate without question. But she did more than this. She accepted with the same absolute completeness his second postulate: that he, William Blake, was an artist of this type with this type of mission. And this of course was of still more service to Blake's sanity. *It enabled him to fix his attention on the source of the inspiration and its externalisation and to ignore the vehicle—himself.*

It is clear that Blake was not an introvert. He was not a morbid romantic primarily interested in himself. At moments when fortune was especially unkind to him he showed paranoiac symptoms and depression. But these temporary characters are explicable by the pressure of circumstance. Everyone admitted to his friendship has told us that simple gaiety and absence of pretension were his habitual characteristics. It is clear that he only talked high-falutin—as distinguished from simple statements of his imaginative experience—to people who doubted or denied his two postulates. It was not till he encountered this resistance that he felt the need to force the pace, as it were, to drive himself to firmer faith, in order to substantiate not only the general concept but also the special application. We see him engaged in this process when confronted with the hostile personality of Reynolds. That path for him was perdition. His wife

147. JOHN MARTIN

Paradise Lost: Adam and Eve and the Angel Raphael—Engraving

148. WILLIAM BLAKE
Paradise Lost: Adam and Eve and the Angel Raphael
Boston Museum, Mass., U.S.A.

by accepting without question not only the general concept of the inspired artist but also its special application in his case absolved him from the necessity of attempting to prove both or either in any way except the right way—*i.e.* by his work; and thus, I feel confident, she saved his sanity. Had his wife been a female Reynolds she would soon, I imagine, have driven him insane.

'Kate, you have been a good wife', he said to her an hour before he died. The tribute was deserved.

3. BLAKE'S ART

'"*Madman*" *I have been called: Fool they call thee.*
I wonder which they Envy—Thee or Me?'   WILLIAM BLAKE.

'*Fable or allegory is a totally distinct and inferior kind of poetry. Vision or Imagination is a representation of what actually exists real and unchangeably.*'   WILLIAM BLAKE.

'*Greatness of Ideas is Precision of Ideas.*'   WILLIAM BLAKE.

'*L'imagination est la plus scientifique des facultés parce que seule elle comprend l'analogie universelle.*'   BAUDELAIRE.

'*A serpent is a honeysuckle with a head put on!*'   JOHN RUSKIN.

'*A spirit and a vision are not, as the modern philosophers suppose, a cloudy vapour or a nothing; they are organised and minutely articulated beyond all that the mortal and perishable nature can produce. He who does not imagine in stronger and better lineaments and in stronger and better light than his perishing and mortal eye can see, does not imagine at all. . . . Men think they can copy nature as correctly as I copy imagination. They will find this impossible; and all the copies, or pretended copies of nature, from Rembrandt to Reynolds, prove that nature becomes to its victim nothing but blots and blurs.*'   WILLIAM BLAKE.

BLAKE, at times, was a terrific artist. He could take a piece of paper and when he had done with it a gale would fill the room. At other times he was tender and exquisite. And at yet other times he failed. To understand his drawings and his pictures we must separate effects deriving from his technical procedures, many of which were experimental, from those which derive from his central intentions, and we must discover the fundamental character of those central intentions.

His technical procedures in the so-called 'tempera' paintings and hand-printed drawings were very varied. Trained as an engraver, he always felt an urge to make a number of impressions of his designs and, as the colour was always an integral factor, he made a number of experiments in colour printing. He had a prejudice against oil painting on canvas to which I shall refer again later; and he experimented with various media, and various grounds, painting on wood, canvas and copper. His hand-printed illustrated books and printed drawings are still in good preservation. But the so-called 'tempera' paintings have partly perished or changed their appearance and some have already been restored. We can now only guess at the original appearance of *Bathsheba at the Bath* (Pl. 143), *The Ghost of a Flea*, *Satan calling up his Legions*, *The Spiritual Form of Pitt guiding Behemoth*, and *The Spiritual Form of Nelson guiding Leviathan* (Pl. 142) which were painted with some kind of glue medium. In *Satan smiting Job with Sore Boils* (Pl. 153), on the other hand—a tempera painting on mahogany—the colours are quite fresh and the outlines are clear.[1]

Blake was not interested in procedures as such. He was not of those who believe that the artist must respect his physical material and collaborate with it. He scorned such 'vegetable' collaboration, which, he would have said, had no more to do with the result than his own hand had—both being merely vehicles for the expression of the universal spirit. The variety of his procedures is thus of no significance for the student seeking to understand his art.

But the great variety in his concepts of form—which must strike everyone familiar with a large proportion of his pictures and drawings—is a matter of real importance which takes us to his mental as distinguished from his material workshop.

[1]This painting once belonged to George Richmond who repainted all the heads on the *Southwold Rood Screen* (cf. below, p. 268).

149. WILLIAM BLAKE
Paradise Lost: Adam and Eve Sleeping
Boston Museum, Mass., U.S.A.

150. WILLIAM BLAKE
Paradise Lost: The Temptation of Eve
Boston Museum, Mass., U.S.A.

Blake's artistic creed was much the same as Baudelaire's and Ruskin's; all three had the concept of the Universal Analogy of form; all three believed that the principles of that analogy can be apprehended by human imagination. Ruskin said: 'A serpent is a honeysuckle with a head put on'; Baudelaire said: 'l'imagination est la plus scientifique des facultés parce que seule elle comprend l'analogie universelle.' Blake said: 'He who does not imagine in stronger and better lineaments and in stronger and better light than his perishing and mortal eye can see, does not imagine at all.' He regarded the so-called scientific approach to the 'vegetable' world as a stony, futile, and sterile activity because he regarded the 'vegetable' world as purely the envelope of the spiritual world. He looked upon this approach in painting as an absurdity which could lead nowhere. 'Men think', he wrote, 'that they can copy nature as correctly as I copy imagination. They will find this impossible; and all the copies or pretended copies of nature, from Rembrandt to Reynolds, prove that nature becomes to its victim nothing but blots and blurs.' He did not, that is to say, stop where I stopped when I pointed out above that Crome's attempt at still-life painting in *The Chapel Fields, Norwich*, was doomed to result in nothing but blots and blurs, or where Ruskin stopped when he said that a painter can imitate an apple or a fiddle but not a tree or the Alps.[1] He went further and said that the man who paints an apple or a violin by the still-life procedure, or by means of so-called scientific knowledge, must inevitably produce a blotted blur or a blurred blot, however clear and illusionist the result may appear to the 'vegetable' eye. I said above, as Ruskin said, that outside a certain radius the still-life procedure is physically impossible—and the same applies of course to any type of scientific procedure in painting—and I have suggested that all intelligent artists have always realised this and avoided these procedures from elementary considerations of expediency. Blake went much further. He said that the results of these procedures are equally approximate, and so equally untrue, within the

[1]Cf. above, p. 203.

smallest and the largest range; he called for the avoidance of the procedures not on grounds of expediency, but as a matter of principle, as an article of faith; he condemned the results as evidence that the artist was concerned with 'vegetable' and not with spiritual values.

What we have then is a man convinced that his mission is to record accurately by drawing and painting aspects of the spiritual world revealed to his own spirit. How could this be done? 'A spirit or a vision', he said, 'are not a cloudy vapour or a nothing. . . . Greatness of Ideas is Precision of Ideas.' How were the ideas to be exteriorised in painting and drawing?

Most original artists concerned with spiritual values have answered the question by putting down their visual experience charged, stressed, or distorted in some way to record the intensity of the experience and its emotional quality. We have encountered examples of this in the course of this inquiry. Other artists—or the same artists at other times—have recourse to transmutation of their visual experience in time and place to record the spiritual significance of the experience. Examples of this too we have encountered. But for Blake both procedures were impossible—or rather to be deliberately avoided. He refused absolutely to regard his visual experience as of any service in his art. He never used his eyes at all. He wrote: 'If you have not Nature before you for Every Touch, you cannot Paint Portrait; and if you have Nature before you at all, you cannot Paint History; it was Michael Angelo's opinion and is Mine;' he also wrote: 'Of what consequence is it to the Arts what a Portrait Painter does?' And by 'portrait' he meant physical-visual experience, and by 'history' he meant spiritual-imaginative experience.

He not only, metaphorically speaking, shut his eyes before he began to work but he tried to keep them permanently closed against physical impressions—as a principle, in service to his faith. But the picture to be made was not to be 'a cloudy vapour or a nothing'. Nor was it to be merely an approximation to the spiritual reality to be recorded; any vagueness or transmutation would be treachery to his mission, a record of half-truths equivalent to lies. The exteriorisation must be entirely unequivocal and precise.

For this reason—and because he had been trained as an engraver—he put his faith in line. He knew as every artist knows that a line must be either true or false. And he laid it down as a principle that artists who do not work by line are liars, hired by Satan 'to depress art'.

The precision then was to be obtained by line. The emotional quality—which was part of the spiritual reality to be recorded—was to be obtained by colour. As he was not a still-life or a scientific painter of 'vegetable nature' he was concerned neither with the local colour of objects nor with their apparent colour in effects of light. As he wanted to use colour, not as an instrument of illusionist effects, but as a vehicle of emotion, he used colours as colours in what modern art criticism would describe as an abstract, or aesthetic, way.

This explains, of course, his prejudice against oil painting, which he looked on as an invention of the devil to tempt man to naturalistic imitation of 'vegetable' phenomena—just as many modern sculptors look on clay as a medium which tempts to naturalistic and romantic procedures. After a certain number of experiments in tempera painting and colour printing he worked exclusively in water colour or with the burin because he found that in the other procedures he could not get perfect precision of abstract lines and colours.

But still the problem of exteriorising his spiritual experience remained unsolved. 'A spirit and a vision are not . . . a cloudy vapour or a nothing.' What forms were the precise lines and abstract emotional colours to create?

Here, of course, he was confronted with an enormous difficulty. He had to make up his mind what he wanted to say as a pictorial artist without using his eyes as a means of providing the material. From the standpoint not only of painters with the still-life approach (be they apple painters, face painters, or landscape painters)—but also from the standpoints of romantic and architectural artists—he was asking himself to make bricks without straw.

In the event he turned to the illustration of the Bible and literature, especially of Milton and Dante, and to the illustration of his own writings. Outside these fields he drew only a few imaginary portraits and a few compositions including the colour-printed drawing *Hecate* and the tempera painting *The Ghost of a Flea*. The water colours called *Fire, Famine, Plague* and *Pestilence: The Death of the First-born* (Pl. 154a) must be regarded as illustrations of the Plagues of Egypt. The celebrated *The River of Life* and the *Pity* (Pl. 146) are both, of course, illustrations, the first to Revelation xxii, 1, 2, and the second to Shakespeare's:

'And Pity like a naked newborn babe,
Striding the blast, or Heaven's Cherubim, horsed
Upon the sightless couriers of the air,
Shall blow the horrid deed in every eye
That tears shall drown the wind.'[1]

The *Hecate* has always seemed to me a failure—a work which if its pedigree were not so invulnerable (it comes from the Butts collection) I should ascribe to some one like Fuseli who was influenced by Blake. As it is we have to set it down, I think, as evidence that working, without straw, even Blake had to fall back sometimes on hack symbolism and even on 'vegetable' experience.

But *The Ghost of a Flea* is truly terrific. Here we have a colossal bestial figure never seen in art before, or in the mind of any other man—(unless it be in the mind of Rowlandson)—with forked tongue extended, and holding a bowl of blood—the Flea in this concept being the terrestrial symbol of the Ghoul or Bloodsucker. No one could pass his life making drawings of this intensity, without straw, and preserve his sanity. Varley says that Blake told him that he *saw* the figure of the Flea's spirit before him. Perhaps Blake said so; and perhaps he did see it. But if he had seen figures *in this way*, out of an inner vision, continually all his life, he would have been either a raving madman all his

[1]'Macbeth', Act I, Scene vii.

151. G. F. WATTS
The Temptation of Eve
National Gallery, Millbank, London

152a. MICHELANGELO
The Creation of Adam

152b. WILLIAM BLAKE
The Elohim creating Adam
Private Collection, England

life or else a genius of a stature with whom no other artist can be for an instant compared—and he was neither one nor the other. It is not the character of the image in *The Ghost of a Flea* but the mechanism of creation in the picture—the attempt to dispense with the whole range of human experience in the normal connotation of the words,—which makes it obvious that Blake could not continuously have produced such pictures in a working life of fifty years.

Blake himself would have said, of course, that his postulates would cover a daily production of bricks without straw in this way. Pressed by a hostile antagonist he would not have hesitated, doubtless, to talk of pre-natal experience, just as pressed by the 'Discourses' of Reynolds he declared that the artist is born complete and can gain nothing from experience within this life. But the fact remains that, as he was neither a raving madman nor an unparalleled unique genius, he did habitually fall back upon something within this life—on the Bible, on Milton, Dante, and Shakespeare—on the works of writers concerned with spiritual values.

Here he found the main material for his art taking him more than half-way to exteriorisation in form. But the authors of the Bible, and Milton, Dante and Shakespeare were not pictorial artists. Blake had the most intimate contact with their spirits; their words called up images and gestures and configurations of form; but these images compared with the precision of the words which evoked them were nevertheless indeterminate and incomplete.

His problem was to remain true to his indeterminate and incomplete images and at the same time to make them visible on paper. In one way he was never untrue to his imagination. He never attempted to make his images appear more complete by the addition of accessories. He never, for example, built up a scene like the *Adam and Eve and the Angel Raphael* by his contemporary John Martin (1789-1854), a professional concocter of enormous *tableaux vivants*, who set this particular scene in an elaborate landscape that would have served as well for another subject because it has no particular connection with this one (Pl. 147). Blake was never tempted to complete his images in this untruthful way. The figures in his drawings are accompanied only by the suggestion of such accessories and such setting as the words read really called up to him, and no more. On the negative side he never found it difficult to be faithful to his vision, to demonstrate that men would find it impossible 'to copy nature as correctly as I copy imagination', to surpass Crome's *Chapel Fields, Norwich* (Pl. 107b), in truth. He was always absolutely truthful in what he left out. But was he always as truthful in what he put in?

Here the answer in regard to the bulk of his work is in the negative. As he excluded visual experience, and disdained to look at 'vegetable nature', he had to fall back on his experience of art. And that experience in his case was most unfortunate. Apprenticed in his youth to the engraver Basire he had become acquainted, as noted, not only with the Gothic monuments which he was sent to draw in Westminster Abbey but also with Basire's engravings after Raphael and Guercino. At the same time he saw engravings after Michelangelo and prints by Dürer, and engravings after the fifteenth-century Italians then habitually referred to as 'Gothic primitives'. He also at this time and afterwards collected prints and engravings. His habit of looking at records of the past began early and continued long. And it almost destroyed him. For this man who scorned to look at the phenomenal life around him acquired early and continued to acquire, unconsciously, images of works of art, which entered his mind and remained there, to reappear with disastrous persistence whenever he started to create.

We can also, and indeed we must, go further, and say that Blake, when he failed to force the image of a figure to precision, when his imagination failed in a hand or a foot or a torso—quite evidently went to his portfolios, and attempted thus to make good the deficiency. It is thus that we must explain the extraordinary variety of formal character in his drawings, the alternations and admixtures of Gothic and Renaissance elements,

153. WILLIAM BLAKE
Satan Smiting Job with Sore Boils
National Gallery, Millbank, London

154a. WILLIAM BLAKE
Pestilence: The Death of the First-born
Boston Museum, Mass., U.S.A.

154b. WILLIAM BLAKE
David and Goliath
Boston Museum, Mass., U.S.A.

of elements that come from the monuments in Westminster Abbey and elements that come from engravings after fifteenth- and sixteenth-century Italian pictures and from the ceiling of the Sistine Chapel (Pls. 142, 148, 149, 152a, 152b).

If we take Blake at his own valuation, as I do, and accept his two postulates, we must say, I think, that whenever he used un- consciously a remembered image from the art of the past, and whenever he opened his portfolios, he was false to his mission as an original artist solely concerned with spiritual values, because by the process he showed mistrust of and thus insulted his own imagination and destroyed its integrity. The exclusion of un- imaged accessories and setting, of all still-life or scientific repre- sentation of phenomena, the rigid insistence on precision of out- line and emotive colour—all this, by his own standards of value, cannot make good these failures in truth. This man who wrote in complete sincerity and simplicity: 'I am under the direction of Messengers from Heaven, Daily and Nightly. . . . If we fear to do the dictates of our Angels . . . who can describe the dismal torments of such a state?' this man who again and again threw up patronage and 'the mere drudgery of business' to preserve his spiritual integrity,—destroyed that integrity again and again by memories of dead men's pictures and a portfolio of prints. Hence, partly, his rage against Reynolds, who exalted thieving to a principle but was himself not damaged by the thefts.

But fortunately for us there were days when neither the memories nor the portfolios intruded, days when Blake could force his imagination quite truthfully to precision and draw things like *Soldiers casting Lots for Christ's Garments, David and Goliath* (Pl. 154b), and *Pestilence: The Death of the First-born* (Pl. 154a); and days when by sheer force of will he forced the memories and the prints into the mould of his own images as in *Adam and Eve Sleeping* (Pl. 149) and the thrilling *Temptation of Eve* (Pl. 150).

More fortunately still as he advanced in life the memories gradually became dim and were more habitually conquered. At fifty he had almost worked through them. By that time the deliberate abstinence from physical experience of form had been compensated by continuous efforts towards complete and precise realisation of images evoked by the written word. As a formal artist he found himself just after *The Temptation of Eve* (Pl. 150) and just before the *Illustrations to Comus* (Pls. 144 and 145), that is, somewhere about 1810 when he was fifty-three. After this the sale of his portfolios in 1821 was of no importance. He sold them because he wanted money. But he also sold them, I feel certain, because he had not opened them for at least ten years. If he had been entirely true to himself he would not have sold them; he would have put them in the fire as temptations from Satan sent 'to depress art' and decoy him from his mission.

In his last period Blake was completely assured and serene; his postulates, reinforced by his group of young disciples, now feared no opposition; no frustrations attacked his sanity; all his faculties were free.

The works of the last period, the *Illustrations to Comus* (Pls. 144 and 145) and the drawings to *The Divine Comedy* (Pls. 156, 157a, 157b, 158a, 158b, 159a, 159b) are truly splendid because they are splendidly true. The engravings illustrating *The Book of Job* which come, in time, between the two—though they represent a great technical mastery of the burin, the result of lifelong practice, a complete domination of the derived material, and the capture of a rhythmic quality to which I refer again in a minute—are not, I think, so exclusively true to his mental vision as either the Comus drawings or the illustrations to Dante. It is in the *Illustrations to Comus* and to *The Divine Comedy* that Blake achieved a final contact with the spirit of the authors, with his own spirit and with universal rhythm. It is in these drawings that he finally found himself as an artist. For here at last he found a pictorial equivalent to the art of words, the fluid art of progression, and thus arrived at the formal exteriorisation in pictures which he had so long been seeking. He had never been content, like John Martin, or the contributors to Boydell's Shakespeare Gallery, to concoct a picture like a scene in the theatre. He had never thought of himself as a

155. WILLIAM BLAKE
Illustration to the Book of Job—Engraving

156. WILLIAM BLAKE
Dante: The Gate of Hell
National Gallery, Millbank, London

theatrical producer arranging a tableau. He had always desired
to achieve not frozen images but an art of progression. He had
always felt that form to be true to his imagination must be fluid
and not static. The floating and flying figures in *The River of Life*
and *Pity* (Pl. 146) are typical of scores of others which occur in
his work at all periods. He had always chafed at the limitations
of the single picture and produced works in series. Moreover in
each series he had always made an effort to preserve a unity of
formal concept; in this, in spite of the memories and the portfolios, he had always succeeded to some extent, and he succeeded more and more as the years went on—all the drawings in
the *Paradise Lost* series (Pls. 148, 149, 150), for example, being
very visibly connected in formal concept without reference to
the subjects. But it was not till he reached the last period that
he really evolved a pictorial equivalent to verbal progression.
In the *Illustrations to Comus* and *The Divine Comedy* he has given
us not a collection of drawings but one drawing that goes on
and on in one continuous progression of vital rhythm which, in
Calvert's phrase (that doubtless came from him), 'transforms
physical truth to musical truth'. To see what Blake really
achieved in the *Illustrations to Comus* and still more in *The Divine
Comedy* we should have to put all the drawings in each series
touching in a row—ignoring of course the nominal subjects
and choosing neighbours by the pictorial form. The rhythm
that pervades these drawings, especially *The Divine Comedy*, is
emotive in the highest degree. It is the rhythm of the most
thrilling architecture, the most enthralling writing, and the most
exciting music.

Rossetti said of Blake's drawings: 'Given without the colour
they cannot be said to embody Blake's intention in producing
them.' This is particularly true of the illustrations to *The Divine
Comedy*. For here the most emotive colour collaborates with
the linear and spatial rhythms; and the colour is not merely
decorative; it is, as Rossetti knew, an integral part of the form
and spirit of each drawing and of the whole series, an integral
part of Blake's intention.

The drawings in *The Divine Comedy*, as Blake left them when he died, are always described as unfinished. But nothing more could conceivably be done to them except elaborations which would render them untrue—in the same way that Constable's later elaborations called *The Valley Farm* are untrue in relation to the so-called *Sketch for the Valley Farm* (Pl. 113). As they stand, taken together as one symphony, they are a complete and final statement of Blake's mission, which in spite of his memories of dead men's pictures and in spite of his portfolios, he thus finally fulfilled.

We should realise his achievement at once if we set these final drawings in the gallery of oil paintings by G. F. Watts (1817-1904) in the National Gallery of British Art at Millbank. For then we should see small pieces of paper converted to great art contrasted with huge canvases which tell us that a man who had the fine ideas contained in *Hope* and the *Eve Trilogy* was ruined by acquaintance with Titian's painting and the Elgin Marbles.

No works by the English School mean as much to the modern student as *The Divine Comedy* by Blake. Paul Nash has found in them the reinforcement of his own conviction that the painter should be concerned not with still-life or scientific imitation but with musical and architectural truth (Pl. 160). And Leon Underwood has found behind them a man whose attitude encourages his own (Pl. 1).

APPENDIX TO CHAPTER I

*

EARLY GOTHIC REMAINS (1066-1377)

In addition to *The Chichester Roundel* (Pl. 2) already referred to, and apart from manuscripts which are outside my subject—and which cannot tell us the appearance of destroyed mural paintings and panel pictures—the principal remains of early Gothic painting presumed to be English can be classified as follows:

(*a*) One well-preserved figure in Canterbury Cathedral, fragmentary remains of other mural paintings there and in other Cathedrals, and in a number of parish churches in Norfolk and Suffolk, at Kempley and Hailes in Gloucestershire, at Clayton in Sussex, at Croughton in Northamptonshire, at Chalgrove in Oxfordshire, and various other places.

To these we can add a *Crucifixion* in the Chapel of St. Faith in Westminster Abbey; and a large repainted figure of *St. Faith* in the same chapel which tells us little of the mediaeval or Gothic painting underneath except, perhaps, its size.

(*b*) The remains of a few paintings on panel, including the *Westminster Altarpiece*, some fragments on sedilia at Westminster, and one or two paintings on the inside of chest lids, and so forth.

The student who wishes to acquaint himself with the surviving mural fragments must travel round the country, and climb ladders, and see what can be seen of them. But he must bear in mind that he is examining not English mediaeval painting but the present condition of fragments of paintings which may have been wholly or partly repainted more than once in the five or six hundred years of their existence.

If he cannot tour the country, he must examine photographs —when such are available—bearing in mind that these photographs are black-and-white records of the present condition of the surviving coloured fragments.

If he cannot get photographs he can look at the watercolour copies made in recent years by Professor Tristram—many of which are preserved in the Victoria and Albert Museum.

In looking at Professor Tristram's watercolour copies, or reproductions from them, he must bear in mind that these watercolours are copies not of the original appearance but of the present appearance of the surviving fragments; that no one can judge of the accuracy of any copies without comparing them with the things they are copied from; and, as before, that the present appearance of the fragments may or may not bear a close resemblance to their appearance five or six hundred years ago.

Authors who find it convenient to illustrate their books with reproductions of copies by Professor Tristram are sometimes tempted to write as though Professor Tristram's drawings and English mediaeval mural paintings were one and the same thing. The cautious student will guard against this confusion.[1]

There is no evidence that any of the surviving fragments of mural paintings are the work of Englishmen. In these early Gothic times the artists, here as elsewhere, were monks and laymen of various nationalities working side by side. The nationality of the painters of the surviving mural fragments is thus a matter of guesswork. But as the fragments are on English walls, it is natural, in the absence of other evidence, to guess that the men who painted them were English.

We cannot arrive, by any means, at a concept of a 'style' specifically characteristic of English mural or panel painting at this period. Attempts to arrive at it by comparing surviving fragments with one another, or with illuminated manuscripts assumed to be contemporary, produce only fanciful results be-

[1]In the same way he will guard against forgetting that the photographs which illustrate this book are photographs and nothing more.

157a. WILLIAM BLAKE
Dante: The Hypocrites with Caiaphas
National Gallery, Millbank, London

157b. WILLIAM BLAKE
Dante: The Devils with Dante and Virgil by the Side of the Pool
National Gallery, Millbank, London

158a. WILLIAM BLAKE
Dante: Homer and the Ancient Poets
National Gallery, Millbank, London

158b. WILLIAM BLAKE
Dante: Tu Duca, Tu Signore e Tu Maestro
National Gallery, Millbank, London

cause they assemble chance survivals without any evidence of connection between them. When we group any two such survivals and call them characteristic of English workmanship we may merely have grouped the work of a Frenchman and that of an Englishman who copied him—or vice versa. The student must read the fanciful-antiquaries on this subject with great caution—distinguishing carefully between their guesswork and their statements of fact.

The following appear to be among the facts which the real antiquaries have ascertained.

From the later years of the thirteenth century onwards there were lay artists as well as artist-monks in England, and both types were employed in mural painting. Both English and foreign names occur in references to artists of this period. Nigel of Winchester, Walter of Colchester, William, Monk of Westminster, Walter of Durham, Hugh of St. Albans, William of Walsingham are among the English names; Peter of Hispania, John of St. Omer, and William of Florence among the foreign ones. In the reigns of Henry III (1216-1272), Edward I (1272-1307) and Edward III (1327-1377) artists were employed to paint walls in Westminster Abbey and Westminster Palace which adjoined it.

Some walls in the Painted Chamber of Westminster Palace and St. Stephen's Chapel still had paintings in 1834—how many times repainted nobody knows. In that year the buildings were destroyed by fire and all the paintings perished, except two or three small and badly damaged fragments from St. Stephen's Chapel now in the British Museum. The student must thus resign himself to ignorance of the appearance of the Gothic paintings which originally covered these walls. And he must not be tempted to assume that this ignorance has been converted to knowledge if he encounters an attractive picture which was shown in the Exhibition called 'British Primitives' at the Royal Academy in 1923 and described as a 'reconstruction' of some of the fourteenth-century paintings in St. Stephen's Chapel.

This reconstruction is the work of Professor Tristram, who

used copies made by J. T. Smith and Robert Smirke shortly before the 1834 fire. The copies made by Smith and Smirke purported to record the appearance at that time of these nobody-knows-how-many-times-repainted paintings. J. T. Smith was the author of the celebrated *Life of Nollekens*, and Robert Smirke was a painter of humorous Academy pictures for engravings. We cannot judge the relation of these copies to the nineteenth-century appearance of the paintings which they purport to record. But we may, I think, assume that the attitudes and procedures of Smith and Smirke were not identical with those of the Gothic artists who painted religious subjects. For Smith began his career as a pasticheur of drawings by Van Ostade; and Smirke, in his best-known picture, illustrated a scene between the painter Carmine and Lady Pentweazle in Foote's comedy called 'Taste', which reads as follows:

'*Lady Pentweazle*. Muster Carmine, I have heard that everybody has a betterer, and a more worserer side of the face than the other—now, Sir, which do you choose?

'*Carmine*. The right side ma'am—the left—now, if you please, the full. Your ladyship's countenance is so exactly proportioned that I must have it all; not a feature to be spared.

'*Lady Pentweazle*. Muster Carmine, when you come to the eye, let me know, that I may call up a look . . .

'*Carmine*. Now, Madam, now if you please, I am come to the eye. Oh that look! that, that, I must despair of imitating.

'*Lady Pentweazle*. O! O! have you found out that. Why, Sir, all my family by the mother's side are famous for their eyes. I have a great aunt among the beauties at Windsor; she had a sister at Hampton Court, a perdigeous fine woman! she had but one eye, but that was a piercer—that one eye got her three husbands.'

We may, I think, assume that the productions by Smith and Smirke were not identical in form and spirit with the pictures of *The Nativity*, *The Adoration of the Magi* and *The Presentation in the Temple* which the Gothic artists painted in St. Stephen's Chapel in the fourteenth century. And the student must remember that Professor Tristram's data for the reconstruc-

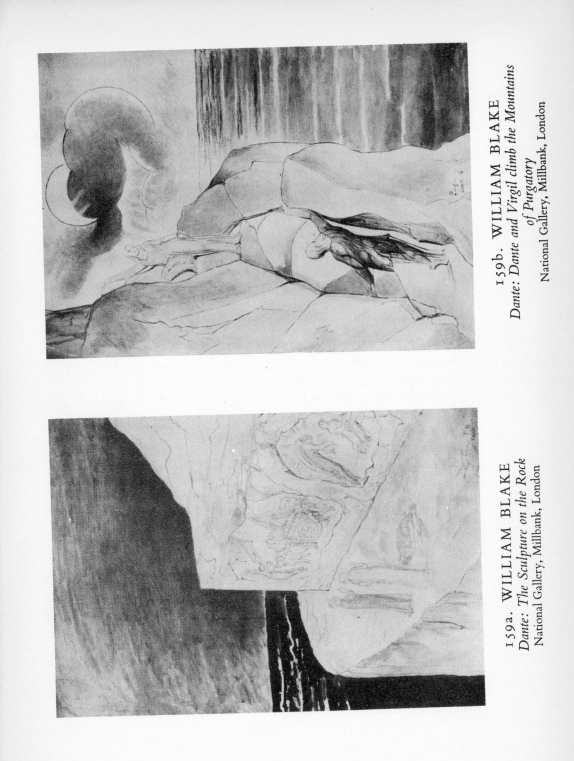

159b. WILLIAM BLAKE
Dante: Dante and Virgil climb the Mountains of Purgatory
National Gallery, Millbank, London

159a. WILLIAM BLAKE
Dante: The Sculpture on the Rock
National Gallery, Millbank, London

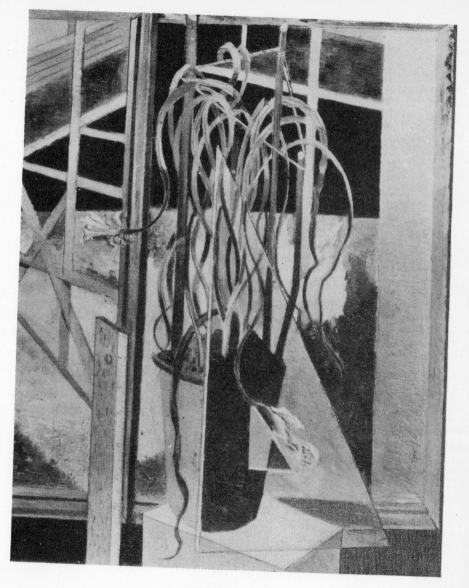

160. PAUL NASH
Still Life

tion of these vanished frescoes were not the perfectly reliable Gothic data which he would have preferred to have at hand.

The surviving fragments of paintings on panel tell us nothing of English easel pictures in these early Gothic times. The *Westminster Altarpiece* is a wreck, and there is no evidence that the artist was English. The paintings on the interior of chest lids are minor productions of no account. The student must resign himself to ignorance on this subject, as on the subject of the mural paintings at Westminster.

The student must also read with caution a fanciful legend that some battered panels from Norwegian churches, now in Norwegian museums, represent the English Gothic style of this period.

The Norwegian legend has been built round the personality of Matthew Paris, monk and historian of St. Albans.

It begins with two facts: (1) Manuscripts of writings by Paris, preserved in Corpus Christi College, Cambridge, and the British Museum, are illustrated with drawings; (2) Paris was sent to Norway in 1248 on ecclesiastical business—the reformation of a monastery.

Then comes a piece of hearsay: Thomas Walsingham, writing a hundred years later, referred to Paris as *pictor peroptimus*.

Then come a series of guesses: (1) that the drawings in the Paris manuscripts are by Paris himself 'or very directly under his influence'; (2) that he also painted mural and panel pictures; (3) that he took with him to Norway examples of his panel pictures; (4) that battered panels from Norwegian churches, now in Norwegian museums, are the remains of these pictures, or others like them, and thus provide us with evidence of a specific 'style' in English panel painting at this period.

The cautious student will carefully distinguish here between the two facts, the hearsay, and the guesses.

There seems to be evidence that English manuscripts and embroideries were imported into Norway at this time. But there is no evidence that Norwegian painters of panel pictures knew or imitated English panel pictures.

APPENDIX TO CHAPTER II

★

LATE GOTHIC REMAINS (1377-1509)

From this period in addition to the *Westminster Portrait of Richard II*, the *Wilton Diptych* (Pls. 3, 4 and 5) and the *Eton Chapel Frescoes* (Pl. 6) already referred to, there are the remains of several altarpieces and of a number of rood screens which some antiquaries assume to be English work. These remains include a *Doom* (Last Judgement) at Wenhaston in Suffolk, an altarpiece in Norwich Cathedral, a *Crucifixion* belonging to Lord Lee of Fareham, and some scores of panels mostly in East Anglia and Devon.

The *Wenhaston Doom* is the remains of one of several surviving examples of the paintings of the Last Judgement called Dooms, which were painted for the chancel arch or, as in this case, on wooden planks serving as background to the rood, in parish churches. This particular picture was plastered over at some time by iconoclasts. It was discovered in 1892 and the plaster was removed. It had originally relief figures of Christ Crucified, with the Virgin and St. John the Evangelist on either side. The remains show fragments of scenes depicting Heaven and Hell—St. Michael weighs a naked soul in front of the mouth of Hell (represented by the mouth of a monster with chained naked souls inside) and St. Peter receives a king, bishop, cardinal, and queen, in Heaven. An inscription (presumed to be Elizabethan) reads: 'Let every soule Submyt himselfe unto the authorytye of the hygher powers for there is no power but of god. The Powers that be are ordeyned of god but they that resest or are against the ordinannce of god shall receyve to them selves utter damnasion. For rulers are not fearefull to them that do good but to them that do evyll for he is the mynister of god.' Nobody knows the name or nationality of the painter of this work.

The *Norwich Cathedral Altarpiece*, consisting of five compartments representing scenes from the Passion of Christ, has been badly battered and partially effaced. In 1643 it was taken from the Cathedral by Puritan iconoclasts and converted into a table (the pictures underneath). For this purpose a strip containing the top of the painting—with the heads of several figures—was cut away. Later the picture was kept in the Cathedral Treasury. It reappeared in the Cathedral in 1847. What restorations were then done to it I do not know. Nobody knows the nationality of the artist. Some antiquaries suggest Italian; others English.

The coarsely drawn *Crucifixion* belonging to Lord Lee of Fareham is an eclectic composition with a Flemish-German flavour. Nobody knows the nationality of the painter. Flemish antiquaries reject him, so do the German. Some English antiquaries claim him. The picture is painted on canvas applied to panel, a procedure known in Italy. It was formerly in the collection of Grosvenor Thomas, artist and expert on stained glass. I can find no record of its history before that time.

More attractive works of this period, assumed to be English, are a number of fragments of panels some of which have now been assembled as a reredos in the church of St. Michael-at-Plea in Norwich. *The Betrayal*, badly damaged, with the faces scratched by iconoclasts, seems the ruin of a once affective picture. An almost obliterated *Annunciation* has the flavour we associate with early Italian art.

On the *Barton Turf Rood Screen* there are the remains, I know not how much repainted, of a number of figures including *St. Apollonia, St. Zita*, and the *Nine Orders—Potestates* with a devil in a chain; *Vertutes*, four-winged with cap, sceptre and feathered body; *Dominaciones*, four-winged, in triple crown, and chasuble; *Seriphyn*, six-winged, feathered body, with girdle of fire; *Cherubin*, six wings, full of eyes, feathered body, hands outspread; *Principatos*, four-winged, girdled with bells; *Troni*, six-winged, holding a church and scales; *Archangeli*, two-winged, in armour in a citadel, with mace and sword; and *Angeli* with almsbox at girdle, holding a spear, with naked souls in prayer on a rock. Edward the Confessor, and Olaf with two loaves, are other figures distinguishable.

On the *Ranworth Rood Screen* there are remains—again, I know not how much repainted—of twenty-six figures. The *Sparham Rood Screen* has the remains of a *Memento Mori*—two skeletons in fashionable male and female clothes, the man carrying a torch inscribed '*Sic transit gloria mundi*' and the woman a bunch of flowers. The *Cawston Rood Screen* consists of twenty panels of Saints apparently painted in three instalments, one group being on parchment stuck on the wood. The figures include SS. Agnes and Helena, Apostles, and Sir John Shorne holding a boot with the devil's head emerging. The *Southwold Rood Screen* has the remains of thirty-six figures. All the faces were repainted by George Richmond, R.A. (1809-1896).[1]

No one knows the nationality of the painters of these screens. It has been suggested that they were done by a group of English artists, equipped with Flemish and German engravings, who moved from place to place.

[1]Cf. above, pp. 244, 250.

APPENDIX III

APPENDIX TO CHAPTER III

★

TUDOR AND STUART PAINTING
(1509-1702)

As noted in the Preface, Professor Constable has drastically disentangled the main facts about the paintings surviving from the Tudor period in 'English Painting of the Sixteenth and Seventeenth Centuries'. He has there chipped away a quantity of surmise surrounding Guillim Streetes, a Dutchman who worked here in the reigns of Edward VI and Queen Mary, and given the scanty information available about John Browne and Andrew Wright, Serjeant Painters to Henry VIII, about the Fleming Johannes Corvus, and the German Gerlach Flick who painted Cranmer, about Lucas de Heere who worked in England between 1566-1576, about George Gower who was Serjeant Painter to Queen Elizabeth and a rival of Nicholas Hilliard, and about Marc Ghaeraedts and other painters of Elizabethan and Jacobean times.

MARC GHAERAEDTS the Younger (1561-1635) was a Fleming. He was brought to England in 1568 from Bruges—(by his father, who had the same name and seems to have won some success as a portrait painter and to have been patronised by Queen Elizabeth). He is known to have painted portraits in England at various times between 1585 and his death in 1635. It is generally assumed that he spent his whole working life in England; but very little is really known about him, and very few existing pictures can be certainly ascribed to him, though scores bear his label on the frames because in the eighteenth century owners of ancestral portraits, who had no records of the painters, labelled the Elizabethan and Jacobean pictures 'Marc Ghaeraedts' much as they labelled the Restoration pictures 'Lely'.

In the phonetic spelling of the sixteenth and seventeenth centuries Ghaeraedts' name was sometimes written Garret or Garrard and it is the fashion now to spell it in that way to create the impression that he was English.

Of the few pictures which he almost certainly painted mention must be made of the *Portrait of a Dead Man* which bears his initials as a signature. *Elizabeth Cherry, Lady Russell,* seems to be the only surviving picture which bears his full signature.

PAUL VAN SOMER (1576?-1621) was born in Antwerp and came to England about 1606. He painted *Queen Anne of Denmark* in 1617 and 1619. In 1730 the antiquary George Vertue guessed the portrait *Elizabeth Lady Tanfield* at Ditchley to be his work. A number of portraits are ascribed to him by Mr. Collins Baker.

JOHN DE CRITZ was a member of a Dutch or Flemish family, established in England in the second half of the sixteenth century, which produced a number of painters in the Elizabethan and Jacobean period and in the reign of Charles I and the Commonwealth. He held the office of Serjeant Painter to James I, and one of his sons, also called John, held it under Charles I from 1641. The functions of this office seem to have been those of the artists attached to Royal and other courts in Gothic times. The holder was curator of the Royal collection of works of art and was expected to superintend all kinds of decorative operations, and take a hand in them, and also to paint portraits. It is recorded that John de Critz painted portraits of James I and his Queen and the Prince of Wales; and that he also painted the royal coaches, and repaired pictures by Palma Vecchio and Titian. The office was held later by Hogarth.[1]

No pictures by members of this family are known to survive except a series in the Ashmolean Museum in Oxford which are Dutch in character.

Mention may be made here of FEDERIGO ZUCCHERO (1542-1609), an Italian decorator, who came to England in 1574. His name is found on the labels of many Elizabethan por-

[1] Cf. above, p. 70.

traits because he had international celebrity and because two famous pictures—*Mary Queen of Scots* at Chatsworth and a *Portrait of a Lady in Fancy Dress* (presumed to be Queen Elizabeth) at Hampton Court were long ascribed to him. But he was only in England for a few months—at a time when Mary Queen of Scots was in prison—and it is not known whether he really painted either picture.

ROBERT PEAKE shared the office of Serjeant Painter to James I with John de Critz. No pictures known to have been painted by him survive, except a portrait of Charles I, as Prince.

SIR NATHANIEL BACON (1585?-1627) was an amateur who painted a full-length seated portrait of himself—an interesting composition much nearer to the creative spirit of the time than other Elizabethan and Jacobean portraits. It is presumed that he had seen portraits by Hals, Rubens or Van Dyck.

Many portraits surviving from this period are traditionally labelled as by DANIEL MYTENS (1590-1642) who was patronised by Charles I as mentioned.[1] His few signed works include *Lionel Cranfield, 1st Earl of Middlesex*, *William, 2nd Duke of Hamilton*, *Elizabeth Duchess of Newcastle* and *Anne Countess of Middlesex* painted late in his career in imitation of Van Dyck. There is no evidence that he was in England before 1618.

Charles I's invitation to GERARD HONTHORST (1590-1656), already mentioned, was in connection with plans for the decoration of Whitehall. This singular and successful artist, who had an enormous influence, was a native of Utrecht, who went to Italy, where he made a reputation as a painter of candlelight effects and won the nickname of *Gerardo della Notte*. He returned to Holland in 1622 where his candlelight pictures influenced Rembrandt, and where he developed a practice as a portrait painter. After his English visit he became attached to the court of the Queen of Bohemia. He died a very wealthy man when both Hals and Rembrandt were bankrupt. In England, where he remained for about six months, he painted *Charles I*

[1]Cf. above, p. 50.

and *Queen Henrietta Maria* and *George Villiers, 1st Duke of Buckingham with his Family.*[1]

Another foreign portrait painter in England at this time was JOHANN PRIWITZER, a Hungarian. He signed and dated (1627) the picture *Lord William Russell and his Dwarf.*

CORNELIUS JOHNSON (1593- *c.*1664) was the son of one Cornelius Janssen who came from Flanders. He himself was born in London and signed his pictures Jonson or Johnson. He painted *James I* and *Queen Anne of Denmark* and *Charles I*; also many other portraits some of which survive and bear his signature. He seems to have been able to 'catch a likeness' even in portraits of women where the minor portrait painter habitually fails; for the faces in signed examples of his pictures are distinctly differentiated. He started, apparently, in the Elizabethan-Gothic tradition; but later, especially after Van Dyck's arrival, he seems to have been influenced by contemporary interest in plasticity. His *Charles I* dates from 1630; and he was possibly fascinated by the full drooping eyelid with high eyebrow that characterised the King, for thereafter he seems to show a tendency to impose this structure, with its affective expression, in his portraits of other sitters both men and women—in *Sir Ralph Verney*, for example, and *Lady Waterpark.* His *Elizabeth Cockaine, Lady Fanshawe* is a frank imitation of Van Dyck.

After Van Dyck's arrival, as already mentioned, Johnson retired to the country, and eventually, in 1643, to The Hague and Amsterdam, where he practised as a portrait painter till his death some twenty years later. In this last period he signed his pictures 'Jonson Van Ceulen, Londini', and seems to have adapted his style to the taste of his Dutch patrons who were then ignoring Hals and Rembrandt and raining commissions on Bol (1611-1681), Flinck (1615-1660) and Van der Helst (1612-1670).

I have mentioned Robert Walker (*c.* 1600-1658) and Samuel Cooper (1609?-1672) as English painters who worked here during the Commonwealth. WILLIAM SHEPPARD (active

[1]Cf. my 'Introduction to Dutch Art', pp. 50-54 and plates 22-25 and 27.

1640?-1665), who belongs to this period, seems to have been a royalist who went abroad during the troubles and returned at the Restoration. Only one picture can be with certainty ascribed to him: the signed portrait *Thomas Killigrew*. This was painted in Venice where Killigrew went in 1650 after two years' imprisonment for royalism; it shows the dramatist writing at his desk with a portrait of Charles before him on the wall.

EDWARD BOWER painted a well-known picture *Charles I at his Trial* (1648). ISAAC FULLER (1610?-1672) painted portraits and decorations with Bacchic themes in Oxford taverns; he also painted altarpieces in Magdalen and All Souls Colleges, described by Evelyn as 'too full of nakeds for a Chapel'.

Other minor contemporaries of Lely were the Scotsman MICHAEL WRIGHT (1625?-1700) painter of *Charles II on his Throne*, and of a number of portraits of English Judges; EDWARD HAWKER (1641- *c.*1721) one of Lely's pupil-assistants who after Lely's death, Walpole tells us, 'succeeded to Lely's house but not to his reputation'; JOHN GREENHILL (1644?-1676), who was also trained in Lely's studio, and is said to have gone to pieces in riotous living; and MARY BEALE (1632-1697) who copied some of Lely's pictures and had a considerable portrait practice of her own.

Those whose curiosity about the minor painters of the seventeenth century is still not satisfied must procure Mr. Collins Baker's celebrated book.[1]

[1]'Lely and the Stuart Painters' already referred to (cf. above pp. 27, 58). The student who uses that work must be careful to distinguish between the numerous and valuable statements of fact which it contains and the equally numerous ascriptions which may be right, but remain for all that in the category of suppositions. Mr. Collins Baker himself does not always assist the distinction in his catalogues at the end of his work and his captions to the reproductions.

APPENDIX TO CHAPTER IV

★

HOGARTH'S 'ANALYSIS OF BEAUTY'

In Hogarth's day this celebrated publication, though it enraged the minor artists and connoisseurs, was treated seriously by intelligent students, like Burke and Lessing, as I have noted.[1] And it is worth more consideration by students to-day than it commonly receives.

Hogarth begins by basing himself on a cryptic statement ascribed to Michelangelo to the effect that a figure should always be made 'Pyramidal, Serpentlike and Multiplied by one, two and three'. He interprets this in the first place to mean that a picture must have movement; and that movement is most essentially suggested by flamelike forms.

Here we may observe that this idea was certainly El Greco's. But we do not know, in El Greco's case, whether it was a consciously held idea or an instinctive preference for this type of form or a preference unconsciously acquired in the atmosphere of Toledo with its frequent *autos-da-fé*.

This flamelike form, Hogarth goes on to say, is represented by the serpentine line which is therefore the essential line of movement and of life and so of beauty.

If Hogarth had stopped here his doctrine could not be regarded as very important because it would only amount to an explanation of his personal pleasure in this type of line on paper. But he did not stop here. Or rather he did not from the beginning think of the serpentine line as a line on paper; he thought of it as the line formed by winding a wire round a cone.

It is for this reason that his treatise is so interesting to the

[1] Cf. above, pp. 64, 65.

student to-day. We may or may not be disposed to agree with him or even to follow him in his judgements of the relative beauty of the line wound in one way or another; but the fact that his concept of the line to be aimed at was three-dimensional and not two-dimensional brings him at once in touch with the aesthetic attitude of our own time, the attitude behind Cézanne's landscapes and the Cubist movement, the attitude heralded in the field of landscape painting by Cotman in *The Normandy River* (Pl. 118).

Professor Herbert Read discussing Henry Moore's sculpture has written recently as follows:

'If you are translating form in one material into form in another material, you must create that form from the inside outwards.'

That also is Hogarth's doctrine, not only for the sculptor but for the painter as well. The only difference is that Read, who is concerned in this passage only with sculpture, means that the sculptor must project himself imaginatively into the centre of the stone he is carving in order to create an equivalent in terms of that stone for his experience of form in another material in life; whereas Hogarth says that the artist must project himself imaginatively into the centre of the form experienced in life in order to be able to create an equivalent in painting.

As an aid to this conception Hogarth recommends the student to make figures of wax, and thrust wires through them in many directions, and thus acquire the habit of three-dimensional realisation. His most interesting illustration of the point reads as follows:

'In order to my being well understood, let every object under our consideration be imagined to have its inward contents scoop'd out so nicely as to have nothing of it left but a thin shell, exactly corresponding both in its inner and outer surface to the shape of the object itself: and let us likewise suppose this thin shell to be made up of very fine threads, closely connected together, and equally perceptible, whether the eye is supposed to observe them from without, or within; and we shall find the ideas of the two surfaces of this shell will naturally coincide. The very word, shell, makes us seem to see both surfaces alike.

'The use of this conceit, as it may be call'd by some, will be seen to be very great, and the oftner we think of objects in this shell-like manner, we shall facilitate and strengthen our conception of any particular part of the surface of an object we are viewing, by acquiring thereby a more perfect knowledge of the whole, to which it belongs: because the imagination will naturally enter into the vacant space within this shell, and there at once, as from a center, view the whole form within, and mark the opposite corresponding parts so strongly, as to retain the idea of the whole, and make us masters of the meaning of every view of the object, as we walk round it, and view it from without.

'Thus the most perfect idea we can possibly acquire of a sphere, is by conceiving an infinite number of straight rays of equal lengths, issuing from the center, as from the eye, spreading every way alike; and circumscribed or wound about at their other extremities with close connected circular threads, or lines, forming a true spherical shell.

'But in the common way of taking the view of any opake object, that part of its surface, which fronts the eye, is apt to occupy the mind alone, and the opposite, nay even every other part of it whatever, is left unthought of at that time: and the least motion we make to reconnoitre any other side of the object, confounds our first idea, for want of the connexion of the two ideas, which the complete knowledge of the whole would naturally have given us, if we had considered it in the other way before.

'Another advantage of considering objects thus merely as shells composed of lines, is that, by these means, we obtain the true and full idea of what is call'd the *outlines* of a figure, which has been confin'd within too narrow limits, by taking it only from drawings on paper; for in the example of the sphere given above, every one of the imaginary circular threads has a right to be consider'd as an out-line of the sphere, as well as those which divide the half, that is seen, from that which is not seen; and if the eye be supposed to move regularly round it, these threads will each of them as regularly succeed one another in the office of out-lines, (in the narrow and limited sense of the word): and the instant any one of these threads, during this motion of the eye, comes into sight on one side, its opposite thread is lost, and disappears on the other. He who will thus take the pains of acquiring perfect ideas of the distances, bearings, and oppositions of several material points and lines in the surfaces of even the most irregular figures, will gradually arrive at the knack of recalling them into his mind when the objects themselves are not before him: and they will be as strong and perfect as those of the most plain and regular forms, such as cubes and spheres; and will be of infinite service to those who invent and draw from fancy, as well as enable those to be more correct who draw from the life.

'In this manner, therefore, I would desire the reader to assist his imagination as much as possible, in considering every object, as if his eye were placed within it. As straight lines are easily conceiv'd, the difficulty of following this method in the most simple and regular forms will be less than may be first imagined; and its use in the more compounded will be greater.'

The rest of Hogarth's treatise is of less interest to modern students, because it becomes autobiographical in the sense that the author is concerned to produce a theory of Beauty which will cover his own work. The theory of characteristic beauty— of beauty residing in expressive character of any kind including ugliness—which would be the real defence of his own work, did not, I believe, appear in European aesthetic till the turn of the eighteenth to the nineteenth century (although it had been heralded at the end of the ancient world by Plotinus). Hogarth in his self-defence did not go all the way to this Romantic concept. He did not even reach the stage reached three years later by Burke who added the 'Sublime', i.e. pleasant horror, as an element of 'Beauty'. But he moved in this direction in his own way. For taking his stand on the old theory of Variety within Unity he laid exceptional stress, as we should expect, on the Variety;

and in his system 'Intricacy' and 'Continuity of Variety' assume more importance than does Unity.

Reynolds as is well known did not accept Hogarth's theory. And of course he could not do so seeing that Intricacy and Continuity of Variety were not features in his own work. And thus Reynolds was led to write to Dr. Beattie:

'Your idea of producing the line of beauty by taking the medium of the two extremes, exactly coincides with my idea, and its beauty I think may fairly be deduced from habit. All lines are either curved or straight, and that which partakes equally of each is the medium or average of all lines and therefore more beautiful than any other line; notwithstanding this, an artist would act preposterously that should take every opportunity to introduce this line in his works as Hogarth himself did, who appears to have taken an aversion to a straight line. His pictures therefore want that line of firmness and stability which is produced by straight lines; this conduct therefore may truly be said to be unnatural, for it is not the conduct of Nature.

'What you have imputed to convenience and contrivance, I think may without violence be put to the account of habit, as we are more used to that form in nature (and I believe in art, too) which is the *most* convenient. Fitness and beauty being always united in animals, as well as in men, they are fit in proportion as they are beautiful, and beautiful in proportion as they are fit, which makes it difficult to determine what is the original cause; as I said before, I am inclined to habit, and that we determine by habit in regard to beauty without waiting for the slower determination of reason.'

It will be observed that Reynolds has not realised that Hogarth's serpentine line was a three-dimensional and not a two-dimensional concept and that he therefore opposes to it not the cube but the straight line. It will also be realised from this letter that Reynolds thought of Beauty as a middle type, the type with which we are most familiar because it most frequently occurs. He was thus further back than Hogarth on the line leading to the Romantic concept of beauty residing in expressive character including ugliness. And this we get also in his writings:

'Every species of the animal as well as the vegetable creation may be said to have a fixed or determinate form towards which Nature is continually inclining, like various lines terminating in the centre; or it may be compared to pendulums vibrating in different directions over one central point; and as they all cross the centre though only one passes through any other point, so it will be found that perfect beauty is oftener produced by nature, than deformity. . . . In creatures of the same species beauty is the medium or centre of all various forms.'

A professional aesthetician's—Bernard Bosanquet's—comment on this is interesting:

'Reynolds evidently thinks that a central or average form in each species represents the purpose of nature. I suppose that if we to-day could attach any meaning to a purpose or inclination of nature, we should interpret it dynamically, and should regard it as likely to be ahead of any existing individual forms, or at any rate as various, and incapable of exhaustion within a single typical or central figure. This influence must obviously force forward our conception of central or essential reality from the species to the individual, and from the "invariable" to the law of variation, which is itself a kind of invariable.'

Blake's comment on this attitude of Reynolds is shorter and more emphatic:

'Reynolds thought Character Itself Extravagance and Deformity.'

APPENDIX V

APPENDIX TO CHAPTER XIV

★

THE BURGHCLERE MEMORIAL CHAPEL

In the year in which I write (1933) Stanley Spencer has completed a series of paintings in a War Memorial Chapel at Burghclere in Hampshire. He served as a private for four years in the 1914-1918 war, at one period in Macedonia; and he spent much of his time as a hospital orderly.

The paintings cover three walls. The side walls carry a series of lunettes depicting scenes in the field; and below a series of oblong panels depicting scenes in hospital. The central wall behind the altar carries the large painting *Resurrection*. I reproduce two of the lunettes, *Kit Inspection* (Pl. 128a) and *Drawing Water* (Pl. 129); one oblong panel *Tea in Hospital* (Pl. 128b) and *Resurrection* (Pl. 130). I should have liked to have reproduced all the lunettes and panels and to have shown details of *Resurrection*, because Spencer's pictures must be read from corner to corner, almost inch by inch. But this was impossible and in any case these pictures can only be properly apprehended in the chapel itself.[1]

The paintings are important in three ways. In the first place they are records of war, as such, by a sensitive man and an artist in touch with the cultural attitudes of his own day. In the second place they are descriptions of and at the same time comments on individual happenings personally experienced; and in the third place—and this applies especially to the central picture *Resurrection*—they reveal Spencer as an imaginative artist.

Spencer's record of war, as such, is neither in the nature of

[1] The photographs reproduced were taken in the chapel and they are not quite true to square. Reduced to the size of this page the degree of error is not great. But I feel bound to record it. The chapel, which should be visited by everyone interested in English painting, is always open to the public.

romantic propaganda in defence of war, nor in the nature of a moralist's protest against it. He has not made use of allegorical procedures deriving from Renaissance pageantry; Mars does not appear, no maidens in Greek draperies bind laurels round the heads of conquering generals. He has also not made use of the romantic method of war propaganda; no wounded men rise on their elbows to shout *'Vive l'Empereur'* as in *Napoleon at Eylau* by Gros (1771-1835). Nor on the other hand has he used the *in terrorem* procedure of the moralist which I have discussed in the chapter on Hogarth. His war is not the nightmare of gibbets and mutilations and flames shown by Callot (1592-1635) and by Goya (1746-1828). In one of his hospital scenes we see the swollen legs and feet of a patient exposed beneath a bedframe which prevents a contact that would be agony—but this is almost the only record of physical pain. Nor, again, does he protest against spiritual pains; there are no *in terrorem* scenes of iron discipline, of martyrdoms for independent opinion; and there is nothing here of the character of *Napoleon in Hell* by Wiertz (1806-1865). War as Spencer shows it is a series of activities of healthy young men who travel, camp, and work in a hundred ways in the open air, in conditions more accurately described as uncomfortable than arduous, and of sick and wounded young men cared for with devotion in hospitals by their fellows much as men are cared for in hospitals in peace time. No concept of war could be less sentimental, less sensational, or less dramatic, or, the reader, who has not seen the pictures, might imagine, less likely to move and enthral.

But in fact these pictures are extraordinarily affective. They appeal with equal intensity and in several ways to several categories and levels of emotion. I felt when I looked at them that every one of the thousand memories recorded had been driven into the artist's consciousness like a sharp-pointed nail. He takes us with him as he moves among this crowd of young men, this vast boarding-schoool of grown-up boys—for all the figures are small men, as he is himself, and all are given a pathetically boyish look. We see them, as he does, at a distance, at close quarters, in groups and singly. Sometimes the impression that came to him was an impression of form observed from the other end of a field or room—the queer shape made by the attitude of a boy combing his hair in a mirror held between his feet, the silhouette of a boy in a blue suit lying on a bed (Pl. 128b); the silhouettes of boys spreading out their blankets, kneeling within them, like people in Canadian canoes (Pl. 128a); or a configuration of helmeted heads with waterbottles to their lips (Pl. 129).

At other times the impression recorded is not one of form seen at a distance but of characters apprehended by close contact—by the eye, by smell and by touch. By the artist's side in this experience we smell the flesh of these herded soldiers, we feel the textures of their clothes and towels, the exact consistency of every object that they handle, the texture and substance of the food they eat. We are not asked to note the difference between one soldier's nose and another's; the artist makes no pretence to portraiture; he tells us that they have heads of various shapes and colours—like the heads of people seen in an omnibus or train; not being engaged in portraiture he makes no pretence to tell us more. There are too many of these boys for portraiture here to have any meaning; if they reveal themselves as individuals it is not by their noses but by their actions—by the choice of post-cards which they pin above their beds in hospital—postcards of ships and sailors in one case, postcards of pretty girls in another. And then by Spencer's side we do the work he did, we kneel on the floor and scrub, and note the pattern of the soapsuds because he chanced to be an artist born in 1892; we get entangled in a linear arabesque of tent ropes and feel the hardness of the cord; we tear up newspapers to light fires and feel the heat and note the shadows as the flames leap up: we cut a sick man's toenails, we carry pails, we make and remake beds; we pass with him through a hundred aspects of his experience, through an endless series of contacts that are almost unbearably acute and intimate.

Here a comparison between this epic—for the Burghclere pictures are nothing less—and the caricature-comment in Hogarth's *Gin Lane*, *The Four Stages of Cruelty*, the Bedlam

Scene in *A Rake's Progress, Scene* 8 (Pls. 16b and 17) and Burra's *Marseilles Bar* (Pl. 88), may be, it seems to me, instructive.

Hogarth accumulates incident and specific detail to reinforce his meaning. But to record the intensity of his ideas he relies mainly, as he himself tells us, on *in terrorem* exaggeration in depicting cruelties and miseries, and on a certain crudity in technique.[1] Hogarth is thus there, in an early stage of English painting, to remind us that sensations, impressions and ideas experienced beyond a certain point of intensity cannot be expressed by literal description of the physical objects and concrete things involved in the experience; that to record *truthfully* in such cases the artist must in some way record the intensity which is the essence of the experience. We have seen Hogarth's way of doing this. Now let us look at Burra's procedures and Spencer's.

To Burra, I have submitted, the experience which eventually became the drawing called *Marseilles Bar* (Pl. 88) was contact with a scene which seemed to him grotesque and unreal. And it seemed grotesque and unreal to him because he was not inside it but remained in amused detachment outside it. The world he recorded is not a world of which he ever formed a part nor a world in which he was ever sufficiently interested to project himself imaginatively inside it. The difference between Burra's experience and Spencer's experience (setting aside the point of magnitude, the difference that is to say between the short series of impressions which went to the making of *Marseilles Bar* and the tremendously long series that went to the making of the Burghclere epic) is that Burra has given us a truthful record of his amused, detached impression by the use of accumulated incident and distortions which work together to suggest the grotesque unreality which was the essence of the impression; whereas Spencer, who lived inside his subject for years, has truthfully recorded his experience by the use of accumulated incident and distortions working together to suggest the terrible intensity of his physical, emotional and spiritual contact with his subject. The types of truth revealed in the two

[1] Cf. above, pp. 85, 86.

283

cases are different in kind and they have accordingly different effects: we are moved to smile in the one case and to deeper and more disturbing emotion in the other; but the mechanism, as it were, in both cases is very much the same; and in both cases it is different from Hogarth's mechanism—though one procedure, the use of the sum of the parts to contribute to their product, occurs in all three cases. The important point is that none of the three thought that categoric still-life description of the physical aspects of experience would be sufficient for their purpose. And indeed it would not have been sufficient, because it would not have been true, in any of these cases.

In the Burghclere *Resurrection* Spencer is in the field of imaginative art. And to understand this work we must recall his earlier imaginative pictures.

In one of his earliest pictures, *The Visitation*, he painted the Virgin as a Cookham kitchen-maid, in a pink cotton dress and newly laundered apron, arriving at her cousin's cottage up the lane. There was nothing funny in the result. Everyone who had read St. Luke's account of the Angel's charge to Mary and her obedience to it knew at once that this picture was a new and truthful concept of *The Visitation*. This picture made it clear to all intelligent students that an almost unbelievable thing had happened in these sophisticated days; that a young man born in a village, who had spent four years in London at the Slade School, had gone back to his village and read his Bible and paid to it so much attention that his mind's eye saw local images in illustration. Here was a man to whom his village was a microcosm, a man to whom the village of Cookham was the world, and the inhabitants of Cookham the human race. Seven years later, in 1920, he painted *Christ carrying the Cross* (Pl. 131) and to those who were following his development it was clear that he was making a great effort to continue this intense close contact with his village. The scene is again localised in Cookham. But the closeness and the simplicity of the earlier contact is no longer there. In *Christ carrying the Cross* the procession passes between rows of railings that are really spears, and rows of figures who are really soldiers standing easy on parade. In this picture the artist, I fancy, was driven to transmute, to change more and more the real village of Cookham (with which he could not recapture contact) to a city without local or even terrestrial significance, a city where the spectators of the procession, who lean eagerly from windows, between fluttering lace curtains, become angels with wings looking down from heaven (Pl. 131). Here the transmutation, I submit, really records a sense of frustration, a sense of failure to recapture the old contact with the village; and the failure was caused, of course, by the four years' experience that had intervened. As truly envisaged by Spencer in 1920, Christ carrying the Cross was Christ carrying the Cross not in Cookham but in Macedonia.

The Burghclere *Resurrection* on the other hand seems to me a completely truthful imaginative picture. The scene takes place in Macedonia. It is the last adventure of the herd of boys with their horses and mules. The boys rise from their graves as though called by the bugle in the morning; they are then demobilised, and each boy hands back his spiritual equipment—his Cross—to Christ who quietly receives it in his arms or at his feet; and the boys then travel on to their final resting place (Pl. 130).

Here Spencer had no more need for transmutation than in the descriptive pictures of the soldiers in the field and in hospital. As a result of those four years of intense experience, and of the incessant ordering of the memories for ten years afterwards (the designs for the Burghclere pictures were made in 1923 and have hardly been altered in the execution which was completed this year), he has localised the idea of Resurrection as the resurrection of those boys in Macedonia. And the result has the simplicity and truthfulness of *The Visitation* localised in Cookham twenty years earlier.[1]

[1] Spencer was commissioned to paint the Burghclere pictures by a gentleman who saw the designs in 1923 and built the chapel that they might be carried out. The work was interrupted in 1926-7 because the artist wished to paint *The Resurrection of the Dead* (now in the National Gallery of British Art, Millbank). The Millbank picture I assume to have been a gigantic effort to externalise finally the Cookham attachments before painting the Burghclere *Resurrection* which could only be carried out by an imaginative return to Macedonia.

INDEX

287

INDEX

INDEX

INDEX